PHENOMENOLOGY, UNCERTAINTY, AND CARE IN THE THERAPEUTIC ENCOUNTER

Phenomenology, Uncertainty, and Care in the Therapeutic Encounter is the latest in a series of books where Mark Leffert explores the therapeutic encounter as both process and situation; looking for evidence of therapeutic effectiveness rather than accepting existing psychoanalytic concepts of theory or cure without question.

Mark Leffert focuses on the uncomfortable fact that analysts and therapists can and do make many mistaken assumptions and false moves within their clinical practice, and that there is a tendency to ignore the significant levels of uncertainty in what they do. Beginning with a discussion of the phenomenology of the self and its relations with the world, the book moves on to explore the notion that interdisciplinary discourse both opens up possibilities in the therapeutic encounter but also imposes healthy constraints on what can be thought or theorized about psychoanalytically.

Phenomenology, Uncertainty, and Care in the Therapeutic Encounter contributes a new understanding of familiar material and brings a new focus to the care-giving and healing aspects of psychoanalysis and psychotherapy leading to a shift in the analyst's identity from that of one who analyses to one who cares for and heals. This book will be of interest to psychoanalysts and psychotherapists, neuroscientists, and academics in the fields of psychiatry, comparative literature, and literature and the mind.

Mark Leffert MD, has been on the faculty of five psychoanalytic institutes and has been a Training and Supervising Analyst at four of them. He has taught and supervised psychoanalysts, psychologists, and psychiatrists for forty years. He is the author of many papers and two previous books, *Contemporary Psychoanalytic Foundations* and *The Therapeutic Situation in the 21st Century*. Dr Leffert has been engaged in an interdisciplinary reformulation of clinical psychoanalysis drawing on postmodernism, neuroscience, network studies, and (among others) heuristics and biases. Present and future work focuses on phenomenology, care, healing, and the self. He is in private practice in Santa Barbara, California.

"Once again, Leffert provides readers with the eclectic scholarship and gentle iconoclasm for which he is justly renowned. Here he sets himself the paradoxical task of theorizing the 'inconvenient truth' of a post-modern psychoanalysis bereft of certainties and grand theories. He deftly does this via a) an accessible account of phenomenology (including all you ever wanted to know about Husserl and Heidegger but never dared ask), in which what patients say at the outset of treatment they want to be different about their lives is taken with utmost seriousness b) showing how transference can be understood in terms of Kahnemanian heuristics and systematic biases c) acknowledging that care and palliation are no less important goals for therapists than the elusive, and largely mythical, 'cure'. Convincing clinical material, buttressed by contemporary neuroscience, keeps the reader's feet on the ground throughout. A must-read for all broad-minded and self-reflexive therapists."
— **Professor Jeremy Holmes MD, FRCPsych**, *University of Exeter, UK*

"Psychoanalytic theory and psychotherapeutic practice benefit from not taking anything for granted. On-the-hand psychoanalytic training is more indoctrination than exploration with a limited interdisciplinary reach. Dr Leffert's book offers an elegant and eloquent corrective to the limitations of our business as usual approach."
— **Arnold Richards**, *Editor of Internationalpsychoanalysis.net*

"This important volume is a part of Leffert's ongoing interdisciplinary odyssey to understand and enrich the therapeutic situation in today's uncertain post-modern world. Leffert persuasively argues for the need for a phenomenologically-informed psychoanalysis, stripped of metapsychological paraphernalia. He investigates the relevance of complex systems and their properties from neurology to social networks in his characteristically clear and erudite way. Leffert explores 'big picture' issues while attending to theoretical and clinical details in his search for an effective therapy focusing on healing, care and what patients want."
— **Douglas Kirsner PhD**, *Emeritus Professor of Philosophy, Deakin University, Melbourne. Author of* Unfree Associations: Inside Psychoanalytic Institutes

PHENOMENOLOGY, UNCERTAINTY, AND CARE IN THE THERAPEUTIC ENCOUNTER

Mark Leffert

LONDON AND NEW YORK

First published 2016
by Routledge
27 Church Road, Hove, East Sussex, BN3 2FA

and by Routledge
711 Third Avenue, New York, NY 10017

Routledge is an imprint of the Taylor & Francis Group, an informa business

© 2016 Mark Leffert

The right of Mark Leffert to be identified as author of this work has been
asserted by him in accordance with sections 77 and 78 of the Copyright,
Designs and Patents Act 1988.

All rights reserved. No part of this book may be reprinted or reproduced or
utilised in any form or by any electronic, mechanical, or other means, now
known or hereafter invented, including photocopying and recording, or in any
information storage or retrieval system, without permission in writing from the
publishers.

Trademark notice: Product or corporate names may be trademarks or registered
trademarks, and are used only for identification and explanation without intent
to infringe.

British Library Cataloguing in Publication Data

A catalogue record for this book is available from the British Library

Library of Congress Cataloging-in-Publication Data
Leffert, Mark.
    Phenomenology, uncertainty and care in the therapeutic encounter / Mark
Leffert.
        pages cm
    Includes bibliographical references and index.
    1. Phenomenological psychology.   2. Psychoanalysis.   3. Psychotherapy.   I. Title.
    BF204.5.L44 2015
    616.89'17—dc23
    2015007732

ISBN: 978-0-415-81259-7 (hbk)
ISBN: 978-0-415-81260-3 (pbk)
ISBN: 978-1-315-70726-6 (ebk)

Typeset in Bembo
by Apex CoVantage, LLC

Printed and bound by CPI Group (UK) Ltd, Croydon, CR0 4YY

on sustainably sourced paper.

For
Ernst Lewy and George Ginsberg
Who
Started me on this path
A very long time
Ago

CONTENTS

Acknowledgments   *ix*

Introduction   1

1   The self and its contexts   9
    Introduction   9
    The self   11
    Collections of selves: network studies   26

2   Phenomenology and existentialism   31
    Introduction   31
    Heidegger the man   33
    Phenomenology and existentialism   35
    Phenomenology, intersubjectivity, and neuroscience   39
    Dasein and being-in-the-world   44

3   Psychoanalysis and Daseinanalysis   47
    Introduction   47
    American phenomenological psychoanalysis   49
    Phenomenological analysis: goals and substance   50
    Clinical phenomenology   53
    Roger's analysis: phenomenologically speaking   63

4   The phenomenological unconscious   68
    Introduction   68

viii Contents

The unconscious and unconsciousness 70
The phenomenological unconscious 74
The relational unconscious 76
Unconsciousness and the uncanny 85

5   The role of decisions made under uncertainty in
    clinical psychoanalysis   94
    Introduction 94
    Uncertainty in contemporary psychoanalysis 95
    Decision-making under uncertainty 101
    Risk 103
    The law of small numbers 105
    Heuristics and Biases 108
    Variants of uncertainty 120
    Why psychoanalysts need to study uncertainty 121

6   Care and suffering in therapeutic situations   123
    Introduction 123
    The nature of care 126
    Care of the medical patient 130

7   So what *is* psychoanalysis, really, and what are its therapeutic
    goals and actions?   152
    Introduction 152
    An expanded perspective on psychoanalysis 155
    Neuroscience: selected issues 161
    An expanded relational perspective 165

References   *181*
Index   *201*

ACKNOWLEDGMENTS

I wish to thank four people who in a very real sense have made this work and the ones that have come before it possible. The first is Kate Hawes, my Editor at Routledge, with whom I began a relationship with her offer to publish this current book. The second is Kristopher Spring, who had been my Associate Editor at Routledge. In it, he guided me through the process of making text into my first two books. I asked him to participate as my personal Editor in the process of making this book happen, and he graciously accepted. Then there is my oldest friend, Marshall Sashkin, PhD, who has supported me in many areas of my life. Finally and most importantly, there is my wife, Nancy Leffert, PhD, who read every word I wrote until becoming a university president made this impossible. Since then she has supported me in every possible way.

INTRODUCTION

This is meant to be a radical and subversive book. Although conceived as an entirely independent volume, it is very much a continuation of an ongoing project begun with *Contemporary Psychoanalytic Foundations* (2010) and *The Therapeutic Situation in the 21st Century* (2013) and now (apparently) to be continued with *Psychoanalysis, Aesthetics, and Well-Being*.

This has in no way been a planned series. It has rather followed from the ongoing development of my thinking about psychoanalysis as the research and writing themselves revealed issues that still needed to be pursued with different lenses and from different perspectives. *Contemporary Psychoanalytic Foundations* (*CPF*) offered a hard interdisciplinary critique of metapsychology in general and of even the *possibility* of any single named metapsychology being able to claim standing. I argued that other disciplines such as neuroscience and complexity theory had much to offer psychoanalytic inquiry into areas such as unconsciousness, consciousness studies, and memory. I posited that a soft postmodern critique of psychoanalysis, one including an integration of the social and the scientific, could offer a foundation for including all of these areas interreferentially into contemporary psychoanalytic thought.

Although *CPF* has held up as a basic science text critical of psychoanalytic hermeneutics and situating psychoanalysis in the wider, interdisciplinary world, it did not attempt to offer any overarching discussion of clinical psychoanalysis or the therapeutic situation as it exists in contemporary times. The eponymous *Therapeutic Situation in the 21st Century* (*TS21*) began *this* project, offering a rudimentary textbook of psychoanalysis in a new language. *TS21* retained a vigorous critique of psychoanalytic orthodoxy and reification. Although clinical innovation in psychoanalysis has always taken place within the framework of *some* metapsychology, it has remained uncertain whether those frameworks helped or hindered clinical advancement. I have generally followed Gill and Holtzman's (1976) observation

2 Introduction

that psychology is not metapsychology and that psychoanalysis involves two theories: a very powerful clinical one and a very dubious metapsychological one. I followed a clinical thread in our literature beginning with Freud in his German[1] voice (as opposed to Strachey's voice, modeled on that of a 19th-century British scientist), progressing through the radical ego psychologists of the 1960s and '70s and coming to rest in contemporary critiques both of and by the relational schools. It treated all of them as local knowledges, that is to say, knowledge with limited standing and limited areas of applicability. It offered a much more fully realized discussion of post-structuralism and, along with it, retained a focus on power and its abuses in the psychoanalytic situation.

If there was a problem with *CPF* and, to a lesser extent, with *TS21*, it was an overly optimistic view that contemporary relational thought could address the problems psychoanalysis had gotten itself into and how those problems limited therapeutic results. It seemed that the Relational School had entered a phase in which second-generation theorists were elaborating their theories in much the same way that second-generation Freudians were doing in the 1940s, '50s, and '60s. If, however, excessive dedication to or reliance on the theoretical precepts of any of the metapsychological schools only limits therapeutic effectiveness, then what sorts of overarching concepts could offer a grasp of the therapeutic situation?

I have set out to recast psychoanalysis in two ways that, while still privileging the centrality of the therapeutic relationship (that, I will argue, is best understood in terms of the doctor-patient relationship), largely breaks with Contemporary thinking. The first is the development of a phenomenological psychoanalysis tracing its roots to the work of Husserl, Heidegger, May, and Boss, and the second is the unfortunately novel concept of focusing the therapy on what the patient actually wants and needs.

Thinking in phenomenological terms frees up our thinking about both the patient and the therapeutic situation. At its most basic level, what it means is that the patient is simply the patient and the analyst is, well, simply the analyst. For both, *reality is always fully deployed*; there are no secret depths to be plumbed in either the patient or the analyst. Admittedly, this goes against the grain of everything we have been taught, but what we have been taught involves a fallacy resting on a misunderstanding. There *are* depths, but they are temporal depths involving the historicity of our being, not some organizational, metapsychological depth. Although it is possible, with some effort, to roughly impose a conscious, temporal scale on our cognitions, no such order seems to exist in memory retrieval into consciousness when such retrieval is possible. There are many sorts of encoded memories that reflect different sources of experiences. Only the most obvious are memories of events: episodic memories, the memories of Tulving (1985/2003) and Schachter (Schacter, 1996; Schacter, Addis, & Buckner, 2008). Then there are the memories

---

1 I have often thought that, as Anglophones, we lucked out with Shakespeare but lost out on Freud.

that encode how we think: the attachment memories of Bowlby (1969) and Main (George, Kaplan, & Main, 1984); the memories of metacognitive knowledge and Theory of Mind, again of Main (1991) and of Baron-Cohen (Baron-Cohen, 2000; Baron-Cohen, Leslie, & Frith, 1985); and the memory of internal working models of Craik (1943/1952) and again of Bowlby (1969, 1973). There are memories that organize perception, how we see (Gregory, 1997; von Senden, 1932/1960); if sight is not somehow present before adolescence, then we are only able to see swirls of disorganized color. The list goes on. But one thing must stand out about all of this: *the existence of memory has nothing to do with consciousness.* Neuroscience has told us (e.g., Baars, 1993/2003b), as narcissistically injurious to our Left Brains as it may be, that consciousness is small potatoes, only a fairly small, slow slice of the activity of the self.

Phenomenologically, there is no way to demonstrate the existence of "an" unconscious governed by repression, as psychoanalysts and psychotherapists make use of the term. There is a robust interdisciplinary literature (e.g., Singer, 1990; Willingham & Preuss, 1995) critiquing such a usage of the term. Things may be hidden, or kept secret, or more specifically kept secret from the Left Brain (Baars, 1988/2003a; Risse & Gazzaniga, 1978). However, these are fairly simple processes, understood in everyday language and addressed through *constructive* deconstructive discourse, as opposed to repression, a putative process. There is no real-world definition of repression as opposed to an "explanation" of it in the arcane language of metapsychology and the equally unsupported assertion that it is undone by interpretation. All that we *know*, and all we can know, is that, as a result of intensive psychotherapy or psychoanalysis, people remember more (that is, Left Brain conscious access to episodic memory) than they do at the start of treatment.

Historicity also takes on an entirely different form; in its evolutionary form, it is phylogeny. Here there is also a kind of temporal layering. However, the time scale here is not one of years but rather of units of geologic time: Periods, Epochs, and Ages (in descending order of duration). In its simplest form, this means that we possess a reptilian brain, on "top" of which there is a mammalian brain, then specialized as a primate brain and further specialized as our human brain. Ontogeny (somewhat) recapitulates this process of phylogeny. The ancient brain is the original seat of emotion that has been demonstrated (Panksepp & Biven, 2012) in cross-mammalian studies to have evolved into seven emotional regulatory systems. More about this later.

The phenomenological hook (so to speak) on which to hang all of this can only be the self. The self in clinical psychology and psychoanalysis is generally thought of as a psychic structure. It even has a location demonstrated in functional neuroanatomy (e.g., Uddin, Iacoboni, Lange, & Keenan, 2007) as residing in the Cortical Midline Structures (CMS) of the brain. Alas, this doesn't work, or, more precisely, it only works if you roll back Western thought almost five centuries and re-embrace Cartesian mind-body dualism. If you don't want to do that (a wise choice), then you must embrace instead a post-Cartesian self that includes, well,

4 Introduction

everything, however "everything" is defined. The CMS do remain, but they remain as centers that consolidate information about self-representation.

The Post-Cartesian self is a bio-psycho-social self, and different epistemological languages describe it in different ways. The first is that mind is not separate from body and does not reside in the skull. The whole body is indistinguishable from mind; the latter is more of a figure of speech for which a quantum mechanics approach, at least as metaphor, is more apropos. The second is that, just as mind and body are inseparable, mind–body and world are inseparable. What we have is a radically disautonomous mind–body that, along with its interreferential connections to the world, makes up a holistic self. Readily available evidence for such a state of being exists in the observation that the use of sensory deprivation tanks results in, after varying periods of time, a kind of disintegration of the self. I have previously (2010, 2013) offered discussions of the self but offer here, in Chapter 1, what I hope is a still more fully realized version of those discussions.

Heidegger (1975/1982) constructed his own language, admittedly arcane sounding to Anglophone speakers, to address these issues. He uses the complex (for him) term Dasein to at once describe the existence of the self and other selves, and the nature of their being there, being in the world. He separates Dasein into three components: the inner world (*Eigenwelt*), the world of being with other selves (*Mitwelt*), and the being of the self in the wider world (*Umwelt*). He also makes a distinction between being-in-the-world in a routine, lifeless, and empty way ("fallen") and being in the moment in an alive, experiencing way ("thrown"). More recently, these separations have come to seem more heuristic than actual. This criticism has, most prominently, originated in the work of the network theorist Bruno Latour (Latour, 2005; Serres & Latour, 1990/2011).

I will offer a discussion of these complex ideas and their utility in Chapters 2 and 3. The discussion in Chapter 2 covers phenomenology as a particular philosophical discipline and describes the work of the major actors in the field and how they interact with each other. It is a discussion of philosophical ideas and can, at times, be difficult. In the interests of clarity, it made the most sense to separate this discourse on philosophy from its *clinical applications* in the therapeutic situation. Chapter 3 will focus on these applications.

The two following chapters address aspects of, for lack of a better term, the landscape of the therapeutic situation, the nature of the workspace in which we and our patients conduct our therapeutic relationship. The first of these, Chapter 4, examines the concept of unconsciousness. In an earlier work (Leffert, 2010, Chapter 5), I leveled a series of radical critiques at the psychoanalytic concept of a dynamic system unconscious held separate from a system conscious by the force of repression. Room was also made for unconscious things that had never been nor would become conscious in this topographical world. I summarized these arguments grammatically in a shift from an unconscious to unconsciousness. This chapter will briefly reprise these arguments before going on to explore the wider phenomenological implications of this shift.

Introduction **5**

In particular, the relationship between unconsciousness and psychopathology can be seen, from the vantage point of the 21st century, to be a relatively small piece of the action. Although conscious discourse between the members of the analytic couple[2] *does* function as one of the entry points of the therapeutic relationship, it is only one of many. Most of what goes on in the therapeutic situation, as in life itself, goes on outside of awareness, *whether or not* it entered the process through conscious discourse.

The work of therapy and analysis has always involved working with episodic memory, the memory for past events, both cognitive and affective. That work has been both interpretive and discursive. I have previously written (2010) on conceptualizing it as the integration of episodic memories into personal narrative, a process that involves memories that start out outside awareness but also unintegrated memories already *in* awareness. This work does remain an important part of the therapeutic process, but it has been joined by more foundational work on, for lack of a better summarizing term, how the self processes information. This includes elements of cognitive neuroscience such as priming, organizations of information like internal working models, and an exploration of personal epistemes, an individual person's rules of knowledge that shape thought. Although some of this work *is* discursive, much of it is experiential and goes on outside of the awareness of both patient and therapist, Right Brain to Right Brain.

Finally, if we are going to talk about unconsciousness, we also have to talk about the uncanny and talk about it in a wider way than is usual in clinical writing.

Most, but by no means all, 21st century psychotherapists and psychoanalysts recognize that there are limits on knowability in the therapeutic encounter. That recognition often results in confusing the concept of limits on knowability with that of uncertainty. The latter usually makes reference metaphorically to the Heisenberg Uncertainty Principle (Wheeler & Zurek, 1983), specifically that the act of measuring or observing something changes it so it can never be known in its original form. This resonates with the postmodern concept of interreferentiality, the concept that subjects are centers of mutual influences that cannot be untangled. I have previously discussed uncertainty and unknowability in these fairly standard terms (2010, 2013). I have also looked at the role of complexity (2008) in rendering predictions of future events based on a knowledge of their antecedents impossible, not because of limits on their knowability, but rather because of the behavior of complex systems. Chapter 5 will offer a relatively brief discussion of these points.

I am, however, after bigger game here, beyond what has been considered by psychoanalysts and psychotherapists. As it happens, there is a robust literature (e.g., Kahneman, Slovic, & Tversky, 1982; Meehl, 1983/1991b; Nisbett & Ross, 1980) in

---

2 The relationship between what the participants consciously *think* is going on and their relationship to some impossibly ascertainable reality of what *is* going on are similarly uncertain.

6 Introduction

the areas of empirical psychology and sociology that deals with the role of uncertainty in human thought and action, not confined to the analyst's thinking about her patient. The fact is that we live in an uncertain world in which we possess incomplete information, whether or not complete information even exists somewhere. These disciplines pursue the study of human inference and of judgments reached under uncertainty. An understanding of these subjects applies to the therapeutic situation in ways that we have not much considered. With reference to patients, it offers a novel insight into how they reach decisions concerning their thoughts and actions. We have, of course, looked at the way issues (I'm being purposely broad here) in a patient's life past and present influence the way they navigate their world, and *its* relationship to the wider experience that we all share. *We have done so even though we have not defined the process in these terms.* What the study of inference and judgments under uncertainty offers us here is a way, in the therapeutic situation, to identify the *systematic errors* that our patients make in determining thoughts and actions and offer them an entirely different perspective on what they're doing. Since these functions long ago became autonomous for them, it offers an approach to an area that otherwise may be almost impossible to get at, much less address.

The second use of the study of judgments undertaken under conditions of uncertainty that is probably of even more importance in the therapeutic situation is that it can help us to better understand how we reach conclusions about our patients and how we decide what we will or will not do as a result. It is inevitable that we will make *some* systematic errors in how we go about this that involve a reliance on particular kinds of shortcuts in our thinking. These shortcuts, called heuristics, are a necessary and often helpful part of our thinking; we can learn to distinguish how the heuristics we rely on can facilitate the therapeutic process or distort it.

Learning and experiencing, again very broadly defined, conscious or otherwise, are processes that we seek to engender in our patients and ourselves through the use of clinical tools. Although they make up much of the stuff of the therapeutic process, they have also tended to become de facto ends in and of themselves. This has happened for a number of reasons. The first is that there is no widespread agreement on what kind(s) of outcomes we should expect at the conclusion of a successful therapy or analysis. We also can't agree on the presence or nature of any distinction between the two procedures. Secondly, a focus on, let alone concerns about, results, goals, and outcomes has been abjured as a restriction of and a constraint on the therapeutic process itself. They have also been seen as placing the patient under some kind of obligation to perform or live up to our expectations, leading perhaps to what have been called transference cures. The way a therapist's value system impinges on the patient (and it is impossible for it not to) is indeed a complex matter that requires ongoing reflection on his part; it should not be confused with goals and outcomes. The problem with this confusion is that if prospective patients thought that there were no particular phenomenological outcomes (as opposed to metapsychological outcomes) that could reasonably be expected from a

Introduction **7**

therapeutic experience, then their interests in undergoing it could be expected to decline substantially.

It is of course true that most patients seek out therapists at least in part to fulfill transference wishes that they are often only dimly aware of. This observation has led to an overarching judgment that such wishes should be elucidated and explored rather than gratified in treatment. However, this has become a much more complex issue in contemporary psychoanalytic thought. It remains relatively clear that, should the patient come to the therapeutic situation seeking the therapist to assume some place in his life *outside* of that situation and her identity as a therapist, this is not what we do. Even in this situation, there is no single way for dealing with these wishes. However, if we take even a small step away from this situation, to, say, a patient who comes to us, knowingly or not, out of a need to get something in the *therapeutic* relationship (as opposed to some imagined external one) that they did not get early in their lives, then we are instantly involved in a century-old controversy. Some number of us (and I include myself in this group) do think that an important curative factor in any treatment does involve providing this very thing to the patient. Some others think nothing of the kind, while still others brand such concerns a form of psychoanalytic heresy (a term with specific psychoanalytic meanings; Leffert, 2010). It is, I think, safe to say that transference per se does not deny the patient the right to have their wishes and needs prioritized in any therapy or analysis.

The first way out of this conundrum is to ask the patient *in the first session* just what it is that they want and, secondarily, whether they have any expectations concerning how that will happen. Perhaps, a little later, it may be useful to inquire about what role they may expect us to play in bringing these ends about. I have no idea how often this is done, but I have encountered many instances in which it was not.

In Chapter 6, I discuss an answer to the question of what psychoanalytic therapy is about that is so old, it has become novel. Therapy is about care *of* the patient. A reviewer of the proposal for this book dismissed this line of inquiry with the observation that "of course [relational] analysts care *about* their patients." My arguments hinge on this very confusion. There are, among others, two definitions of care. The first of these (*Merriam Webster's Dictionary*, 2004) is of care as attention and solicitude, and, yes, this form of care *about* has been with our profession since its beginnings.[3] Care in the second sense is very much a different matter. It means (*Oxford English Dictionary*, 1989) "the attention and treatment given to a patient by a doctor or other health worker." This is the piece that is largely absent from psychoanalytic writing, discourse, and, explicitly at least, from the therapeutic situation.

---

3 I recall a supervisor of mine in the 1970s who believed in being as close to completely silent as possible with his patients. Even at the time I knew he was simply wrong-headed about this, but I also had no doubt that he cared deeply about his patients.

8 Introduction

This chapter is about the role of care in the psychoanalytic encounter and the centrality of relief of pain and suffering in its practice. This concept dates back to ancient Greece and the *iatroi*, healers, drawn from a range of different disciplines. If this *is* what we are about, then it requires a very different way of thinking about psychoanalysis and psychotherapy, and it is those ramifications that are explored here.

Chapter 7, the last chapter, undertakes two difficult tasks. The first is to draw together all of these disparate arguments into a single coherent whole. By the very nature of such a project, at best only partial success is possible. What it does offer is a different and, I hope, valuable way of thinking about psychoanalysis. The second, that these arguments are meant to inform, is a serious look at how psychoanalysis cures, heals, and relieves pain and suffering. It should be surprising how little we think about or write about these processes that *ought* to be at the very center of what we do. I also offer two appended discussions. One is of the Placebo Effect, which is typically depreciated and poorly understood by most health professionals, including psychoanalysts. I offer a re-assessment of it based on the newer literature that does bear on what we do.

The second discussion presents a sort of caveat suggesting that we need to think about the secular limitations some of the people who come to us for help have that interfere with their ability to engage us and the process (our own limitations are inevitable but hopefully open to a personal struggle to surmount them). Although in some cases these problems can be successfully addressed as "grist for the mill," there are others for whom there is no procedure, no theoretical adjustment, no correction of a therapeutic inadequacy, that can change such parts of a patient's very being.

This book raises complex arguments concerning the very nature of psychoanalysis and the world in which it lives, its ontology, if you will. For those readers without much past exposure to Phenomenology, Chapters 2 and 3 will require careful reading. The book offers novel (or at least fairly novel) views of the psychoanalytic situation and approaches the latter in ways very far removed from the familiar metapsychological points of view. Indeed, it strenuously criticizes the twin concepts they implicitly rely on: that *deeper* psychological truths exist and that they can be posited or discarded based on the evidence drawn from data of very poor quality whose collection is governed by the "truths" it is expected to "prove." I have instead posited that truths, by their very nature, are phenomenological and, with respect to psychoanalysis, require interdisciplinary confirmation.

September 1, 2014
Santa Barbara, California

1

THE SELF AND ITS CONTEXTS

Introduction

William James (1893/2007), for perhaps the first time in modern psychology, offered an expansive definition of the conscious, empirical self as "*the sum total of all that* [a man] CAN *call his*." He went on to include in this total "not only his body and his psychic powers, but his clothes and his house, his wife and children, his ancestors and friends, his reputation and works, his lands and horses, and yacht and bank account" (p. 291). James had, rather shockingly for the times, and still not seen all that much today, offered up a post-Cartesian definition of the self, whose essence is that of a social and physical creature, inseparable from its social matrix.

Taking the first of several narrative turns, in 1987 (one of two years in which the Minnesota Twins ultimately won the World Series), I went to a playoff game with my family at the Hubert H. Humphrey Stadium. Sitting halfway up behind the third base line, I looked across the stadium and saw a band of people, perhaps ten seats wide, begin to stand up and then sit down, moving clockwise (perhaps that's why clockwise *is* clockwise) around the stadium. When this phenomenon, a so-called human wave, reached me, I stood up and sat down as well, feeling at once free, happy, and not at all in control of my actions. If you knew me, you would know just how odd this was.

The question we have to ultimately concern ourselves with is how these two ways of being – ontologies of being, if you will – can approach each other. We are already beyond the post-Cartesian critique of the self-in-isolation that still characterizes some of current (as opposed to Contemporary) and all of past psychoanalysis. James (1893/2007) had leapt past this critique even as Freud succumbed to a theory of the analysis of an intrapsychic self that only responded defensively to impingements upon it and later became only an *element* of a psychic structure dealing with other internal structures (objects as mental representations). What we

10 The self and its contexts

are about here is first to flesh out and set in context James's definition of what constitutes a self, and second to consider the nature of human waves in Network Studies and neuroscience terms along the lines that I have previously suggested (Leffert, 2013).

Psychoanalysis has not as yet approached the gap between the self and human waves;[1] indeed, it has been treated as one of Lyotard's (1983/1988) *différends*: conflicts between parties with such radically differing epistemologies that no agreement – even in how to resolve their differences – is possible. These differences include, among others, the nature of therapeutic discourse and its contents, dialogue, accessibility to consciousness, neuroscience, hermeneutics, and network studies. I will posit that instead of *différends* what we are dealing with is a matter of *différance* (Derrida, 1978, 1972/1982), in which the two strands – one of selves, the other of human waves – remain but are braided together in a kind of sheaf, distinct *autres*, always in relation to one another.

The world of clinical psychoanalysis should be a world of selves and their overlapping social networks. It is not. It is a world much taken up with theory; it should not be. There is little agreement among diverse authors concerning the nature and location of the self and, despite the appearance of the new science of Network Studies (Barabási, 2003, 2005; Christakis & Fowler, 2009), as yet little understanding of the nature of the bonds between individual selves that form these networks. Instead, psychoanalysts and psychotherapists[2] usually consider social relationships in terms of relational dyads (attachment pairs, analytic couples) or, at most, triads. New developments in the neurosciences should be taking up more of our time as they relate to clinical psychoanalysis. Since I last wrote on these subjects (Leffert, 2013), neuroscience and Network Studies have begun to approach each other, recognize that each has much to offer the other, and start to exchange information (Sporns, 2011). A new, very fast form of functional brain imaging, diffusion tensor imaging (DTI) (Assaf & Pasternak, 2008; Le Bihan et al., 2001), shows a promise of being able to map changes in the brain in response to its activities in real time. In addition to what all of these approaches will tell us about the self, they will also put therapists who prefer to think hermeneutically about their patients[3] under increasing pressure.

---

1 This is as true for the Relational and Intersubjective schools as it is for the Freudians and Kleinians.

2 I find the distinction between psychoanalysts and psychodynamically oriented psychotherapists of little practical merit, in that whatever particular clinical procedures we may be talking about, we will find some members of both groups carrying it out.

3 Throughout this book, I use the term *patient* to refer to the people that come to see me for help. I do so only in part because, as a physician, I grew up with the term. But far more important to me is that it refers to people who come to us for help and healing, concepts that will recur in the chapters ahead. *Client* seems (to me at least) cooler and distant from healing and care. My only regret is that contemporary clinicians with other degrees are not trained to use it. However, it is worth noting that both Rollo May (1958b) and Ella Freeman Sharpe (1950/1968), the gifted second-generation psychoanalyst who was originally trained as an English professor, both use the term *patient* to refer to the people they treated.

The self

Heinz Kohut (1977, 1984) introduced contemporary American psychoanalysts and psychotherapists to the idea of a depth psychology of the "tragic man" (1977, p. 132), manifesting a damaged self and impaired selfobjects, existing beside the older, more usual psychoanalytic depth psychology of the "guilty man" (p. 132), beset with anxiety. The former involved a self that was, perforce, located within the psychic apparatus, while the latter involved a psychic apparatus taken up with isolated drives whose expression was inhibited by intrapsychic conflict. Kohut's healthy self is a continuous self; discontinuity involves fragmentation and should always be guarded against. This danger, he said, led him to terminate the second analysis of "Mr. Z" (Kohut, 1979). Kohut had chosen, in effect, to mount a conservative critique of ego psychology and libido theory, perhaps in the hope that traditionally minded psychoanalysts would find it more palatable. But what if he was wrong about all of that *except* for the central importance of the self?

I would argue first, as I have in the past (Leffert, 2010, 2013), that what Kohut terms "depth psychologies," and I call competing schools of metapsychology, represent collections of artificial and unstable constructs operating as closed systems, unsupported by direct observation and unable to survive deconstruction. In keeping with this view, Roy Schafer (1979), in a not recent paper cited only eight times in our literature, observes procedurally that "what makes each school a school is its having a substantial body of literature and eminent members who make persuasive claims as to their special vision of the psychoanalytic truth and the results to be obtained by those who share this vision" (p. 346). Truth does seem to be in the eye of the beholder and in no way guaranteed by its partisan connections. There are many thoughtful and sensitive clinicians in our field who have had important and clinically useful ideas, but to make these into metapsychologies at the pinnacle of truth only offers constructs that beg for subsequent deconstruction.

Second, along with James (1893/2007), I would contend that the self is not simply a psychical structure, cannot be just a psychic structure;[4] just what it is we will discuss shortly. Third, selfobjects are also constructs, and the real self as opposed to the constructed self is, or attempts to be, very much taken up with objects in the external world, *not* their internal representations. Finally, tragic man (or woman) and guilty man are, to the extent that they exist, existential states of the self, not representatives of competing metapsychological doctrines.

When we try to get a fix on the self in order to talk about it, we find psychoanalytic authors (as well as neuroscientists and philosophers) in a jumbled confusion of self, selves, bodies, and self-representations. As if that weren't enough, there are more problems. *Experientially*, most of the self is wrapped up with consciousness and has been with us in that capacity for a very long time. Then there is the problem of the relations of the self with its world. This too is complicated by the fact that we mostly experience ourselves autocentrically (Schachtel, 1959) as quite

---

4 I'm getting ahead of myself here, but that would make it a self-representation.

12 The self and its contexts

separate from others and unique, since our experience of other selves is different. Sullivan (1938/1971a, 1950/1971b), in an oft-referenced comment, observes that any such thoughts of uniqueness are entirely illusory. But I think that he misses the point. It is not that most of us not of a narcissistic bent do not know that there are other people around who are quite like us (a kind of normative knowing), but rather that our means of knowing and perceiving them results in a different kind of awareness than we have of ourselves. What, then, have psychoanalysts made of this jumble?

The self in psychoanalysis

To begin contemporaneously and then work backwards, Stephen Mitchell (1991) was aware of the definitional problem and lack of consensus surrounding it.

Stern (1997) illustrates the problem when he describes Sullivan's ideas about the self as involving "multiple and discontinuous selves *or* self-states" and "most particularly the idea that a self *or* self-state can be understood" (p. 147, italics added) in terms of multiple interpersonal fields. The problem is with the "ors." This particular conjunction means to say that selves and self-states are equivalent, that they have fundamental properties in common; *they do not.* Where, then, is the self located, what is the nature of its states, of its multiplicity, of its representations, and where do they reside?

What Mitchell (1991) and Stern (1997) are most concerned with is defining the self as a relational self, inseparable from its interpersonal field. Bromberg (1996), Mitchell, Stern, and Sullivan (1938/1971a, 1950/1971b) share the view that the concept or the experience of a unified self is entirely illusory. It is worth noting that *none* of them offer us a definition of what a self might actually be. Stern (1997) goes so far as to posit a "multiple-self-theory" (p. 149), to wit, that selves are multiple and discontinuous. He further attributes widespread acceptance for such a hypothesis. We will have to see. Although they are able to free the self from consciousness as James (1893/2007) was unable to do, there remain two fundamental problems that cause these authors difficulty: navigating the real distinction between self and self-representation that they blur, and the location of the self.

Despite these assertions, the radical ego psychologists of the mid-twentieth century better understood the problems of a psychical self than many authors today. Rapaport (1957/1967) was very much aware of both the distinction between and the difficulties inherent in the concepts of self and self-representation.

> The self in subjective experience is something which can observe itself. [The problem is that] The self will have to be so defined in the psychological apparatus that it is observable by an ego function which is at the same time defined as a subsidiary organization within the self. [Yet] *The self cannot simply be re-defined. It is a concept that has been with man for a long time. . . .* [Instead] the self will have to be so formulated within the psychological apparatus that it

The self and its contexts **13**

is amenable to observation, though not necessarily to full inspection, because
many parts of it may be, like Erikson's identity, unconscious.

(*p. 689, italics added*)

Rapaport, unlike many authors who consider the self and some of its properties
without actually defining it, gets most of it right. He acknowledges its murkiness, its
relations with narcissism and identity, and is not as ready as some (Bromberg, 1996;
Mitchell, 1991; Stern, D.B., 1997; Sullivan, 1950/1971b) to abandon its common
usage. The one thing he does not consider, as other authors with the exception of
James (1893/2007) do not, is the possibility that the self might not reside within the
psychic apparatus, and what might follow from an acknowledgement of a different
location. I would posit such a change in location to be unavoidable.

George Klein (1976), in a rather business-like way, dispenses altogether with a
self-representation. The self is the single psychic apparatus of control, "the focus of
which is either an integration experienced in terms of a sense of continuity, coherence, and integrity, or *its impairment, as cleavage or dissonance*" (p. 8, italics added). As
far as the question of how conscious or unconscious of itself the self might be, Klein
observes (as he does about other psychic processes) that it is as conscious of itself (or
not) as it chooses or as it is compelled by internal or external circumstances to be.

Schafer (1976) viewed the widespread interest in the self appearing in the work
of mid-century psychoanalytic authors as arising out of a growing sense of failure
in what was then standard psychoanalytic theory and technique. He observed, "in
recent decades particularly, many psychoanalysts have become increasingly dissatisfied with the apparent remoteness, impersonality, and austerity, as well as inordinate
complexity of modern ego psychology" (p. 191). He goes further, however: "What
I am suggesting comes to this; the popularity of concepts of self and identity is
symptomatic of a fundamental shift toward a modern [contemporary] conception
of theory making and a modern psychological concern with *specifically human phenomenology*" (p. 192, italics added).

Among those authors, Winnicott (1952/1975a, 1945/1975b) and Kohut (1971,
1977) are best known for their interest in the self and their willingness to deal with
its definition. At this distance, it is hard to remember that, while Winnicott was
accepted in Britain, both authors were, in their day, considered heretical by orthodox American audiences. Winnicott observes developmentally that "the basis of a
self forms on the fact of the body which, being alive, not only has shape, but which
[sic] also functions" (1971/1989, p. 270). He is dissatisfied with his efforts at definition but perseveres, observing, "there is much uncertainty even in my own mind
about my own meaning. . . . For me the self, which is not the ego, is the person who
is me, who is only me, who has a totality based on the operation of the maturational
process" (p. 271). He believes (Winnicott, 1952/1975a) that the self does not start
out as an individual but rather differentiates out of an individual-environmental
matrix. This position, favored by both Middle Group analysts in Britain and later
Relational theorists here in the United States, has not stood up in the face of

14 The self and its contexts

developmental research into infant attachment (e.g., Ainsworth, Bell, & Stayton, 1974; Bowlby, 1979[1977]/1984, 1991).

Kohut (1971), early on in his writing, attempts to define the self as a structure within the mind, cathected with psychic energy and represented in the various psychic structures. In his later works (Kohut, 1977), he refers to the self as "the center of the individual's psychological universe . . . not knowable in its essence" (p. 311).

It is subjectivity and the limits of knowability that are ultimately of importance to Kohut, concerns that, as Teicholz (1999) observes, move him towards the postmodern camp.

The holistic self – towards a definition

Contemporary psychoanalytic authors have been justly critical of both Freud and the classical metapsychologists that followed him for attempting to deal with the mind in isolation. Stolorow (2011) in particular has labeled the shift from a mind in isolation to a relational mind as involving a similar shift from Cartesian to post-Cartesian thinking. The problem here is that Descartes's (1641/1999) quarrel was not with a relational mind – it was with the idea of mind being connected to body, and led to his positing a dualism of mind and body. Descartes believed that mind was a non-physical substance. True post-Cartesian thought dictates that self must inseparably include mind and body, a seemingly obvious point the ramifications of which have not been much considered.

One such ramification is that we are seeking a systems definition of self as a holism, comprising a single complex system (Laszlo, 1972/1996).[5] What this means is that although the self can for heuristic purposes be divided into subsystems, these systems lack ontology, they do not signify, and the whole of the self is both different from and unequal to the sum of its parts. As I have found in the past (Leffert, 2010, 2013), a good place to start in seeking to define self is Walter Freeman's (1995) definition of what he calls the biology of meaning:

> The biology of meaning includes the entire brain and body, with the history built by experience into bones, muscles, endocrine glands, and neural connections. A meaningful state is an activity pattern of the nervous system and body that has a particular focus in the state space of the organism, *not* in the physical space of the brain. (p. 121, italics added)

I would highlight two particular elements of this definition. The first is that the history of the self is encoded both in its physical elements and in its particular neural connections. The second is that a "meaningful state" comprises an "activity pattern" of the whole works. This is important. What we are up against is the

---

5 For a discussion of complexity theory, see Marion (1999) and Coburn (2002).

The self and its contexts **15**

obvious tension between a process view of self as opposed to a physical structural view. A number of approaches are open to us in dealing with this problem. The easiest one is to simply say that there is a dialectical relationship between the two and leave it at that. Not entirely satisfying. Another approach is to posit that this is a manifestation of *différance* (Derrida, 1978; Malabou & Derrida, 1999/2004) and that the two are *autres*. Also not satisfying. Still another way is to observe that a self is alive, that life bridges the gap and without it we have only *remains*. Life needs to be in our definition. A final approach would be to draw on quantum mechanics as a metaphor (maybe more than a metaphor) – that, depending on our view, we are describing either a process or a structure. This is not as whimsical as it might first appear. The entire self is a creature in motion; one has only to specify that the motion in question is taking place on many levels: atomic and molecular, intra- and extra-cellular, and, finally, motion of the self in the world. I believe that all of these possibilities are operative in our self and its *existence* or *being*, about which we will have much more to say in the two chapters that follow.

Contrary to personal experience, the self *is* largely unknowable. There are many reasons for this. On the simplest of levels, it has properties that we are as yet unable to measure. As a complex system, its behavior is at best partly predictable and unpredictable based on knowledges of its antecedents, even if the latter could be entirely known. Finally, the postmodern concepts of irreducible subjectivity and interreferentiality render it indeterminable and immeasurable. Before moving on, however, there is more to say about the body's participation in the holism of self.

Evidence from the body side of the holistic self

It is a matter of some interest how psychoanalysts who think or write about the self manage to consider the body as if it were only an *object of the self*. For some, who are of a hermeneutic bent, considering the body would make such a metatheory of technique impossible. Although overlooking the body in considerations of self may have been possible prior to the mid-twentieth century, it was no longer possible a half-century later, let alone in 2015.

If the body is thought of only in terms of being operated by the mind, there *perhaps* remains some option for leaving it out of the self. In the face of current neuroscientific and neurohormonal evidence (see, for example, Panksepp, 1998; Porges, 1998, 2009; Schore, 2009) that the body *profoundly* influences the mind, and that the two are deeply interreferential, even this position becomes untenable. I have previously covered this material in considerable depth (Leffert, 2013) and will approach it again here, but from a somewhat different point of view.

There is a growing body of literature, both on a macro and a mid level, in all of these areas that we could subsume under the general umbrella of Neuropsychoanalysis, much of which requiring that we consider the body as a part of the self. On a macro level, Schore (2002), in his critical discussion of self psychology, raises some of the very issues we have been discussing here. He observes that "when self

16 The self and its contexts

psychology, like psychoanalysis in general, *discards the biological realm* of the body, when it overemphasizes the cognitive and verbal realms, it commits Descartes's error" (p. 437, italics added).[6] We have already discussed how psychoanalysts have, in general, failed to comprehend the exact nature of Descartes's error. Schore appropriately refers us on to Antonio Damasio (1994), who has built a popular series of neuroscience books on this very subject and who describes this error as "the separation of the most refined operations of mind from the structure and operation of a biological organism" (p. 90). Damasio was also aware of the intimate connections between emotional and cognitive processes and the body, both of which were constantly resynthesizing or reimagining themselves.

Diffusion Tensor Imaging (Le Bihan et al., 2001) has come to offer a cogent illustration of how these two processes function intimately in parallel. DTI is able to map magnetic resonance images in three dimensions as it registers the movement of water molecules through neuron bundles, their axons, and their myelin sheaths. It makes possible the study of white matter[7] architecture. It provides heightened image contrast and the ability to map white matter pathways in two and three dimensions (Assaf & Pasternak, 2008). A recent paper (Sagi et al., 2012) that is of particular interest uses DTI to study the time scale of events in brain structure remodeling that accompany the emotional/cognitive events that demonstrate neuroplasticity. Long-term structural changes had been previously mapped over periods of weeks. The authors wished to explore what happened structurally in the brain in response to functional changes occurring in an individual adopting new procedural memories (Schacter, 1992, 1996) over a period of minutes or hours. These investigators were able to detect microstructural changes in the hippocampus and parahippocampus after a period of training as short as two hours. For our purposes, this finding demonstrates that the physical and psychological changes as a result of learning are aspects of the same process. One would have to also conclude that such changes need not be confined to the brain.

The information about the interrelations between mind and physical body (including the brain) is equally compelling. Stephen Porges (1998, 2009) has studied the X Cranial Nerve, the Vagus, that is comprised of efferent, unmyelinated, slow parasympathetic nerve fibers that control the heart and the smooth muscle of the gastrointestinal tract, as well as afferent fibers that communicate the states of these organ systems to the brain (Leffert, 2013). The Vagus is present across all classes of vertebrates. Porges posited a Polyvagal Theory of reciprocal function between brain and body: "It describes an evolving Vagus nerve and its role over the course of vertebrate phylogeny that begins in the lower classes of vertebrates with regulation

---

6 The same critique can also be leveled against Relational and Intersubjective psychoanalysis. It does not apply to phenomenological or existential psychoanalysis.

7 White matter is composed of axons and bundles of axons that transmit information from and between parts of the brain and the body.

of the heart and gastrointestinal tract and is co-opted in mammals, the order of primates, and then humans, for social purposes" (Leffert, p. 157). A second system operating in complementary fashion with the Vagus in fight-or-flight situations is comprised of the sympathetic nervous system. Unique to mammalian species is the addition of fast, myelinated fibers controlling heart rate and motor neurons, present in the Vagus and other cranial nerves, that control speech and facial expression. In primates and humans, the system grows in size and complexity. Along with the central nervous system and the facial muscles, the Vagus forms a brain-heart-face circuit (BHFC) that mediates social engagement through speech and facial expression.

The Polyvagal Theory (Porges, 1998, 2009) offers evidence of two forms of intimacy – courtship, and the formation of enduring social bonds between adults – in the mind-body self. Although unstudied as yet, it is entirely plausible that this system would behave similarly in the formation of enduring bonds between mother and infant. While courtship involves the BHFC (here operating as an intersubjective signaling system), bond formation is even more interesting. Briefly, the slow, unmyelinated visceral Vagus is co-opted by the BHFC and acquires a new function. The slowing of the heart and metabolism becomes associated with feelings of safety and trust. The BHFC also triggers the release of oxytocin and vasopressin (Panksepp, 1998) by the hypothalamus, which influence the source nuclei of the visceral Vagus in the medulla of the brain and facilitate both sexuality and the formation of longstanding relationships. In addition, oxytocin, released post-coitally in both partners, influences the cerebral cortex to facilitate bonding (Freeman, W.J., 1995; Panksepp, 1998). "Specifically, learning functions like priming (Schacter, 2001) that determine our beliefs, feelings, and perceptions are loosened and re-form around new, mutually determined, shared content" (Leffert, 2013, p. 121). This is not an argument for the neural specificity of emotions (Porges, 2009) but rather for the brain, mind, and body being subsumed under the holism of the self.

A striking further piece of evidence demonstrating the affective interreferentiality of body and mind as components of a holistic self appeared recently (Finzi & Wasserman, 2006; Wollmer et al., 2012). Unsurprisingly, some significant percentage of depressed individuals demonstrates glabellar[8] frown lines. What *is* surprising and indeed very interesting is that when Wollmer and associates locally administered botulinum toxin (Botox) to relax the frown lines of their depressed subjects in a double-blinded, placebo-controlled research protocol, those individuals felt significantly better and their depressions were ameliorated. Given Porges's (1998, 2009) work on the brain-heart-face-circuit (BHFC), are these findings really all that surprising?

It is important to add a further word about where emotions fit into all of this. Self/mind/brain researchers of whatever scientific discipline take the position that emotions reside in the head and often rely on brain ablation or injury studies to

---

8 The glabella is the smooth area of the forehead located between the eyebrows.

18 The self and its contexts

prove it. We are saying something quite different, and Wollmer and associates (2012) offer but one instance of it. Freeman (1995) describes emotions as self-states in the state-space of the *entire* organism. Emotions are emergent properties of the self, *not* the mind or brain. It is the self who feels, just as it is the self who is conscious.

Self-representation and self-perception

If, as I have argued, we acknowledge the clear distinction between the self and the self-representation/self-perception system, the many problems associated with smushing all three of them together as intrapsychic phenomena disappear. Although it requires some reformulation of psychoanalytic ideas melded into clinical theory, it brings with it the tremendous advantage of offering a starting point for a psychoanalysis that actually *exists*.[9] As opposed to a construct or series of constructs, it provides a reliable subject of observation, measurement, and therapeutic discourse.

Although I have previously (Leffert, 2013, Chapter 4) talked about self-representation and self-perception independently as separate subjects, I find that I am no longer able to do so for two reasons. The first is that the two are intimately connected and continuously interreferential. The second, following from this, is that this system is a *process* entity; it is not about structures, although there is some (but only some) concentration of these particular process activities in the brain's cortical midline architectures (as we will discuss in the section on neural hardware). Perception is a continuously changing representation, which, in turn, changes what is being perceived.

It is through this system that the self chooses to be aware or unaware of itself or parts of itself. The self is both the subject and the object of these inquiries. They take place when we are inactive, in the autocentric mode, or in what neuroscientists (Molnar-Szakacs & Arzy, 2009; Spreng, Mar, & Kim, 2008; Uddin, Iacoboni, Lange, & Keenan, 2007) refer to as the default state. They are variously accurate or precise. Only parts of the system can become conscious; aspects of representation and perception become conscious or have consciousness thrust upon them (as a result of external or internal physical events) out of choice or necessity.

This is perhaps a good point at which to reconsider briefly the multiple-self hypothesis and the notion of the illusory nature of the experience of a unified self raised by several authors (Bromberg, 1996; Mitchell, 1991; Stern, D.B., 1997; Stern, S., 2002; Sullivan, 1950/1971). By *observing* that the self is not a psychical structure (as has been so messily posited) but a singular mind-body holism *distinct from its representations*, we can dispense with speculations about multiple selves. However, we must situate the multiplicity that, if not part of self, nevertheless exists. At any

---

9 Clinical theory taken up with treating the "ego" or the "bipolar self" or the "unconscious" should be at once more obviously problematic than it has seemed (beginning with Freud) over the decades to be.

The idea that the experience of a unified self is illusory is also not quite on the mark. Illusions are designed and perpetrated to deceive or mislead; the perception of a unified self, an outcome of *representation*, is a product of integration, of synthetic functioning. We are and remain the same person (even though we behave and represent ourselves to ourselves and to others as different at different times and in different circumstances) and know that we are. It is a great necessity in allowing us to operate in the world in the same ways that sensory perceptions (not collections of recordings of light or sound waves) allow us to do.[10] Indeed, failures of these integrative and synthetic functions do occur. Whether caused by psychopathology or by licit or illicit drug use, they are accompanied by varying degrees of dysphoria (more often greater than lesser) and notably impair many kinds of normative psychical function. Extreme forms of such failure exist in the fragmentation of self-representation/perception occurring in acute psychotic processes, in splitting observed in persons suffering from borderline personality disorder, and in multiple personality disorder. Failure of representations of the body can reach psychotic proportions, such as what is seen in anorexia nervosa (Bruch, 1962). Somewhat less severe deficits in self-representation/perception exist in dissociative states occurring acutely or chronically in response to trauma.

The self (often? mostly?) is *experienced* singly and in isolation. However, experience is not being. The self is radically disautonomous; if truly isolated, in a sensory deprivation tank for example, its cognitive activities and sense of having boundaries begin to decay fairly quickly. This is not an experience of self without world or other, but rather an experience of unstable boundaries, loss of time sense and decay of cognitive function. The *experience* of self is situated in consciousness; unconsciously, all kinds of complex information is always entering and changing the self, which then sends out information of its own. For any of this to make sense, self and self-representation/perceptions must be processes, not structures.[11]

The self-representation/self-perception system has another, singularly important property. In keeping with its process nature, its components are active rather than static and capable of past and future simulations (what happened then/what will

---

10 Perceptions are integrative in the following manner. Any given visual image that we perceive as being out in the world is comprised of 20% information moving upstream from the retinas and optic nerves and 80% information moving downstream from the cerebral cortex, a product of prior sensory experience (Gregory, 1997).

11 This is in no way some radical, contemporary idea. Contrary to the Strachey translation and despite his unfortunate sketch, Freud (1923/1961a), as Brandt (1966) tells us, viewed ego psychology as a process model. Rapaport and Gill (1959) also defined psychic structures as "configurations of processes with slow rates of change" (p. 157). Processes can also include physical elements; bone, for example, is a configuration of processes with a slow rate of change. Finally, being is a process.

20 The self and its contexts

happen if). What we are talking about are internal working models (IWMs). We have become so accustomed to the usage of this term by attachment theorists (see Ainsworth et al., 1974; Bowlby, 1973; Main, 1991; Main, Kaplan, & Cassidy, 1985) to describe infants, caregivers, and their relationship that we fail to recognize or remember that it has an earlier and broader origin in a short work by Kenneth Craik (1943/1952), *The Nature of Explanation*. He describes IWMs in a couple of different ways, but this is the more thought-provoking:

> By a model we thus mean any physical or chemical system which has a simi-lar relation-structure to that of the *process* it imitates. By "relation-structure" I do not mean some obscure non-physical entity which attends the model, but the fact that it is a physical working model which works in the same way as the process it parallels, in the aspects under consideration at any moment. Thus, *the model need not resemble the real object* pictorially . . . but it works in the same way in . . . essential respects. (p. 51, italics added)

This was pretty sophisticated thinking for 1943.

IWMs within the self-representation/self-perception system are multidimen-sional models that display at times contradictory properties. They contain spatial, relational, and temporal information; they are contextual and phenomenologi-cal. They are largely unconscious, with parts of them coming into consciousness as global contexts dictate. Parts of the models are constantly being updated with new internal, external, and cognitive information that is being processed both consciously and unconsciously. They are the objects of metacognitive monitor-ing (Main, 1991) that include planning and checking outcomes. (Metacognitive monitoring remains phenomenological.) Incorporated into these models of self and other is a synthetic function, Theory of Mind (ToM). Its major characteristic is the ability to formulate a sense of others as being more or less like us, having their own centers of cognition and motivation just as we do, being able to think like us or have their own separate thoughts (even though our manner of experiencing them *is* different than our experience of ourselves). It offers the ability to empathize, to cooperate, to see things from another's perspective, and to deceive; it is uniquely human (Gallagher & Frith, 2003). Severe failures in developing a ToM exist in autism (Baron-Cohen, Leslie, & Frith, 1985), while less severe but also debilitating failures exist in narcissistic conditions and in Asperger's syndrome.

With such processes in operation, we would expect the models to be at least roughly accurate. Alas, this is not always the case. Distortions can be introduced as a result of isolated perceptual errors or, more systematically, as a result of develop-mental psychopathology. Deficient attachment experiences at the hands of caregiv-ers manifesting severe relational failures lead to faulty IWMs, which cannot model a sound relationship between self and intimate others. In severe cases, a single model cannot contain the disparate attachment experiences of the child, resulting in dis-organized, self-containing, multiple, fragmented models. IWMs are metastable and highly resistant to change. This is all well and good – but how do we understand this stability without the usual recourse to repression and regression/fixation[12] and without producing only circular arguments? We can answer this question from outside of both psychoanalysis and attachment theory if we think in complex and postmodern terms.

Complex systems (such as IWMs and the mind/brain) manifest phenomena called strange attractors that draw other parts of the system towards them.[13] These attractors, in this case of a normative or faulty IWM, are arranged in basins. One *can* shift them out of these arrangements, but in the absence of a true phase shift, they will return to their original architectures (Freeman, W.J. & Barrie, 2001; Freeman, W.J., Chang, Burke, Rose, & Badler, 1997). We have all observed this process clinically, when a change in a patient's thinking or feeling shifts in response to an intervention, only, after a time, to return to his old patterns. These arrangements of attractors can shift for good or ill as a result of effective psychoanalysis or major life-changing events. Although *less intensive* forms of psychotherapy can be highly beneficial, they cannot, almost by definition, change these fundamental architectures.

It may be occurring to some readers to be asking: What *is* the point of this conversation about the self and its ramifications? A case illustration[14] should help to bridge these discussions of the properties and contents of the self and their clinical appearance.

Roger was a physician early in the first year of his psychiatry residency when he was referred to me by a psychoanalytically oriented attending physician on the ward where he was assigned. It seemed that his going about his business on the ward irrespective of the feelings or concerns of the staff had caused something of a minor uproar. As Roger told me in our first meeting, he had little interest in these issues that, he thought, grew out of their inability or unwillingness to take care of his patients' needs in a prompt fashion. He felt this grew out of their laziness or incompetence and, as he told me, he "may have mentioned this 'fact' once or twice." While somewhat aghast at his obliviously narcissistic delivery, I was not inclined to entirely dismiss his views out of hand. It should be noted that, however he treated the ward staff, he *cared* for his patients, often difficult, psychotic people, in a sensitive fashion. However it might have looked, this was not simply some narcissistic problem.

---

12 Again, contrary to Strachey, Freud always used the concepts of repression, regression, and fixation together (Leffert, 2013, Chapter 5) as parts of an inseparable single process.

13 The reader can find a more complete discussion of what follows in Chapters 3 and 4 of Leffert (2010).

14 In the present volume I will, as I have in the past, offer composite case illustrations. I do so for two reasons: first, in the interests of preserving confidentiality, and second, because this material is offered for illustrative purposes, and the clearer the illustration, the better. Many psychoanalytic authors offer case material out of the mistaken notion that they are offering clinical proof of some hypothesis they are asserting. While clinical evidence, depending on how it is collected, *can* prove some hypotheses, the inevitably subjective case vignettes appearing in our literature do not constitute such evidence.

22 The self and its contexts

But what Roger *wanted*, why *he* had come to see me, and what I focused on, was a fulfilling relationship with a woman he could love (no mention of her feelings here, I noted). The few relationships he had had (one of which had led to an unfortunate marriage and divorce) were painful and disappointing. He was deeply unhappy. He had seen a very supportive analyst weekly during his internship in another city, felt he had been helped, and wanted to go further. Although he hadn't mentioned it, he was thinking of an analysis and readily agreed to my suggestion that this would be the best course of action for us to pursue. A modest trust fund, left to him on his mother's death, made this financially feasible, albeit at a somewhat reduced fee. All this was quickly accomplished in a businesslike manner. Although he appeared to have no interest in me at all, it was clear that he listened very carefully to whatever I said, mulled things over, and asked thoughtful questions. I did not doubt that, in the process, I had passed muster. Had I been the sort of analyst that met questions with silence, I think he would have soon been gone.

In the months that followed, I learned a number of things about him. He tended to be solitary and surprisingly reserved, given the dramatic circumstances of his referral. He was the only child of a mother who was fiercely loyal and caring to him while being covertly seductive. When he was six months old, she began to experience a series of illnesses and surgeries that made her physical and psychological availability unreliable. She died of a heart attack when he was in college. Roger had felt very little at the time and had been unable to mourn her. A partial diagnosis of organized, insecure attachment readily suggested itself. Roger's father was a bright but passive ne'er-do-well of a man who was highly ambivalent towards his son and later envied his accomplishments. The successful, albeit depressed men in his mother's family provided the boy with his only useful role models and mentoring. Unfortunately, they also offered themselves up as subjects with whom he could depressively identify. A question about his early schooling yielded the information that when he changed schools in second grade, he had been unwilling to go unless a parent accompanied him and stayed with him for a while. He did not know, then or now, why this was so, and hesitated to call it a school phobia because he had *felt* nothing. The latter was a frequent reaction in emotionally difficult situations. He understood that his choice of a career in medicine had much to do with fantasies of curing his mother; his captivation by psychiatry had more to do with his own interests. Descriptively, Roger was a rather bruised self, focused on itself, with some shakiness of boundaries.

His relations with women were startlingly similar. He would find himself attracted to a woman, but he would not be sure why. He would ask her out, feel immediately committed to her, and make his "feelings" known. Once this had occurred, he began to feel secure in her presence and anxious in her absence. She would usually be taken aback by his excessive connection and end the "relationship." He would feel considerable pain and anxiety at the loss. When I asked him what he thought these women had felt about him, he responded with surprise that he had never thought about it and had no idea. Unfortunately, some years before

The self and its contexts **23**

the analysis, he had met Janet, a borderline woman in search of a husband (never mind who), and three months later they were married. They had a tempestuous relationship characterized mostly by her affective storms, which Roger had felt showed she cared for him. Janet walked out on him several times before leaving for good after two years. He was devastated and tearful each time and unable to function for several days. Roger (while still definitely being Roger) was a very different person in his relationships with women as compared to how he was in his work, with me, and in other areas of his life. As I write about him here, as a self in relation to women, the resemblance to Quoyle, the protagonist in Annie Proulx's (1994) *The Shipping News*, seems unmistakable, as is that of Janet to Pedal, his borderline wife (played by Cate Blanchett in the screen version of the book).

My purpose here is not to provide a therapeutic account of Roger's analysis (that will come later when we return to Roger in Chapters 3, 5, and 6), but rather what we came to understand about him, his attachments, and his feelings as they unfolded over the course of our relationship. Over the next several years (paralleling his didactic studies in psychiatry and psychoanalysis), it became clear that a substantial amount of clinical theory did not apply to his emotional afflictions or lead to any observable changes in his life.[15] Looking at what conflicts he did have, considering his narcissistic injuries, or casting his life in terms of an unresolved Oedipal nightmare that dominated him thereafter led nowhere in the analysis or out of it. In the absence of their utility, I referenced his illness to the self, as I have been defining it. Two of the problems pertaining to the self, or particularly to its representational/perceptual system, *were* highly relevant. His attachment models were deficient, reflecting his wildly mixed experiences of his mother's uncontrollable unreliability, her manipulative seductiveness, her loyalty to him and his welfare, and, in the present, his anxious clinging to any woman stepping away from him. An attachment based therapeutic encounter,[16] as cogently described by several authors (Eagle, 2003; Holmes, 2010; Lichtenberg, 2003; Slade, 1999a), would need to include an understanding of Roger's limitations in the development of a ToM, a function of the self and a hope to modify his Internal Working Models. Slade (1999b) has observed that both the mother's representations of her own attachment experiences and of her relationship with her child affect the quality of *his* attachment experiences. What is required developmentally is a "link between the quality and coherence of parental narratives and the child's capacities for affect

---

15 Our field has seen much discussion of our subjectivity and the severe limitations it places on our ability to know what is actually taking place in the therapeutic situation (Leffert, 2013). As a result, I tend to follow Renik (2007) in this matter of the proof of the pudding and look for changes in a patient's life to confirm that an analysis *is* taking place and is on the right track.

16 As will be discussed in Chapter 7, by an attachment based therapeutic encounter, I do *not* mean to suggest the possibility of re-opening and repairing the original attachment experience. What I do mean is an approach that takes cognizance of Roger's attachment issues as they are observable phenomenologically and can be approached in the present.

24 The self and its contexts

regulation and symbolization" (p. 801). The child's ability to represent himself and his inner experience grows out the mother's ability to represent him. The relationship between mother and child's representational processes involves "metacognitive monitoring, reflective functioning, and mentalization" (p. 801). Failures in these processes (occurring for Roger as a result of the sporadic availability of his mother and the competitive disinterest of his father) result in limitations in the awareness of the child's, and later the adult's, own thoughts and, even more importantly, feelings, as well as those of others.

So I thought this back to Roger. I returned to two of my early observations: his interaction with the ward staff that had led to his seeking analysis with me, and the failure to register in his descriptions of women he wanted to date what they might think or feel. Roger had only thought of his own feelings. It was not that he didn't know that other people had feelings, feelings with the same names as the feelings he had. It was that he did not know *whether* they felt them, that what they felt *could* be (or not be) more or less what he felt at a given time. This was to be sure an empathic failure, but one of a very particular kind. Suffering was perhaps the first feeling he grasped in his work, could feel in himself, and could and did empathize with. It had taken a long time for him to experience feelings within himself. He then progressed to being able to identify them in others. What eluded him (for some time it eluded me that it eluded him) was whether having the feelings felt the same to them as it did to him. This proved to be the key that made us able to turn the subjects of his relationships into real people like him. Two observations confirmed this: The narratives in his sessions became livelier, and he began to *have* relationships in his life. Actually he became quite popular.

Roger's problems can be understood in a number of complementary ways. He suffered from a failure of a capacity for secure attachment that continued to plague his contemporary relationships with women (but also with men). His IWMs were problematic, but in highly focused rather than global ways. The threats to the self, and the suffering he endured resulting from these failures, produced a defensive narcissism manifested at times by overt grandiosity and defensive aggressive behavior. From a postmodern perspective, he remained mired in the childhood rules governing the acquisition of knowledge (in this case about relationships), and the episteme of that period with its autocentric focus continued to dominate him in the present. He was often confused when recourse to this episteme failed to help him understand what was happening in the relationships around him. From a phenomenological perspective, he lacked useable context for situating himself and, as we will discuss in later chapters, his ways of being in the world and the quality of his embeddedness in it were also impaired.

A brief look at the neural hardware behind these processes

There is certainly physical evidence of a self for those who would look for it, a self given to occasional lapses, it is true, but one that is of a piece and fits the rubric of a complex collection of processes with highly variable rates of change. But what can we say about the self-representation/self-perception system? Do we have any neurocognitive evidence for its existence outside of that obtained from attachment research and psychoanalytic observation? Indeed, two large-scale neural networks (distributed processing systems, Rumelhart & McClelland, 1986) have been separately identified as operating jointly in the representation and experience/perception of self and other (Uddin et al., 2007). The mirror neuron system (MNS), already familiar to psychoanalytic readers (e.g., Iacoboni, 2007; Iacoboni et al., 1999), acts to form a bridge between self and other, and is mobilized when an action performed by an other is performed or observed by the self. The right cerebral hemisphere, particularly the orbital pre-frontal cortex, is a center of MNS functioning.[17] The MNS inputs sensory perceptions of facial expression and motor activity in self and other. It outputs mirroring activity of facial expression and body movements or intrapsychic simulation in IWMs.

A neuroscience literature has been accumulating in the latter half of the last decade (Molnar-Szakacs & Arzy, 2009; Spreng et al., 2008; Uddin et al., 2007) concerned with the functional neuroanatomy of the self-representational/self-perceptual system. In a review article, Molnar-Szakacs and Arzy note in particular that the brain has a "default mode" that includes awareness of self-representation that is suspended when goal-directed behavior is undertaken (the autocentric/allocentric dichotomy). It is apparently possible to be self-aware *or* active, not both. Spreng and colleagues (2008) performed a meta-analysis of neuro-imaging studies and identified a group of cortical midline structures (CMS) that comprise this default network. They identified four higher-level functions of the self-representational/self-perceptual system: autobiographical memory, navigation,[18] theory of mind, and default mode. As they put it, "The MNS together with the 'default network' have been hypothesized to represent abstract and concrete aspects of the self, respectively, and interact to give rise to a unified representation of the self as a social being" (p. 369). Self-representation "emerges as an integration of representations across the domains of time, space, physical embodiment and social cognition" (Molnar-Szakacs & Arzy, 2009, p. 365). The CMS project laterally into all the lobes of the cerebral cortex, and are also responsible for two related high-level synthetic functions of self-representation: self-projection, the ability to place oneself in simulations of different times and places; and scene construction, the ability to mentally construct fictitious scenes and experiences. Both these functions can include representations of others as well as the self (e.g., my representations of Roger and me).

---

17 Although perhaps unnecessary to state, it should be noted that such statements in no way mean to imply that the brain is a system of independent modules, but rather a holistic system including areas manifesting some degree of concentration or specialization of function.
18 Navigation is our very own GPS system. It maintains topographical orientation and a perception of where we are, where we're going, and the route we will take to get there. This hard-wired sub-system functions better in some individuals than in others.

26 The self and its contexts

These affective and cognitive representations of self and others, along with all the bells and whistles we have been describing, are easily capable of being brought to consciousness; the hardware behind them, the CMS and the MNS, are not. The activity of these combined systems pretty well encompasses the processes we psychoanalysts have been writing about from intersubjective, postmodern, and relational perspectives for the last 30 or more years.

Collections of selves: network studies

One can almost say that the only social networks that have interested psychoanalysts per se are those encompassed developmentally by the Oedipal triangle and contemporaneously by patient and therapist. True, for a time in the 1960s, some of us became interested in groups (concurrent with an interest in existentialism), but that interest largely waned long ago. Although the disautonomy of the self has been the subject of some current psychoanalytic interest (Hoffman, 1996; Stern, D.B., 1997; Stolorow, 2011; Stolorow, Atwood, & Brandshaft, 1994; Stolorow, Orange, & Atwood, 2002), that interest has been mostly confined to the areas of subjectivity, unknowability, and reductive critiques of postmodern thought dependent on a neo-pragmatist concept of self as an unstable identity category. I have argued elsewhere (Leffert, 2010, 2013) for both the disautonomy and interreferentiality manifest in social embedding that nonetheless both allows for and mandates an ontologically stable self. There has been little interest in postmodern and neuro-biologically based critiques of knowability (as distinct from subjectivity) and the disautonomy that they also mandate. The fact that the self is ontologically stable should not be taken to mean that it can be separated from the social matrix in which it is embedded.

The relatively new discipline of Network Studies looks at and quantifies social connections between individuals across multiple relational dimensions. It looks at many disciplines: biology, epidemiology, social science, and neuroscience, to name but a few. Network Studies looks at how individual members of networks (called nodes) are connected to each other and pass information (called contagion) from one to another. If multiple nodes are directly connected to the same individual, that individual constitutes a hub. Networks also demonstrate connections between nodes at wider degrees of separation; contagion generally peters out after three degrees of separation. Social networks can be made up of people, animals, automobile traffic, and the World Wide Web. We (parents, children, patients, and therapists) are members of many different social networks that affect us mostly outside of our awareness and influence what happens in an analysis and its course in ways we haven't yet thought much about. As I observed – controversially, I thought – "we are (mostly) prisoners of our networks, our mothers (mostly) get us into them, and our analysts (sometimes) loosen our ties to them" (Leffert, 2013, p. 138).

I can only offer a brief overview of Network Studies here. Like any new field of study, it is awash in disagreement and acrimony, and some of the material I'm discussing here will undoubtedly look different in a decade or so. I am drawing primarily on the work of Christakis and Fowler (Arbesman & Christakis, 2010; Bauer, 2003; Cacioppo, Christakis, & Fowler, 2009; Christakis, 2004; Christakis & Fowler, 2007, 2008, 2009) at Harvard.

Christakis and Fowler

Christakis and Fowler study single-contagion mid level networks; much but not all of their work has involved data collected as part of the Framingham Study (Christakis, 2004; Christakis & Fowler, 2007, 2008) begun in 1948 to study heart disease among the residents of Framingham, Massachusetts, and now in its third generation. Because of the ongoing records, including questionnaires containing unstudied data, they were able to study the spread of individual behaviors independent of concerns of sample choice bias.

They (Christakis & Fowler, 2009) develop a number of important concepts about social networks, their organization, and behavior. They are looking at social networks in the range of 160 nodes, the limiting number of the size of a functional group of human beings determined by Dunbar (1993) and bearing his name. Christakis and Fowler do not look at the effects of larger organizations or the smaller ones that are considered by Sporns (2011) and Nunez (2000). They also do not consider the fact that we are members of *multiple* social networks of different sizes, and that totality must influence how an individual behaves or feels in a particular network she belongs to. They do use the provocative term "superorganisms" to describe these social networks, which hints at the properties of complex systems; networks can behave in ways its members do not know about or are incapable of knowing about. The same may be true for network observers, that is, us. They rightly insist that, "to know who we are we must understand how we are connected" (Christakis & Fowler, 2009, p. xiii). This speaks directly to the importance of contextuality that has been of much interest to contemporary psychoanalysts (e.g., Stolorow, 2011; Stolorow & Atwood, 1992) but makes possible its study on a much broader level.

Christakis and Fowler (2009) proceed to define a number of network properties and characteristics common to social networks. They refer to a member of a network they are studying as an *ego* and an individual they are connected to or influenced by as an *alter*. Networks form and re-form based on homophily, how their members resemble each other. They do not consider the role of power relations (Lukes, 2005), which can determine what networks we are *allowed to join* and what connections to alters we are allowed to have. Social networks are characterized by positional and situational inequalities. Networks are connected in ways that we do not know, and knowledge (contagion) passes through a network unconsciously. We know lots of people but are generally close to only a few of them. We often don't know some of the members of our networks. "How we feel, what we know, whom we marry, whether we fall ill, how much money we make, and whether we vote

28 The self and its contexts

all depend on the ties that bind us" (p. 7). It makes sense to wonder how we could possibly participate in a psychotherapy or a psychoanalysis without acquiring fairly detailed knowledge of a patient's social networks (and our own). Our networks shape us, both on a moment-by-moment basis and in deeper, more long-term ways. We are influenced by our friends' friends *even if we do not know them.* This influence, this passing of contagion, is called *hyperdyadic spread.*

Christakis and Fowler (2009) posit that network properties need not be perceived or controlled by its members. Indeed, they observe that networks are best studied if their members are treated as zero-intelligence units. We would translate this as meaning that the members of a network are unconscious of the spread of contagion from one node to another. However, beyond a certain point, a network's properties are unknowable by its members *and* by individuals studying it. This follows from the fact that social networks are complex systems with all the properties of complexity, unknowability, and a whole greater than the sum of its parts that such systems manifest (Leffert, 2008). *Social networks manifest emergent properties.* They have lives of their own and act in ways their members are unaware of.

Critiques of network theory

Critiques of Christakis and Fowler's (2008, 2009) work have begun to appear in the literature. Three groups of authors – Lyons (2011), Noel and Nyhan (2011), and Shalizi and Thomas (2011) – believe that their statistical methods are flawed and unable to demonstrate the existence of contagion. In addition, Noel and Nyhan and Shalizi and Thomas believe that there is a secular problem here: that homophily confounds contagion. To a degree, this may be so. However, all of these authors, including Christakis and Fowler, fail to consider that contagion is defined as an unconscious process taking place between nodes; homophily is a different sort of process, at least some of which a network's members are aware of.

My own concerns center on the fact that we are all members of multiple social networks, some of which overlap, and this multiplicity affects behavioral outcomes and the spread of contagions in ways we cannot know or study. For example, I am a member of multiple social networks, three of which come immediately to mind. One such network is the psychoanalytic institute whose faculty I am a member of. A second network is my practice in which I am the single hub my patients are all connected to. A third is a social network of nodes to which I am connected through my wife's position at a university. The institute network has multiple hubs that could be mapped. There is some slight overlap with my practice network. At various times, there have been connections between my patients as well as through me. The social network involving my wife has lots of hubs and different connections, and it is independent of the other two. But all kinds of contagion can travel through me from one network to another, and the final outcome of these connections, how, for example, what I might learn at a scientific meeting affects what I say to patients, is very hard to know or quantify.

Clinical considerations

As clinicians, we have so far been largely unattuned to the role of social networks in our work with patients. This is entirely understandable, as it concerns a discipline scarcely a decade old. Regardless of theoretical orientation, as psychoanalysts and psychotherapists, we mostly approach our patients by affectively and cognitively studying their mostly dyadic relationships with a few significant others: parents, spouses, romantic partners, friends, and ourselves. These relationships exist on differing time scales. We do not consider how both ourselves and our patients are constantly being bombarded with information from multiple social networks each made up of many people, not just the customary two or, occasionally, three. As analysts we prioritize the individual, often a rare trait in the caring professions in these times of managed care. Network Studies asks us to shift our perspectives to also consider our patients as parts of larger groups that affect them in ways that they are at best partly aware of. What are we to make of all this information, and how are we to make use of it clinically?

I previously described (Leffert, 2013) working with a young woman who suffered from bulimia. She was very much a member of a social network of women also suffering with a variety of eating disorders at the college she attended. (We have all observed for decades how women often seemed to "catch" bulimia from each other.) She and they were aware of this homophily, but were unaware of its possible significance. Despite this awareness, I believed that they were *not* aware of the contagion spreading through the network about individuals' eating behaviors. Contagion is, by definition, unconscious (Christakis & Fowler, 2009). A year or two into the therapy, during which the patient's binging remained unchanged, I began making every effort I could to talk to her about the eating behaviors of others in her group, as well as how they interacted with each other. (I otherwise carried on the therapeutic work in my usual way.) I had posited that making the contagion conscious could loosen its control of my patient. What I found was that over the next few months her bulimia first lessened and then disappeared. Had I proved anything by altering my technique and then seeing a clearing of the symptom? Of course not. However, I do think the results were provocative.

More recently, a middle-aged attorney, James, came to see me with a history of largely superficial failed relationships. He was not aware of their superficiality but only that the woman he was most recently interested in had wanted nothing to do with him. He had played rugby at Cambridge with considerable success and still maintained contact with many of his teammates and classmates. This social network maintained itself on the basis of homophily. His university connections gave him something he was unable to get from his parents: a sense of belonging. With their success in their sport had come easy access to women, and this had continued, regardless of their marital status. I identified problems in his parents' marriage that included constant bickering and multiple infidelities on both their parts. We looked at their relationship but were unable to see beyond the intellectual to the emotional;

30 The self and its contexts

the treatment had no traction here. I again looked to the social network. When, as he often did, he talked about his friends, their marriages, and their relationships, I began to ask about and explore their behavior, connecting it to what was missing in his own life. No dramatic change occurred, but two things happened. He began to have a sense of something amiss with the relationships with women in his life, and his feelings about his parents, which had resisted engagement, started to become a focus of his interest. Again, proof? No, but I find in my clinical work that I have started looking for social networks and sometimes find them.

In this chapter, I have offered a definition of the self and how it is situated in its social and physical environment. We cannot consider self without world, as Heidegger (1927/2008) first posited and Stolorow (2011) and Orange (Orange, 2009; Orange, Atwood, & Stolorow, 1997) have since commented on. These considerations require a number of things of us. They set us on a path of phenomenology that will take us to new and very different places. In the area of our clinical work, these definitions require connections to the world that have only partly been thought about, among them that a therapy cannot be a closed hermeneutic; it can be an *open* hermeneutic, but some will not be pleased with that. Although psychoanalysis has not much considered the ontological basis of the self and its embedding in the world, they have been a central focus of Heidegger's as well as the phenomenologists that came after him. They are embodied in his concepts of being-in-the-world and of Dasein. It is in order to think together the self and the social and physical world that we now turn to phenomenology, Heidegger, and phenomenological psychoanalysis.

2
PHENOMENOLOGY AND EXISTENTIALISM

Introduction

Perhaps the best way to introduce this difficult chapter is by describing my own bottom-up path to phenomenology, rather than an immediate plunge into the murky waters of Continental philosophy.[1] I studied psychoanalysis in the 1970s, first as a psychiatric resident at Bronx Municipal Hospital Center, and subsequently as a psychoanalytic candidate at the then new San Diego Psychoanalytic Institute. The former largely consisted of an immersion in pure Freud,[2] while the latter, during the second half of that decade, saw the appearance of new ideas at an institute that was a component of the very orthodox and then still powerful American Psychoanalytic Association. This was an unusual time in that both students *and* faculty were simultaneously being introduced to the British Middle School, Self Psychology, and Object Relations theory.[3]

My own experience of the next two decades was less cloistered than it had been and more in keeping with the growing wider world of psychoanalysis. Relational Psychoanalysis and Intersubjectivity Theory made their appearance in the 1980s and brought with them a shift from one-person to two-person psychologies along

---

1 I am writing for a bipartite audience composed of readers who are already well read in these areas and others who are just coming to them with much interest but less familiarity.

2 I don't think any of us then realized, as many still do not, that a part of what we were reading was Strachey, *not* Freud, and that many (but not all) of the criticisms mistakenly leveled at the latter really belonged to the former. I have previously discussed this issue and others concerning reading Freud in considerable detail (Leffert, 2013, Chapter 5).

3 We were *not* introduced to the Existential analysis of Rollo May, or the Interpersonal analysis of Harry Stack Sullivan (both were taught then at the so-called independent institutes and are now of much wider interest). Neither were the ideas of Melanie Klein or Karen Horney ever mentioned. At the time, Relational Psychoanalysis and Intersubjectivity Theory did not yet exist.

32 Phenomenology and existentialism

with the first winds of postmodernism. Things would never be the same. Indeed, by the early 1990s, Mitchell (1992) had, in effect, pronounced classical psychoanalysis dead, or at least said it was no longer worth fighting about or discussing (which, after all, amounts to the same thing). But then a strange thing happened. Although some of the civil discourse between these new disciplines that Mitchell had forecast did take place, rancorous battles for standing, territory, and power appeared, just as they had in the not-so-good-old days.

In the first decade of the new century, two things gradually emerged. The first was that none of the several schools of psychoanalytic metapsychology could lay claim to the kind of standing they wished for or validate their knowledge claims. The second was that the newer schools were as bad as the old with respect to the kinds of knowledge claims they wished to make.[4] What these competing psychoanalytic theories of psychopathology and therapeutic action most closely resembled was a series of competing heuristics.[5] I began to pursue alternatives. I studied power and its inevitable relation to knowledge (Foucault, 1980, 1979/1995; Lukes, 2005), as seen in these competing theories and the organizations that clung to them. If all our theories lacked particular standing, I looked to (among other things) the analysis of narrative and meaning through the use of deconstruction within the clinical situation and, outside of it, turned to postmodernism, attachment, neuroscience, complexity, and systems theory (this is, and can only be, the briefest of sketches). The result was the two volumes (Leffert, 2010, 2013) that I have already cited too often that offer a series of discourses on therapeutic action and its relationship to these other disciplines. What I was about were the beginnings of a particular kind of psychoanalytic phenomenology that was cognizant of outside, extra-hermeneutic ontologies that simply could not be ignored as they were when Husserl (1913/1983) began writing about phenomenology early in the last century.

So why might we need phenomenology in general and Heidegger (1927/2008, 1927/2010) in particular? If we recognize that the premises derived from the existing psychoanalytic metapsychologies are fatally unstable local knowledges (Foucault, 1980), and that any new premise derived from some new metapsychology will be equally unstable and local, we are offered a limited number of options. One is to desist in our search for wider meaning entirely, and retain the plurality of local knowledges we now have (a majority of psychotherapists and psychoanalysts have, I think, implicitly done just that). After all, given the distinction between what therapists say and convey nonverbally and what they think theoretically, at

---

4 I recognize that this is not exactly a popular statement, but it should not be taken to mean that all of these schools did not have many good ideas (along with some bad ones, of course).

5 *Heuristics* (Kahneman, Slovic, & Tversky, 1982) is a very old term that dates back to the fourth century; there will be much more to say about it and its relation to psychoanalysis in chapter 5. The *OED* ("*Oxford English Dictionary,* 1989) defines a heuristic as a process that *may* solve or offer a shortcut to solving a given problem but gives no guarantee of doing so and, in fact, may also lead down a blind alley.

Phenomenology and existentialism **33**

the end of the day it may not really matter all that much. However, if we aspire to more, and if in some number of cases it actually *does* matter, then our search for wider meaning must turn to more stable knowledges of the subjective – that is, to a phenomenology of the therapeutic situation and its backdrop in neuroscience, complexity, and network studies. However, phenomenology brings with it its own share of problems – not the least of which is that, in philosophical terms, it is the study of the subjective experience of consciousness (at least for Husserl, 1913/1983; Heidegger, 1927/2008, did not so confine it), and we are very much interested in also studying *unconscious* experience as it can be understood today. For the present, suffice it to say that the experiencing subject is the self, not necessarily the *conscious* self, and that this problem has not gone unnoticed. A number of responses to it have been suggested (Boss, 1963; May, 1958b; May, Angel, & Ellenberger, 1958; Stolorow, 2011; Stolorow, Orange, & Atwood, 2002), some of which will be discussed here and some in Chapter 4, which provides[6] a more thorough look at unconsciousness and where it might reside.

If we are going to talk about Heidegger, phenomenology, and existential analysis, two issues must be considered: one more particularly about him, and the other being of a more general nature concerning the nature of philosophical discourse. The first involves how our view of Heidegger's work and our thinking about it are influenced by his being a member of the Nazi Party (Faye, 2009; Safranski, 1999/2002)[7] from 1933 until it was dismantled at the end of World War II. He could be considered a sympathizer for some years before 1933, and he never publicly apologized or recanted. This really leads into the wider question concerning the relation of an author to his text; postmodernism already has an answer to that – the two are to be considered independently – which we are free to subscribe to or not.

Heidegger the man

Heidegger's Nazism has been hotly debated from the postwar years into the 21st century; it has been minimized by some, while he has been personally vilified and his work discredited for it by others. A moral issue nevertheless remains here to be considered and judged by anyone approaching his work, as did Safranski (1999/2002) when he subtitled his Heidegger biography *Between Good and Evil*. The question is further complicated by the presence in his writings (Heidegger, 1927/2008) of ideas that clearly lie on the path to his later political beliefs. Dealing with the wide questions of Heidegger's life or offering a psychobiography is clearly

---

6 An earlier discussion of the problems inherent in thinking about unconsciousness in relation to classical topographical and structural psychoanalytic theory can be found in Leffert (2010, Chapter 5).

7 Boss, in his introduction to the Zollikon Seminars (Heidegger, 1987/2001), says he had the same reaction when first exposed to Heidegger's work. He first wanted to look into Heidegger's Nazi Party involvement before being willing to consider his philosophy or contact him.

34 Phenomenology and existentialism

beyond the scope of the present chapter. However, if we are to accept some of his contributions as uniquely important, we must also investigate aspects of his political and psychological life in order to separate the man from his work.

Heidegger (1927/2008) developed a phenomenology that began in his first work with Husserl (1913/1983). This came to involve being-in-the-world, which in turn involved first being part of a group, then a national group, then a national group with a charismatic leader (the *Führer* principle). How this progress may have been influenced by or enmeshed in the German defeat in World War I, the rise of National Socialism, and with it that of Adolf Hitler, remains a subject for speculation. He was much taken with National Socialism (Safranski, 1999/2002), and on May 1, 1933, ten days after his election as Rector of the University of Freiburg, he joined the Nazi Party. His rectorial address, as he planned the event, was to be preceded by the singing of the *Horst Wessel Lied*; afterward *Sieg Heil!* was to be shouted by all. In the address, Heidegger says that science must be the power that shapes the German university. But it soon becomes clear that, by science, he means to include some full and primordial essence of science that includes knowledge of the people (*das Volk*) and the destiny of the state, both as one with a spiritual mission.[8] He goes on to speak of three services: "labor service – military service – service to knowledge" (Safranski, 1999/2002, p. 246). He was much taken with the military spirit, and asked Professor Stieler, a former naval commander, to draft a code of honor for the university staff. Heidegger endorses the draft in which Stieler writes that the goal is to "cleanse our ranks of inferior elements and thwart the forces of degeneracy" (p. 253). He made subsequent appearances in Leipzig, Heidelberg, Tübingen, and Baden and spoke in a similar vein. He resigned the rectorship a year later and *ceased to be politically active* after that point, as one narrative goes (Safranski). According to Safranski, beginning in 1936, he began to speak out critically against the seductions of power offered by National Socialism – referring to it as a perversion of power – and was under surveillance by the Gestapo. However, he did not resign from the party, and at denazification proceedings held under the supervision of French occupying forces in 1949 (at which he neither recanted nor asked for forgiveness), he was stripped of his professorship and forbidden to teach. The ban on teaching was lifted in 1951.

Safranski (1999/2002) notes that Heidegger had portrayed his involvements with the Nazi government as less harmless than they in fact were. Faye (2009) indeed comments that to have a philosopher of Heidegger's international standing in their camp was a great political plum for the Nazis, even though his work was probably incomprehensible to nearly all of them. Although Heidegger did undoubtedly ally himself with evil, one has to ask how this was worse than the behavior of millions of Germans who did more and suffered less (or nothing) after the war as a result of their affiliations.

---

8 Foucault (2000b) and Lukes (2005) would argue (as would I) that Heidegger is simply being honest and explicit about the power relations inextricably intertwined with the acquisition of any knowledge.

Much has indeed been made of Heidegger's postwar silence concerning his Nazi past. Safranski (2002) explains (but does not justify) Heidegger's position: for him to distance himself from the murder of millions of Jews on public demand was to acknowledge that the public considered him to be complicit in their murders. The only *private* comment of Heidegger's that we have on the subject occurred when, sometime after the events of 1933–1934, he was asked by a former student how he could have done such things; he is said to have replied that it had been "the greatest stupidity of my life" (Petzet, 1983/1993, p. 37).

Postmodern thought maintains that author, text, and reader are separate and should be treated that way. The argument has been made (and I see some justification in it) that there *is* no text, only a series of readings, each different, even if they are by the same person. A further argument is that the meaning of a text derives exclusively from the thing itself, irrespective of the circumstances of its creation, authorship, or subsequent deployment. *Being and Time* was published in 1927, a half-dozen years before the full flowering of Heidegger's National Socialism in 1933–1934. I believe that we must accept that both positions – the text in isolation and the text in context – must be allowed to stand simultaneously as *autres* and manifestations of *différance*.

So what are we to do with this narrative that displays some of the confusion we have to struggle with if we are to think Heidegger? It does tell a story that, in the case of the behavior of so prominent a man, must be considered more than what countless Germans did or ignored. Stolorow (2011) offers a chapter-length psychobiographical explanation (apology?) for Heidegger's actions, but I don't think it works very well. Interpretations cannot trump morals. Adding to the confusion, two Jewish philosophers, Hannah Arendt and Jacques Derrida, both defended Heidegger after the war. And Heidegger's philosophy remains of importance. Safranski (2002), near the end of his biography, offers us an anecdote that sums up the problem. In the summer of 1967, the poet Paul Celan gave a reading of his work in Freiburg. He and Heidegger had known of each other, studied each other's work, but had never met. They did so very cordially at the reading. Afterwards, someone wanted to take a photograph of the two of them together, but Celan jumped to his feet and refused. He later said that he found it difficult to be with a man, however much he admired his work, *whose past he could not forget*. The answer, for myself (and one that I would recommend) is to read, of course, but also to *remember*.

Phenomenology and existentialism

Phenomenology and Existentialism must be approached with a number of caveats. They are at once difficult to define and have been taken to signify different things by the various authors writing on the subject: Husserl, Heidegger, Sartre, Merleau-Ponty, and Derrida, for example. They in no way comprise any sort of organized movement, and these authors' positions differ considerably. When one comes upon these terms in writings outside of philosophy, one often finds them

36 Phenomenology and existentialism

"tossed off" as if their meaning is simple and clear to all, with no explication given or required.

There exists great disagreement about the relation between Phenomenology and Existentialism. At mid-century, there was much uncertainty concerning not only their relationship but also their compatibility. In more recent years, the distinction between the two has seemed to be of little importance or even non-existent. It is fair to say that today they connote different areas of thought residing under the same general umbrella. Phenomenology is more about methodologies, while Existentialism focuses to a degree on the body and on emotion; engagement with the world can take place *within* the individual.

The views of the many authors writing and working under the broad umbrella of Phenomenology do have much in common. First among them, perhaps, is a foundation based on a critique of Cartesian dualism. A post-Cartesian ontology simultaneously means a number of things. As psychoanalysts, we know it mostly as a critique of mind in isolation (e.g., Damasio, 1994; Stolorow, 2011; Stolorow et al., 2002), that mind is inseparable from world and from its relationships with others. Body is considered not at all here, despite the importance of *embodiment* to Existentialism.

As a beginning, the editors of *The Routledge Companion to Phenomenology* (Luft & Overgaard, 2012) posit three paradigms as central to Phenomenology. The first is that it is a *first-person* ontology; it is about the "I" and what I experience, both the subjects and the objects I experience. This experience is subjective, but there is much objectivity in it if it is *intersubjectively validated*. It is about human beings. This "I-ness" does not address the unknown and unknowable subjectivities of the self. The second is that Phenomenology *describes* first-person experience. It is thus a bottom-up sort of discourse. This describing attempts to hold in abeyance distorting historicities, but cannot entirely know which elements of history are distorting. It attempts to avoid all prior theories, beliefs, or biases. It places the object in space, time, and relationality; that is to say, this describing is *contextual*. Third, there is a directedness of consciousness (and as we will come to on our own, a directedness of unconsciousness as well); *intentionality* is central to Phenomenology. Intentionality involves the directedness of attention onto the world (including the self). In this sense, psychoanalysis is both phenomenological and intentional. Given the difficulty of this subject, it is certainly fair to ask why we as analysts and psychotherapists need it at all in our work. The simple answer is because we either continue to make use of theories that lack stability or substantiation to guide us clinically in a top-down fashion, or else come to rely instead on this bottom-up series of methodologies based on a conceptually stabilized subjectivity.

Phenomenology is descriptive, not hypothetical and not explanatory. It attempts to offer an objective study of our perceiving or grasping of things subjectively.[9] The

---

9 *Study* is not entirely the right word because some understanding is derived from a "study" that is pre-operational and pre-reflective in nature, occurring from birth, prior to the development of adult capacities for reflection and cognition.

key feature of Phenomenology is that it sets aside the existence and relevance of deeper explanations that are not observed but posited or hypothesized; it eschews metaphysics as it attempts to explain description or intentionality. To the extent we can speak of a Phenomenological movement, Heidegger and Husserl began it.

Heidegger and Husserl

Although Heidegger's (1927/2008) and Husserl's (1913/1983, 1931/1999) positions in Existential Phenomenology are markedly different, they are still seen today by contemporary phenomenologists as being of great importance. Heidegger offers a path through his formulation of Dasein and Being-in-the-World that is directly relevant to psychoanalysis. Husserl, who began with his "pure" phenomenology (the objective study of subjective experience) and an early interest in perception, had been taken up by Merleau-Ponty (1945/2012) and Sartre (1943/2003), leading today to the integration of phenomenology into the cognitive sciences and (I would argue) the neurosciences as well. Both of these contemporary phenomenological subjects will be discussed in the sections of this chapter that follow, but before doing so, we should first consider the similarities and divergences of Heidegger's and Husserl's work.

Husserl (1913/1983) was in pursuit of what he called a "pure" phenomenology. The disagreements that he and Heidegger shared had to do with the "principle of phenomenology," a principle that Carman (2006) saw as having three distinguishable versions. The least objectionable (to Heidegger) of these, Husserl's call to arms, was for a "return to the things themselves" (pp. 98–99). Heidegger (1927/2008) certainly accepts this maxim, although not necessarily what Husserl says that follows from it. By this, Husserl meant concrete (hence important) perceivable matters (*Sachen*). These concrete things are susceptible to description, as opposed to hypothesis and explanation; they are worthy of interpretation in their own right, rather than merely being surface phenomena with metaphysical depths to be sought out below them. Husserl was thus critiquing the creeping natural science of the Enlightenment.[10] Thus both Husserl and Heidegger were positing a bottom-up research methodology from the things (*Sachen, choses*) and the problems connected with them, rather than the top-down theory-philosophy-psychology. It is descriptive, not hypothetical or explanatory. At this point, Heidegger fielded two major criticisms against Husserl's work. One was the absence of historicity in the latter's thinking. The other was that Husserl was still rooted in the philosophical traditions of the 17th and 18th centuries and a methodological insistence on philosophy constituting its own rigorous scientific discipline. In its own way, this was also a form of creeping naturalism. It must be understood that the current debate over the relevance of neuroscience to the theory and practice of psychoanalysis is not about the creeping naturalism of Husserl, but rather about Heidegger's search for meaning.

---

10 This seeking out of the depths is at the heart of metapsychological psychoanalytic thinking.

38 Phenomenology and existentialism

A second, refined reading (version two) of Husserl's principle of phenomenology identifies the things themselves, the phenomena, with appearances (*Erscheinungen*). These appearances are what Husserl describes as the contents of consciousness, not the things in the world appearing in consciousness. Phenomena are then subjective, and phenomenology is the study of subjectivity. This path leads us to issues of knowability, irreducible subjectivity, psychoanalysis, and neuroscience that are of considerable interest to us. However, it is not a path that Heidegger could countenance. For him (1927/2008), appearance depends on *Sachen* showing themselves; *phenomena are not in any way subjective*.[11] Heidegger is not interested in *superficial* appearances (*doxa*). Although phenomena do have surface appearances, their major characteristics are hidden or even secret. Hidden and secret *do not mean deeper* (this distinction cannot be over-emphasized). What is hidden or disguised is, for Heidegger, "rather the *being* of entities" (p. 39). It is not separate but belongs to what first shows itself.

Heidegger (1927/2008) considered the study of phenomena (i.e., phenomenology) to be interpretive; its interpretations were not derived through recourse to deeper meanings, but rather from meaning derived from observation and deconstruction. Although descriptive, phenomenology is not limited to observation. This is different from the descriptively "pure" phenomenology posited by Husserl (1913/1983). Meaning is to be found on the same level as experience, a concept that flies in the face of psychoanalytic interpretation as it is implicitly and explicitly taught.[12] The parallel, phenomenological approach to psychoanalysis, then, is to eschew metapsychology, a path that – although many of us have taken it – is controversial. For Heidegger, interpretation presents a hermeneutic phenomenology, but unlike the closed hermeneutic circle of some psychoanalytic theories of technique, it is an open hermeneutic with constant recourse to the *Sache*.

Heidegger (1927/2008) posits that our understanding of being is pre-conceptual, prior not just to reflection and introspection, but to conceptual and propositional attitudes as well.[13] The question, then, is how it is to be determined what is to be experienced as the thing itself in accordance with phenomenology. Is it consciousness and its objectivity, or is it the being of entities in their unconcealedness or concealment?

Phenomenology is not metapsychology

In offering up Phenomenology to inform our clinical work, how is this different, and, in particular, how is this not simply another metapsychology? The shortest

---

11 At this point, it should be becoming clear that as we examine their ideas, a choice *between* Husserl and Heidegger is not one that we would care to make, and that we had best maintain both as a sheaf of interwoven strands of *différance* (Derrida, 1972/1982; Leffert, 2010) to which we will be adding other authors drawn from Network Studies and the neurosciences.

12 As psychoanalysts, we are accustomed to seeking meaning in the depths, that things are either superficial or deep. I would suggest that depth is metaphorical rather than positional, and that what we seek out in meaning can be concealed or unformulated but is not deeper. Certainly some mental events are older than others, but *older* does not signify *deeper*. There will be more to say about this.

13 Now, we would date it to the early Right Brain-to-Right Brain mother–child relationship.

answer is that phenomenology is a descriptive study of meaning specifically dealing with human beings and how they are in the world, with each other, and within themselves. It does not pretend to offer either a structuralized theory of deeper meaning and/or any sort of theory at all. This descriptive study frequently involves exploration, but at the same level of meaning; nothing deeper is implied. "God created the Universe" is a meta-theory; it is not necessarily valid, just as other meta-theories are not necessarily valid. Roger saying, "I sometimes catch myself acting like my father" is a subjective descriptive statement of exploration made to another person, in this case me. It may be of great clinical and phenomenological importance (or not, as the case may be), but it is not a meta-statement of anything.

If the study of Being is direct and not derived from underlying principles, then it is far away from the methodologies of the natural sciences and metapsychology as described in psychoanalysis beginning with Freud. However, the natural sciences, at least the neurosciences, cannot be so quickly dismissed from the study of Phenomenology.

Phenomenology, intersubjectivity, and neuroscience

A problem arises in contemporary phenomenology that did not exist during the first half of the 20th century, when the first-generation phenomenologists were at work. That problem derives from the advent of the study of mind, brain, and self through the disciplines of cognitive neuroscience, functional neuroanatomy, social networks, and complexity, as they developed in the latter half of the century. They are all very much with us today and of great importance to the study of human beings, a term that has much to do with the origins of Heidegger's phenomenological concept of Dasein. We will have to consider the role of these disciplines in any phenomenological project, and question the validity of a separation of this particular science and phenomenology.

What is of interest to us are the ways in which phenomenology, intersubjectivity, and neuroscience mutually inform one another, and how they might further illuminate psychoanalysis and its *praxis* in the *absence* of metapsychology. This interest is shared by contemporary phenomenologists (e.g., Ratcliffe, 2006/2009; Romdenh-Romluc, 2012; Zahavi, 2012).

There is an approach that will allow us to go on to consider phenomenology, neuroscience, and subjectivity, and their relations at the same time and with the same level of standing. Beginning from the position that attempting to separate the social from the scientific is an impossibility, the relatively new field of Science Studies (e.g., Latour, 1991/1993; Serres & Latour, 1990/2011) has considered just the problem we are interested in – how to bridge the gap between the two.[14] It will also allow us to deal with the conflicting ontologies of the modern and the postmodern

---

14 I have discussed science studies elsewhere in considerable detail (Leffert, 2007a, 2010) and will offer only the briefest of overviews here.

40 Phenomenology and existentialism

and come up with an alternative possibility. Latour observes first that the social and the scientific are interreferential, that the acquisition and deployment of knowledge are inseparable from the social circumstances in which they take place. I would further observe that events taking place within the self and in its relations with other selves also involve social and scientific components that cannot be separated.

Latour (1991/1993) goes on to argue that these failures to separate the social from the scientific grow out of the application of two entirely different procedures called translation and purification, which must be sequentially employed and never thought about together if one is to be truly modern *or* truly postmodern. Translation involves taking all the ontological elements related to a given thing and functionally linking them together into networks, branched hybrid structures of nature and culture. Purification involves then separating these elements into two "boxes," one holding all the elements of humans/culture and the other holding non-humans/nature. Latour refers to this as the "modern critical stance" (p. 11). These procedures produce two mutilated categories: the modern and the postmodern. The result of applying the two procedures works ontologically very poorly, but it does work, *so long as we don't think together about them*. If we do that, the effort collapses, as does the distinction between modern and postmodern. The way out of this dilemma is the formation of an amalgam composed of the *constructive* elements of both ontologies. Among them are the acceptance of the existence of very large networks, the rejection of the social-scientific dichotomy, and the acceptance of a constructive deconstruction that expands meaning. Why are we interested in this here? You see, this amalgam will lead us to a solution to the problem the contemporary phenomenologists have been struggling with: thinking about and working with elements of self, subjectivity/experience, neuroscience, and world.

Intersubjectivity is phenomenology

Intersubjectivity occupies a position at the center of phenomenology.[15] Husserl is the first to have made use of the term (*Intersubjektivität*); he used it at least as early as 1925 (Husserl, 1925/1977), but greatly expanded his discussions of it toward the end of his life (1937/1970). Husserl talked first about "I" and "us" as living in the world together, and that our perceptions of the world are in part shaped by that living together.

Intersubjective discrepancies occur, to be sure, but Husserl sees them as being resolved in "the overarching community consciousness which has grown up through [social contact]" (p. 164). The thing itself is never perceived through a fixed experience because experience is always multiple and always changing from moment to moment. The problem with the phenomenological precept of validation through

---

15 It should be noted that the contemporary psychoanalytic school of intersubjectivity developed seemingly without any awareness of either phenomenology or its intersubjectivity and came to that awareness later on in its development.

intersubjective concurrence is that it does not account for group distortions of thought and being. Ironically, one such distortion is Nazism, which held sway in Germany when and where Husserl (who was Jewish and was ultimately deprived of his academic standing by the Nazi regime) was writing these very words.

The problem of intersubjectivity is really the problem of other minds and other selves, as we have direct (and partial) access only to our own. However, normal development leads us to an adequate theory of mind (ToM) (Baron-Cohen, Leslie, & Frith, 1985; Baron-Cohen, Tager-Flusberg, & Cohen, 2000; Gallagher & Frith, 2003), through which we are able to know that the other self is both like us and different from us. The term encompassing these various knowledges as they exist in the wider world is *folk psychology*. Such knowing must involve decisions made under uncertainty through the use of Heuristics and Biases (Kahneman et al., 1982). Much of this takes place unconsciously, which is a problem for a majority of phenomenologists who have placed a premium on consciousness.

Zahavi (2012) describes a central problem faced by phenomenologists: The knowledge of other selves is always mediated by perceptions of their bodily behaviors. The question, then, is one of exactly how these perceptions give information about another self. A classical attempt to answer this question is by deploying an argument by analogy based on self-observation; our self-observations can be used *directly* to simulate our observations of others. This argument leads to its own conundrums. It requires cognitive self-reflection at an advanced level beyond common usage and beyond what children, who also employ empathy, are capable of. Another problem arises in that deciding consciously what someone is experiencing through their facial expressions means that we are already presupposing what we are trying to prove. Finally, what we want to ascertain about others is not something in their depths but rather, in the tradition of phenomenology, something directly observable. Zahavi, drawing on Husserl's unpublished manuscripts, notes that the latter believed that true objectivity could only be found through an ongoing intersubjective process.

Intersubjectivity draws on the face-to-face encounter and the fact that self and other live in a shared world. At the same time, it depends on a maintained distinction between self and other (even though, as we know, the boundary is not always a sharp one).

Zahavi (2012) posits three points as essential to phenomenological accounts of intersubjectivity. The first is that, without denying the intersubjective nature of language, pre- and extra-linguistic forms of intersubjectivity are of decisive importance. The second is that intersubjectivity exists not as any kind of structure (as in object relations theory) but rather as a *process relation between subjects*. This implies an intimacy between subjectivity and intersubjectivity rather than a competition between the two concepts. Finally, any treatment of intersubjectivity requires dealing with the relations of subjectivity and world, and this involves the essential interrelatedness of self, other selves, and world. This treating and dealing constitutes *doing* phenomenology.

42 Phenomenology and existentialism

Neuroscience is phenomenology

Although there were no alternatives outside of philosophy available to first- and second-generation phenomenologists, in 2015 this is no longer the case. Contemporary findings in areas other than orthodox phenomenology speak to the very issues Zahavi (2012) is raising and offer their own interrelatedness. Recent Neuroscience findings offer two complementary explanations of how this feat is mediated: one is through the mirror neuron system (MNS) (Bråten, 2007; Ferrari & Gallese, 2007; Gallese, Fadiga, Fogassi, & Rizzolatti, 1996); the other is through the brain-heart-face circuit (BHFC) (Porges, 1998, 2009). And, once again, both these systems operate outside of consciousness.

The relationship between neuroscience and phenomenology can be – if some of their respective practitioners are interested – one of mutual re-interpretation. Neuroscience can and already does make use of phenomenological descriptions of experience obtained from research subjects to correlate with functional neuroanatomy. This trend dates back to the split-brain studies of the 1960s (Bogen & Vogel, 1962; Galin, 1974; Sperry, Gazzaniga, & Bogen, 1969; Wolford, Miller, & Gazzaniga, 2004). As a treatment of last resort, patients suffering from intractable epilepsy had their left and right cerebral hemispheres surgically separated via a commisurectomy (the treatment, as it turned out, was highly successful). When these individuals were studied afterwards, it was found that they, surprisingly, behaved and functioned quite normally and described quite usual subjective experiences. The surgery had, however, produced a functional separation of the two cerebral hemispheres. It was then possible to "interview" each hemisphere in isolation, using techniques drawn from cognitive science methodologies. Language ability, in right-dominant individuals, resides in the left hemisphere. It was found that the latter could, in isolation, offer normative narratives. Although the right hemisphere was unable to access language, it could, however, communicate nonverbally with the researchers through gestures and symbols. The result was two different conversations with two different subjectivities.

The MNS and the BHFC together represent the biological engine of intersubjectivity. The MNS was only discovered 20 years ago (Gallese et al., 1996; Rizzolatti, Fadiga, Fogassi, & Gallese, 1996) in Macaque monkeys. In humans, mirror neurons are found in the prefrontal motor, visual, and somatosensory areas (Iacoboni, 2007; Iacoboni et al., 1999). It is a shared processing system in which the same cells process images of self and other. It is a system that operates functionally to produce embodied simulation, the mechanism that makes intersubjectivity possible. Further, the infant comes endowed with a functional MNS, active almost from birth and capable of subject-subject interaction with the mother.

Ferrari and Gallese (2007) define embodied simulation as "an automatic, unconscious, and pre-reflexive functional mechanism, whose function is the modeling of objects, agents, and events" (p. 74). Simulation is a fundamental component of our epistemic grasping of the world. It is not necessarily the result of willed action and is not consciously directed at the hidden meanings of others' behavior. In other words, as a mechanism of intersubjectivity it is exactly what phenomenologists (Heidegger, 1927/2008; Husserl, 1937/1970, 1913/1983) say it should be. It, too, operates unconsciously.

We understand the observed actions of others through resonance in the MNS, a process facilitated by our already having that motor action in our repertoire (Ferrari & Gallese, 2007). The MNS operates independently of whether we actually repeat the action or simply think about it. It does more than grasp a motor act per se. The function or purpose is also grasped, and different groups of cells respond to a group of acts that accomplish the same task. This replaces the older idea that mirror neurons code only the what, not the why. The MNS discriminates between identical motor acts embedded in different functional sequences. Different neurons will thus code the same act differently, depending on its goal. Before initiating a series of actions, we already have in mind our goal, the *action intension*. The observer is able to grasp the action intension – that is, to predict the goal of an observed action.

Mirror neurons also function to mirror emotion and facial expressions, such as disgust (Ferrari & Gallese, 2007). Witnessing an emotion in others or experiencing it in oneself both activate the same area of the brain, the insula. This suggests that the first- and third-person experiences of emotion depend on the activity of a shared mental substrate. That raises the interesting question of how someone who is, for example, happy, *looks* happy – and what does it mean to look happy, anyway? This brings us back to Porges's (1998, 2009) work on the Vagus nerve and his polyvagal theory. One of the circuits he posits is the BHFC (which has vagal components). The face part of the circuit involves the innervation of the facial muscles, which contract in different ways to signify different emotions. The information telling them to do so comes from complex connections within the brain, the afferent and efferent fibers of the autonomic nervous system and the cranial nerves. Facial expression, then, plays an important role in intersubjectivity, and this raises the question of just how the infant starts off on his or her own intersubjective path.[16]

Before moving on to being-in-the-world and Dasein and drawing the connections between the neuroscience and the philosophy, there is another point to add. There are not one but two kinds of ToM and MNS function. One sort is an everyday sort – it is casual, and much of it is unconscious. It allows us to operate in the world fairly automatically, not requiring much attention. However, there is a second sort that operates on a much higher level of conscious scrutiny. It too is partly unconscious, but it is active and attentive, very much in keeping with Heidegger's (1927/2008) use of the word "thrown." We will discuss it shortly.

---

16 It is significant that humans are uniquely able to convey complex patterns of emotion through their facial expressions yet we seldom reflect on this or the way that these patterns, over time, *permanently* alter facial expression.

44 Phenomenology and existentialism

Dasein and being-in-the-world

Heidegger (1927/2008) can be differentiated from other phenomenologists by his use of two concepts – Dasein and being-in-the-world – and the centrality of their position in his phenomenology. These concepts are of importance to us because they offer new ways of thinking about and clinically approaching the self and its relations with its social and physical world. If we are not going to do psychoanalysis based on some metatheory, then we need a different sort of clinical theory, one that is immediately grounded in description and experience. The two concepts – Dasein and being-in-the-world – are intimately bound up with one another. They are also complex to the point of seeming impenetrability; one must accept Heidegger's meaning with at least some degree of uncertainty.

Dasein directly translates as "existence." Two other common German words for existence are *Vorhandensein* and *Existenz*; many authors use these terms more or less interchangeably. In colloquial German, Dasein means "to be present" and usually applies to people. Heidegger also took the term as "being there," applied to human beings (the term *human being* has a similar double meaning). His more recent translators (Heidegger, 1927/2008, 1927/2010) have retained the German term (but dropped the italics), so Anglophone readers are met with a strange foreign word to get their heads around while German readers start with a colloquial one. I think they have an easier but not necessarily a better time with it. Heidegger is concerned with being and how human beings exist. Dasein is the term for the being of a human being. Although not explicit, I take him to mean "exist mentally," but freely, not purely, and not as *opposed* to "physically." Human beings are also physical and connected to the world through action and perception, but this is not the kind of *being* he is concerned with. He also applies *Existenz* to human beings. These are the only forms consistent with Heidegger's stated position that there is a fundamental difference in humans' mode of being and that of non-humans, for which he reserves the term *Vorhandensein*. Dasein is the name of the being (*das Seiende*), while *Existenz* designates its mode of being (the *Seinart* or *Seinweise*), and "phenomenology is the science of the being of beings – ontology" (Heidegger, 1927/2010, p. 35).

Dastur (2012) identifies two reasons for the return to the German Dasein from the English "being there" (and the French *être-là*). First, Dasein signifies a comprehensive relation to being, not the traditional opposition of subject to object. Although the term originally meant "being there," Heidegger is reserving it for the intrinsic relation of the human being to being. In keeping with this, he originally spelled it Da-sein. The Da conveys a number of things: a spatial (there *or* here) and a temporal location, and an unveiling and disclosedness of Dasein's true being. Second, as Heidegger (1927/2010) puts it, this disclosedness involves a self-finding or "attunement, understanding, or discourse" (p. 173) (*Befindlichkeit*). Heidegger is after a new consideration of the being of human beings, thus he pushes aside all the baggage of previous philosophical designations. Dasein has a priority over all other beings because it alone has an understanding of being itself.[17] It alone has the understanding of its own being and the being of the other beings. Heidegger considers Dasein to contain the fundamental ontology on which other ontologies (such as anthropology) are based.

This brings us to the next great question: the nature of Dasein's being-in-the-world. Heidegger (1927/2008, 1927/2010) identified two very different ways of being; he has more to say about the first than the second. The first he describes as the "average everydayness" of being at home in the world. Everydayness is in itself not a failed state (although in special circumstances it can become one); as it came first, it is the original state of being human. Everydayness is, well, it's about going about the usual business of living, which varies with the individual (my everydayness at the moment consists in composing this chapter and referring to my notes; soon I will go out for coffee). However, Heidegger goes on to posit other properties. In a state of everydayness, Dasein loses its individuality and becomes *entangled* with other selves. It is dispersed.

For the everyday Dasein, there is only the surrounding world to discuss or the useful things that can be found "at hand" in it because *everyday Dasein can have no experience of the world as such*. It involves being-with (*Mitsein* and *Sein-bei*) and caring for (*Besorgen*) and being-toward beings encountered in the world. "Taking care of" refers to things like food or clothing or as a part of some social institutions like nursing or psychoanalysis. Everydayness is the equivalent of the allocentric position.

It is well worth noting that Heidegger's concept of everyday being-in-the-world travels to the field of Network Studies. It signifies the same thing as Christakis and Fowler's (2009) connectedness, with the same properties as their social networks. Everyday Dasein is similar to their concept of an ego, a zero intelligence unit. It does not know about the properties of the network of which it is a member, and only knows about those alters that are "at hand." Both are receiving information (contagion), unconsciously, that influences their behavior, *their* being-in-the-world. Network Studies offers a powerful tool for inquiring about the everydayness of a particular Dasein beyond what Heidegger had to offer.

In addition to everydayness, there is an alternate way of being-in-the-world that is quite different. Strangely, Heidegger does not discuss it at length; perhaps it was to be covered in additional divisions of *Sein und Zeit* (Heidegger, 1927/2008) that were never written. It is a state of "thrownness." Dasein does not enter this state by choice but is "thrown" into it by circumstances. As Stolorow (2011) observes, trauma is one such circumstance, but there are many others that shift us into an autocentric mode. Many of the things that Dasein is in this existential state of

---

17 To code this concept of Da-sein with the relevant neurobiology, think of Tulving's (1985/2003) auto-noetic consciousness (Leffert, 2010, Chapter 6) with the emphasis not on consciousness, but the particular kind of consciousness (*self* consciousness).

46 Phenomenology and existentialism

thrownness are simply what it is not in everydayness. It experiences itself in its authenticness. It knows the world as a holistic whole beyond simply those useful things that are near at hand. Dasein is thrown into the world and finds its singularity.

So there are to be two states of being-in-the-world: everydayness and thrownness. These states are clinically identifiable. Both are shaped by the self's irreducible subjectivity (for our purposes, the patient's and the analyst's); as we will discuss in the next chapter, the analysis of Dasein – the analysis of being – involves the analysis of that subjectivity. Perhaps unsurprisingly, this same conclusion was reached by much of psychoanalysis sometime in its second half-century. What this Daseinanalysis offers us is an ontologically based psychoanalysis as opposed to a theory-based analysis resting on artificial constructs.

What comes with thrownness is consciousness of the finitude of life. Death contains the possibility of an impossibility of Dasein having any existence at all. This knowledge requires the choice of a life with meaning, lived to the fullest, or a life that is already dead. The anxiety that comes with it is grounded in the collapse of everyday experience and the uncanniness that accompanies that collapse. Death, then, is a possibility towards which we have been thrown, a being-towards-death. The everyday world makes death only something general – that is, defensive, inauthentic, happening to others, and always capable of being postponed. (In the 21st-century United States, many are focused on desperately seeking that postponement for themselves and sometimes come to us as a result of it.) The grasping of death is replaced by the everyday social rituals that accompany it.[18]

The failure to grapple with death is not the only challenge conveyed by thrownness. Countless personal challenges face all of us in life. Our ability to master them or succumb to them depends on our developmental experiences, described phenomenologically, not in terms of metatheory. This is only what Erikson (1950/1963) offered us in *Childhood and Society* and its eight ages of man that was so little understood at the time. In each age the individual is thrown into a developmental challenge that could be successfully mastered or failed. In the face of such failures, there is a return to everydayness, but this time it is not normative but pathological; it is a falling back into a "fallen" state of everydayness. As just one example of this falling, in the face of an inability to grapple with trauma alone or without care from others, there is a falling back to everydayness and with it the trauma is transmuted into PTSD. The latter becomes resistant to amelioration and can become life-shaping.

This sketch should convey some sense of where we are headed – towards just what phenomenology and existentialism actually have to do with the understanding of psychopathology and the clinical practice of psychoanalysis and psychotherapy. In the next chapter, we will look at these clinical applications.

---

18 Thrownness towards death is also a grounded form of the unstable concept of a death instinct.

3

PSYCHOANALYSIS AND DASEINANALYSIS

Introduction

Before we take the ideas of the last chapter out for a clinical test-drive in psychoanalysis, there are issues of terminology that we have to deal with. What we will be talking about, essentially, is Daseinanalysis, but that won't do in the wider world for a number of reasons. Although the term worked well for Boss (1963) in Switzerland, it does not signify for an audience of Anglophone psychoanalysts and psychotherapists 50 years later. For us, it is and remains arcane and cannot *comfortably* find its way into what we do and talk about clinically. Its use would indeed suggest the formation of still another unstable school of psychoanalysis which, for reasons already discussed, is the last thing I would wish to propose. I want instead to simply talk about how we do non-theory-based psychoanalysis of self and other, and the modes of listening and reflecting that we employ. This is and has been pure phenomenology, and many of us may well have been implicitly practicing this way for some time as we have grown dissatisfied with the outcomes of theory-based clinical work.

In *The Therapeutic Situation in the 21st Century* (Leffert, 2013, Chapter 6), I offered a fairly novel discussion of therapeutic action. Among other points, I posited that *all* psychoanalysis is relational.[1] I also suggested that the stuff of therapeutic action involved working with emotion, meaning, and narrative. However, I did not offer any suggestions concerning what exactly the goals of an analysis or a psychotherapy might be. By goals, I do not mean theoretical goals like "where id was there will ego be" (Freud, 1923/1961a) or the restoration of the self (Kohut, 1977, 1984). In

---

1 For clarity I use relational with a small "r" to signify that element of a therapy or analysis of any orientation that focuses on the relationship between the analytic couple while using Relational with a capital "R" to denote the Relational school of psychoanalysis.

48 Psychoanalysis and Daseinanalysis

practice, such concepts often turn out to be excuses for therapeutic failures rather than any sort of palpable therapeutic goals.

As May (1958a) began an essay on existentialism:

> In recent years there has been a growing awareness on the part of some psychiatrists and psychologists that serious gaps exist in our way of understanding of [sic] human beings. These gaps may well seem most compelling to psychotherapists confronted as they are ... *with the sheer reality of persons in crisis* whose anxiety will not be quieted by theoretical formulae. (p. 3, italics added)

May (1964) went on to note (50 years ago) the striking lack of creativity in our psychoanalytic language, something that has been somewhat improved over the intervening years.[2] He instead located creativity in the *act of encounter* – that, I would add, involves thrownness and being. Growing numbers of us have been becoming aware of the fact that our theories of therapeutic action as well as our terminology have become deficient; this in turn has led to a quest for what, for lack of a better term, has been called "something more" (Stern, D.N. et al., 1998) in contemporary attempts to conceptualize technique. It may be time to move on from something *more* to something *else*. I'm talking about what is currently the novel question one almost never hears posed in a case presentation or finds in a case write-up prepared for purposes of progression at a psychoanalytic institute or for "certification" by the American Psychoanalytic Association (APsaA): "What does the patient want?" This refers to a particular patient, *not* a generic one. This was almost the very first thing I told you about Roger in Chapter 1: He was referred to me because he was driving his ward staff crazy, but he could not have cared less about that. What he really *wanted* was a satisfying relationship with a woman, and he was afraid he couldn't have one. I would suggest that a phenomenological approach to psychoanalysis is uniquely qualified to address such goals, and metapsychological approaches are uniquely qualified *not* to. Now, it is certainly true, as many would object, that patients often come to us with little idea of why they have done so. So be it. But if that is the case, as opposed to the patient having told us and we just didn't *hear* her, then the first task of the therapy is to figure out what they want and why they are with us.[3] And – this once, to make the term a little less arcane – I will say that this is the first step of a Daseinanalysis.

In this chapter, we will talk about phenomenological goals and analysis, including the work of Boss (1963) and May (May, 1958a, 1958b; May, Angel, & Ellenberger, 1958). We will also spend some time on the *Zollikon Seminars* (Heidegger, 1987/2001). Then, we will discuss what specifically goes into a phenomenological psychoanalysis, and finally return to Roger and what his analysis looked like. But

---

2 Unfortunately, much recent Contemporary analytic writing has become filled with its *own* jargon.

3 Psychoanalysts *really like* doing psychoanalysis. Unfortunately, for all kinds of reasons, getting a patient into analysis can become an end in itself.

before embarking on this agenda, something should be said about the history of phenomenological and existential analysis, their relations with psychoanalysis, and the usage of this terminology in the United States.

American phenomenological psychoanalysis

With the publication of *Existence* and other works, Rollo May (May, 1958a, 1958b; May et al., 1958) brought phenomenological psychoanalysis to American audiences. Originally, this material came through Sartre (1943/2003), as Heidegger was not readily available to American readers. This changed when Medard Boss (Boss, 1963; Heidegger, 1987/2001), the Swiss psychiatrist working at the Burghölzi Psychiatric Hospital and the University of Zurich Psychiatric Clinic, visited the United States in the early 1960s, where he and Ludwig Binswanger (1958)[4] exchanged ideas with May and others. Each had developed his own forms of Daseinanalysis. Boss in turn acknowledged *his* debt to *them* in his own book and in the *Zollikon Seminars*, which he edited extensively.

It appears that as the 1960s waned as a social phenomenon in America, so did a direct interest in phenomenological psychoanalysis. However, May was a major force in the psychoanalytic left, and, in 1966, was president of what was then the William Alanson White Psychoanalytic Society. Without difficulty, we can find the *implicit* presence of phenomenological thought in Interpersonal Psychoanalysis (e.g., Sullivan, 1954/1970, 1938/1971, 1950/1971, 1953/1997) and later in its descendants, the Relational and Intersubjective Schools. If one does a PEP-Web search for the terms *Phenomenology, Phenomenological*, and *Existentialism* in the titles of psychoanalytic papers from 1960 on, we get about 100 hits. In the majority of these papers, their authors use the terms as adjectives that signify the manifest or revealed nature of some subject they will be discussing that has nothing to do with phenomenology or phenomenological analysis per se. However, some of these papers are of interest. It appears that although Jung and Heidegger regarded each other with considerable disdain and personal antipathy, later Jungian authors (Adams, 2000; Brooke, 1991) found reasons to become interested in phenomenology. I gather, although it is not made explicit, that they realized that central concepts in Jungian theory and practice (such as complexes, archetypes, and Jungian dream analysis) lack ontological standing, and that treating them in an explicitly phenomenological fashion constituted a way around that problem. However, it did nothing for the Jungian formulation of "Depth Psychology" which also seems to be founded on little if any evidence of actual depth and, as a result, is more of a metaphor or a construct.

---

4 Binswanger developed his own form of Daseinanalysis, distinct from Heidegger and as a critique of Freud's psychoanalytic theory and method. He was the only analyst with whom Freud maintained a lifelong cordial relationship in spite of his dissidence.

50 Psychoanalysis and Daseinanalysis

A number of articles and books have appeared (e.g., Coltrera, 1962; Hanly, 1979; Renik, 1985) over the years comparing psychoanalysis (Freudian) and existentialism, criticizing the latter and finding the two incompatible. Major critiques seem to center on existentialism being a philosophy that would rob psychoanalysis of its scientific nature [sic] and its ability to prove or disprove. They focus their critiques mostly on Sartre (Coltrera *does* have something to say about Heidegger, but not about Boss) and his work as it appears in that of May and his colleagues (May et al., 1958). If we examine how the terms existentialism and phenomenology have come into common contemporary usage by both philosophers and psychoanalysts, it is difficult (if not impossible) to formulate a stable distinction between the two. As far as the standing of psychoanalysis as a science is concerned, by 1985 it was already being called into question in the raging debates between Edelson (1984) and Grünbaum (1984) that had nothing to do with either existentialism or phenomenology. Although many analysts (most of whom are members of the American Psychoanalytic Association) insist to this day that psychoanalysis *is* a science, many do not. As I have argued extensively in the past (Leffert, 2007, 2010), psychoanalysis represents a hybrid of the social (including the philosophical) and the scientific, as described in the field of Science Studies.

The implications of these criticisms of an existential/phenomenological approach to therapy or analysis are that such an approach contains no search for meaning and no analysis; anything is only pretty much what it appears to be. In addition, nothing of relevance is unconscious. I cannot speak for Sartre, but Heidegger (1927/2008, 1927/2010) is very specific about meanings existing but mostly being hidden or secret and requiring an analytic process to reveal or formulate them. I have been flagging the aspects of a phenomenological worldview that *are* unconscious and deferring that discussion to the next chapter. The singular difference in a phenomenological approach to psychoanalysis is that it would not be based on or defer to any metapsychology; it would be based on what is observable or on what can be derived from what is observable. It would eschew theory derived from artificial (that is, created) constructs, hypothesized by analysts or groups of analysts (very much in the manner that Schafer, 1979, describes) that have morphed over the years into revealed truths.

Phenomenological analysis: goals and substance

The relationship between phenomenology and existentialism, on the one hand, and psychoanalysis, on the other, is at once complex and multidimensional. At first glance, first- and second-generation phenomenological and existential authors appear to have had little use for psychoanalysis. However, at that time, they were unable to draw any distinction between psychoanalysis and Freud. One would have to say that they had little use for the latter, although their reading of his work was limited and hardly thoughtful. I think it is also fair to say that they would have maintained a similar view of the other early psychoanalytic orthodoxies: those of Carl Jung and Melanie Klein.

Phenomenological and existential critiques of psychoanalysis

As Askay and Farquhar (2006, 2012) observe, two authors in particular – Heidegger in Phenomenology and Sartre in Existentialism – go to considerable lengths to make their criticisms of both Freud and his work known in print. Along with Husserl, Heidegger and Freud would seem to have had much in common. Brentano and his ideas influenced them all. As Askay and Farquhar (2006) so eloquently put it, "Husserl and Freud undertook a regressive, archaeological inquiry into the affective histories of individuals and into the hidden recesses of the psyche" (p. 166). Although he used different language, Heidegger viewed historicity as an essential component of Dasein along with the need to explore hidden or secret meanings in order to fully reveal its *still phenomenological* nature. (Heidegger did not view this revealing of meaning as anything other than that – in other words, it did not involve a search for a new, *deeper* meaning.) We deal with a patient's historicity all the time, but we just refer to it with different terminology. Historicity shapes the self *in the present*. We tend not to think of this phenomenologically, but the problem is in the present. Patients often seek us out because they are, in effect, prisoners of their own historicities and, although the historicity remains, our therapeutic aim is to lessen its hold on the self.

Heidegger's criticisms of Freud and psychoanalysis did not appear until relatively late in his life. They can be found mostly in the *Zollikon Seminars*, a series of lectures and discussions that were organized by Medard Boss (Heidegger, 1987/2001) and mostly held at the latter's home, Zollikon. There were 21 seminars in all, given irregularly in pairs separated by a day or two, over a 10-year period (1959–1969). Boss later assembled them into a book, adding further notes, correspondence, and conversations between Heidegger and himself. Boss believed that Heidegger's commitment to the project grew out of his interest in educating the participants, usually around 50 psychiatrists and other therapists, in his ideas so that they could make use of them in their clinical work. Heidegger's criticisms of Freud fell into a number of areas. What is perhaps most interesting about them is that psychoanalysts practicing some form of what we have been calling Contemporary Psychoanalysis would agree with them. For example, a major critique leveled against Freud by Heidegger is directed at the former's insistence that psychoanalysis is a science – not just any sort of science, but a science in the spirit of Descartes's scientific method, Newton's scientific positivism, and Helmholtz's Neo-Kantianism[5] (Askay & Farquhar, 2006).

---

5 I'm not at all sure that Heidegger would have offered the same criticisms of 21st century science, involving as it does complexity theory, uncertainty, quantum mechanics, and science studies. Indeed, Heidegger (1987/2001) himself comments on the theory of relativity as consistent with bodily being-in-the-world.

52 Psychoanalysis and Daseinanalysis

A particular observation of Heidegger's in the Zollikon seminar of July 6, 1965, stands out:"Modern science is based on the fact that the human being posits himself as an authoritative subject to whom everything that can be investigated becomes an object" (Heidegger, 1987/2001, p. 94). This is precisely the issue that contemporary psychoanalysts have been discussing (irrespective of Heidegger) for some time. Goldner (2002), Benjamin (1988, 2000), and myself (Leffert, 2010), among others, have focused on the fundamental shift from the Freudian subject who studies the patient-object, to an emphasis on the subject who theorizes, then to the relational context through which knowledge is created. The therapeutic situation becomes a thing of relating subjects, subjects who are influenced by their varying epistemes and social embedding – in other words, subjects who are being-in-the-world (here, the aspect of being-in-the-world that Heidegger termed the *Mitwelt*).

An equally important distinction between Freudian (let us rather say first- and second-generation) psychoanalysis[6] and the kind of therapy[7] Heidegger would have endorsed (that we would call phenomenological analysis) is the presence of a meta-psychology in the one and the absence of it in the other. Remember that Freud, in his paper "The Unconscious" (1915/1957), proposes "that when we have succeeded in describing a psychical process in its dynamic, topographical and economic aspects, we should speak of it as a *metapsychological* presentation" (p. 181). The genetic (i.e., developmental) aspect was considered to be implicitly present, and most psychoanalysts subsequently added the structural point of view to obtain a fifth metapsychological perspective.[8] So what's not to like here? Heidegger would certainly accept the genetic perspective, as we do, given his commitment to the historicity of Dasein. His acceptance would have been based on privileging archaeology and narrative[9] rather than a clinical search for a singular developmental paradigm, such as the Oedipus complex. (Indeed, Contemporary psychoanalysts accept a multiplicity of developmental paradigms without assigning special standing to any one of them.) I believe that he would have accepted the psychodynamic point of view as a process rather than a static concept. The phenomenological analysts of mid-century (Boss, May, and others) as well as the contemporary ones (a group that must include Orange, 1995; Stolorow, 2011; Yalom, 1980, but is otherwise harder to pin down) have certainly thought similarly.

Heidegger would not, as many of us from a wide range of therapeutic orientations would not today, have had any use for an economic or quantitative theory of

---

6 These theoretical positions have persisted into the present, often under the rubric of Modern American Ego Psychology.

7 Heidegger objected to Freud's choice of the word "analysis," which he took in the Greek sense of unraveling or dissolving something into its elements.

8 However, in his "Autobiographical Study" (1925/1959a), Freud stuck with the original three, in spite of its appearing more or less concurrently with the more advanced monograph, "Inhibition, Symptom, and Anxiety" (1926/1959b).

9 For a thorough discussion of narrative, archaeology, and genealogy, see Leffert (2013, Chapter 2).

psychoanalysis. Indeed, as Freud carried it forward – first into the instincts, then into the topographic and structural points of view – he became hopelessly mired in a mutually contradictory reliance on the *laws* of thermodynamics and brought the worst of Newtonian physics to psychoanalysis. For all of this, as well as the fact that the economics of psychic energy was cogently criticized from *within* psychoanalysis (Rosenblatt & Thickstun, 1970; Rosenblatt & Thickstun, 1977) 40 years ago, economic concepts are studied to this day in many psychoanalytic institutes. Brandt (1966) has observed that the Freud of the *Gesammelte Werke* (1991a) meant id, ego, and superego as a rough sketch, far from the reified heights they attained in the United States by mid-century, and as a series of process concepts rather than structures. In this form, and understood descriptively rather than metapsychologically, they do not appear to be in direct conflict with a phenomenological reading of the self. However, as central structures of an intracranial mind-in-isolation, it is much harder to find any place for them other than as anachronisms of an earlier psychoanalytic epoch.

Turning to Sartre, we find his views of Freud to be more complex, undergoing a change from repugnance to ambivalence over the course of his career (Askay & Farquhar, 2006). He was critical – as I would argue he should have been – of a biomechanical basis for human being, the placing of an unconscious at the center of a psyche, and psychic determinism. He saw in Freud's adherence to a Cartesian mind-body dualism an adherence to a Cartesian concept of a mind-in-isolation. Sartre believed that everything was conscious and knowable but at the same time maintained that, in effect, much was unknown or unknowable (Sartre, 1943/2003). He credited psychoanalysis (and Freud) with the discovery and pursuit of hidden meaning and hidden motivation for action. To the extent that this did not mean to imply any metaphor of depth, Sartre here is quite consistent with Heidegger's (1927/2008) position that to grasp the meaning of a thing, one must reveal what is hidden or secret about it.

Clinical phenomenology

Guignon (2006), as a Heidegger scholar rather than a psychotherapist, is perhaps able to notice something that many of us may know but seldom think about. For many people, perhaps for fewer than in the past, psychotherapists and psychoanalysts have become the new moral authority. Like Stern (2012), Guignon also situates us as being an authority on "what constitutes the good life and how we can be at home in the world" (Stern, D.B., 2012, p. 270).[10] This is a position that, over the years, we have been loath to accept. However, I would posit that it has been implicit all along, even if we have chosen to willfully ignore or act against it.

Such a view of what we are about as analysts would also include care and relief of suffering. However, this would be a hard position to maintain if we see ourselves

---

10 This is a position that requires considerable discussion. I only mention it here; it will be one of the subjects of a future volume.

54 Psychoanalysis and Daseinanalysis

as dispensers of applied behavioral science or, as a colleague was wont to observe about himself, "I'm the driest tit in town." What follows from such ideas is that what we are at best about is offering instrumentality and freedom (from what?) on a means–ends, cash-and-carry basis. It offers absolutely no help concerning what sorts of ends are actually worth pursuing. We can consider such things as living at a higher level, thrownness versus falling into life, and authentic versus inauthentic, which all bring us back to Heidegger. Still another dichotomy is mindfulness versus mindlessness, beginning with Heidegger and heading East towards Buddhist teachings. Guignon (2006) observes that human experience involves an "irreducible moral condition" (p. 271). We certainly do not learn to address this condition as part of our clinical training, although perhaps our psychoanalytic descendants will have that opportunity. Another goal I would suggest is that of seeking out an authentic historicity consistent with one's personal archive and not still governed by developmentally early epistemes.[11]

Continuing in this vein of a phenomenological as opposed to a theoretical psychoanalytic language, we are brought to a number of concepts of our ways of being that psychoanalytic authors have lost sight of over the whole of our history. One can, I think, make a case that Freud's three major discoveries were the existence of unconsciousness (Freud, 1900/1953a; 1911, 1915, 1915, 1915, 1925, 1927, 1940/2005; 1899/2006), the nature of inhibitions, some manifested in the form of symptoms or anxiety (Freud, 1926/1959b), and the discovery that dreams have meaning (Freud, 1900/1953a, 1899/2006). The best description of *Die Traumdeutung* is as a discourse on the phenomenology of dreaming upon which Freud attempted (in chapter 7) to graft a "scientific" explanation of the process.[12] Having made these discoveries, however, he turned psychoanalysis inward to the drives and the analysis of the mind in isolation. It took a half-century for existential and phenomenological authors to get us outside again; their work was then lost and is only now being "rediscovered."

In turning inward, he also turned away from certain things fundamental to the being of man. By ceding control of man to the drives and their expression or inhibition, he turned away from the *will* (May, 1966; Wheelis, 1956). The will to act or proceed, in an analysis or in life, is of singular importance. Will is *not* the opposite of inhibition; indeed, it can act in the face of inhibition, and we often rely on it to do so. A related concept is that of intentionality, which, as has already been said, traces its roots back to Brentano (1874/1995), from whom Husserl (1937/1970) claimed it for phenomenology. As May observed, many of our patients come to us *suffering* from an undermining of will and intension, and while it would seem that our goal ought to be the relief of that suffering and the restoration of the two, some of us do something else entirely – we attempt to lead the patient into a state of "therapeutic"

---

11 Note the shift in language. However true it might be, it is at once so much more experience-distant.
12 I leave to the reader the evaluation of the success of this endeavor.

regression.[13] Although regressive elements *do* appear and may need to appear in order that they may be felt, understood, and integrated or re-integrated into the self, procedurally and clinically that is entirely a different matter.

Boss (1963) takes us to the other aspect of Dasein. What man is fundamentally about is being out in the world. The great majority of his thinking is also about the world and how he is (or isn't) in it. Heidegger (1927/2008, 1927/2010) offers three components that together define the world we are in: the *Umwelt*, the physical environment itself; the *Mitwelt*, the environment composed of all of those human beings we are with in the world; and the *Eigenwelt*, the taking of ourselves as subjects of introspection. (The latter is the closest to what we find in orthodox psychoanalysis.) We often implicitly construct the therapeutic situation as if to suggest that the world begins and ends at the door of the consultation room, when in fact what we are offering – and very importantly offering I would add – is a new piece of world to *be in* that is and becomes connected to the rest of it over the course of a treatment.[14]

What we as therapists ought to be interested in should be the nature of our patients' being-in-the-world and, equally importantly, their thoughts, feelings, and fantasies *about* being-in-the-world. What we sometimes find is that someone comes to us with a small repertoire of stereotypical behaviors that have not been reflected on and are leading her nowhere in life. Carol, a young attorney who officed in a building across the street from mine, had come for analysis the year before, suffering from boredom and a life that did not exist outside of her 90-hour workweek. In the session I am thinking of, she was talking about wanting to look for a desk lamp that was modern and colorful. For Carol, this was new and remarkable, but I kept silent about that. As the thought began to trail off, I asked her if she had looked in Crate & Barrel, a store around the corner from us. She replied with interest that she didn't know of the store or where it was. Being careful not to be critical or to say anything that could be construed as something wrong with her, I just said it was down the block and around the corner. She told me she never went that way. I did not comment about any of the things her revelation (the first time she had said anything like that about the *substance* of her life) suggested about her life; I just listened towards her. After waiting a moment for me to say something, she told me that she parked in her building, took the elevator to her office (where she ate her lunch), and only left it to go home or to cross the street to see me. There was no anxiety or inhibition directly behind her actions. I eventually concluded instead that this was simply her way of being-in-the-world – an everydayness, but an everydayness that she had fallen into and could not get out of. Only when I was sure of this did I ask

---

13 I have elsewhere argued at length (Leffert, 2013, Chapter 1) that to encourage a state of regression, rather than being therapeutic, constitutes an exercise in power relations.

14 This view of the clinical office as such a space is closest to what Bachelard (1958/1994) described in *The Poetics of Space*.

56 Psychoanalysis and Daseinanalysis

her if she wanted to do more, and when she told me she didn't know how, I told her that I could help her to learn.

There were obviously many other things I could have said or done, and if I felt Carol was phobic, or depressed, or suffering from PTSD (to name just a few possibilities), I would have done them. Instead, we came to know that in Carol's first being-in-the-world with her mother, whenever she became interested, excited, or exploratory (able to be thrown into the world), her mother, who was depressed, would – for lack of a better term – *still* her. This attachment variant led her to do that to herself whenever she was in the world. My first approach was then to see if there remained any will that could be tapped into and whether I could recruit her to join me in using it.

Carol was an extreme case. But this kind of lifeless narrowing into everydayness is much more frequent on a less striking level in a great many of our patients if we only look for it. It can be one productive strand of a therapy so long as we don't approach it in a way that carries overtones of disapproval or criticism or follows some metapsychological approach to psychopathology.[15]

Depth and time

I have already called into question the existence of actual depth in our being or in our psychologies, suggesting that it is a comfortable metaphor (that has become a form of everydayness for most us) rather than any sort of ontology of being. Most of us *do* think psychologically in terms of depth, but what do we really mean by it? I would suggest that depth is a stand-in for two very different sorts of concepts, one of which is a construct and the other an aspect of Dasein, the self whose being is in the world. The first is that of an unconscious that exists *below* what is conscious, separated from the latter by repression. That unconscious is also somehow layered. So what we have here is a spatial metaphor construed as a representation of psychological depth. It exists only in sketches first drawn by Freud but nowhere in the self or its neuroanatomy.

However, there is something *like* depth that does exist and very possibly is also what we have been meaning all along when we use that term – that something is time. Time certainly is not a construct, and when we speak of the past or a particular Dasein's past, we are talking about a kind of depth. Temporality is individual; each subject has her own. Depth can be measured here subjectively or intersubjectively against the familiar calendar that is in the world as only a reference point. The calendar (also watches, portable electronics, etc.), although objective, is also subjectively impinged on by things like daylight savings time (which does not exist in Arizona) and leap years. And, of course, under the rubric of "the past," we are used to expending a lot of therapeutic energy on it.

---

15 Attachment Studies is very much a phenomenological, observation-based discipline, not a metapsychology.

Psychoanalysis and Daseinanalysis **57**

Heidegger's (1927/2010) thinking on the subject of time was not fully developed in his magnum opus *Being and Time* (despite the title), but he returned to the topic in *The Basic Problems of Phenomenology* (1975/1982). He considered it to be of central importance: "Temporality is the condition of the possibility of all understanding of being; *being is understood and conceptually comprehended by means of time*" (1975/1982, p. 274). By "understanding," Heidegger means to hold oneself in a state of possibility in which the self projects itself into what it can be in the future; it is an unveiling of what can be. To add something, and say it slightly differently: parts of what I am in the present are what I once was and what I will be. Now, clinically, both of these ideas are interesting. If we think of it, many of our patients come to us sometimes with hope, but often without this possibility of "can be" and also lacking a coexistence in Dasein of past, present, and future.

A number of disciplines can be brought to bear on this issue of time. A failure to grasp time constitutes a failure to understand, and in phenomenological language, that is to fall into an everydayness made up of a limited number of stereotypical ways of thinking about it.[16] Heidegger (1975/1982) is talking about the same capacity that Tulving (1985/2003) – perhaps the most important of the modern memory scientists – is describing as the autonoetic memory system or autonoetic consciousness. Tulving is talking about the system capable of being *self*-conscious that is found only in humans. Not everything in this system is conscious at once; it is only capable of being so. He coined the phrase "mental time travel" to describe its capacity to think back into the past, and it is also capable of travelling into the future; it is aware of *possibility*. What Tulving and his colleagues did not consider was that this memory system contains an additional element that is of importance to us as psychoanalysts and psychotherapists – fantasy. We can retrieve fantasies into consciousness from the past, we can create them in the present, and we can fantasize about the future; they make up a component of mental time travel. We manage this autonoetic system by making use of a series of heuristics and biases. For the sake of completeness, we should include in these systems functioning Internal Working Models (IWMs; Craik, 1943/1952). The point is that this subsystem of Dasein, described in all these different ways by all of these disciplines, can fail wholly or partially in many ways as a result of developmental failure, attachment deficits, and trauma. What we have here are multiple ways of diagnosing the problem and offering treatment and care.[17]

I want to offer another weaving of concepts, both clinical and theoretical, with which to approach this matter of possibility, understanding, and "can be." When clinicians think about the past or its memories, we typically leave something on

---

16 Having no future in both short and long terms is highly dysphoric, hence the punishment function of imprisonment.

17 Critical to this argument is that if a concept is developed and evolved by different disciplines in truly different ways, drawing on unrelated data, particularly if they use different names (signifiers) for it, we have considerable basis for relying on its validity and reliability.

58 Psychoanalysis and Daseinanalysis

the table. I have previously discussed epistemes. Foucault (1969 & 1971/1972, 1961/2006a) used the term to describe not knowledge itself, but rather the particular set of rules, conditions, and discursive practices that govern the formation of knowledge at particular points in history. Epistemes refer to cultures and particular periods of time, such as the Enlightenment. I took up the term and used it to apply to individual human development; we all form and pass through a series of personal epistemes that are historically retained in our personal archive. They consist of the conditions and practices that govern the acquisition of personal knowledge, where that knowledge is as much emotional as it is cognitive and perceptual. Epistemes are shaped for good or ill; they are individual but must overlap if they are to allow us to function in our society. Erikson (1950/1963) made this point in purely developmental terms; he referred to it as mode epigenesis. He described how each society shapes the solutions individuals come up with in response to universal developmental challenges (he described eight) that prepare that individual for life in a particular society. Trauma can distort development and the formation of epistemes. In severe cases, the process gets stuck, and early epistemes remain active into the present. We have been calling such an event fixation, but this description (I hope) tells more about how it actually happens.

One set of discursive practices involves how we relate to others as both objects and subjects. In an extreme example, they all might appear in the present as difficult to distinguish from parents, either actual or fantasied. This weaving clearly involves transference, but transference that includes *what was and what is* and is both subject-subject and subject-object. In the therapeutic situation, this is limited to the therapeutic partners, but in the *Mitwelt*, many people are involved. I am treating transference here as a descriptive, phenomenological concept unaccompanied by a metapsychology of displacement, projection, or identification. It is an aspect of experience and being that involves a temporal dimension, certainly, but not spatial depth. It is not a pure culture of some past relationship.

Taken together, these practices lead to the conclusion that, in transference, *nothing* is transferred. Phenomenologically, the "transference" relationship exists in the present between patient and analyst (as does countertransference). That relationship has both history and meaning that can be explored. These explorations reveal the patient's or analyst's personal history of relationships and their meaning. All of this is as much about emotions, often painful emotions, as it is about cognitive understanding. The relationship, however, as it exists in the therapeutic situation is between analyst and patient in the now; *it is not between anyone else* (although other past and present relationships influence it). May (1958b), in responding to the classical definitions of transference from the past, finds little use for the concept and replaces it with the powerful term "encounter."

Anxiety from a phenomenological standpoint

Classically disposed psychoanalysts understand anxiety in two ways: in terms of the structural relations of ego psychology, or pegged to libido theory and its stages

Psychoanalysis and Daseinanalysis **59**

of psychosexual development. In the world of contemporary psychoanalysis, both approaches are seen to be flawed (e.g., Holmes, 2010). Phenomenologists understand anxiety neither in structural terms that lead to a formulation of the ego signaling itself (that is, after all, what is entailed) concerning some form of intrapsychic danger nor in terms of a developmental problem. Anxiety is ontological in nature (May, 1958a). It is a process response that probably exists at least across mammals and perhaps across all vertebrates as a threat to *being there* (Panksepp, 1998; Panksepp & Biven, 2012). I say "being there" and not "life" because it is easy to imagine threats to being not appraised as a threat to life. "Anxiety" is still another place where the Strachey translation lets us down (Leffert, 2013, Chapter 5). Freud, with at least some understanding of these issues, used *Angst*, a term that does not translate well. It is powerful, meaning something like anguish or dread. German does not draw a distinction between anxiety and dread, nor a distinction between anxiety and fear. Anxiety is certainly weaker; Freud could have used *Sorge* (having a care or worry) if he wanted something weaker, but he didn't. I am not meaning here to elide the distinction between normal anxiety and anxiety as an illness, although trying to distinguish the two is not always so easy.

Let me illustrate (not prove) what I am trying to say about *Angst* by describing a series of experiences I had with my now 34-year-old son during the first few months of his life. Jonathan slept in a crib in his own room next to ours. He would awaken us crying loudly in the morning; I would rush in, change his diaper as quickly as possible, and bring him to his mother who nursed him. Initially, he cried loudly throughout these procedures, and it took a few moments for him to stop crying and begin to nurse. All was then well. He acted overwhelmed by the combination of negative stimuli, hunger, dirty diaper, and whatever else he was enduring that he had failed to mention. Whatever these *physical* experiences, this was also a psychological-emotional experience – *Angst. I* may have known that he was going to feel better shortly, but *he* certainly didn't. I took to picking him up and hugging him before changing him, talking to him in a soft, comforting way, and murmuring endearments through all of this. I also took to calling out to him that I was coming as soon as I heard his cries. He must have been 4 months old, give or take, by the time I figured all this out. Then, one morning, when I picked him up and held him, he stopped crying. The rest of the procedure was then accomplished quickly in the usual manner, but without further comment on his part.

Something important had obviously happened. His feeling comforted by my physical presence and his developing ability to formulate some kind of knowledge that help was on the way led to his being able to psychologically master his pain. A maturing body and autonomic nervous system may also have been involved. But there is more to tell. A short time later (I cannot remember just how long) Jonathan awoke crying; I called out to him by name that I was coming, and he stopped crying. My wife and I looked at each other. Two things had happened phenomenologically. First, communication in some form had taken place. It was not just an event in the present but one that had drawn on some sort of historical memory

60 Psychoanalysis and Daseinanalysis

already extant at circa four months. Second, Jonathan had also developed an as yet limited capacity to calm himself when he knew that he would shortly be cared for.

I offer this as a prototypical good enough experience that, for other children and other parents, could have occurred in much the same fashion or have been mishandled and gone wrong in all kinds of ways. They involve a beginning that would be followed by countless events, experiential and developmental, that would determine the ultimate nature and place of anxiety in any given human being. From the earliest experiences onward, the occurrence or absence of anxiety is a byproduct of the regulation or dysregulation of relational emotional systems (Renik, 2000; Schore, 2009). These systems, beginning with the primary intersubjectivity (Bråten & Trevarthen, 2007) of the mother-child dyad, represent nonlinear holisms that are inseparable from the wider subjective emotionality of the *Mitwelt*.

The earliest occurrences of anxiety are linked to events of mind being overwhelmed by experience and sensation. As cognitive development progresses, less intense anticipatory anxiety appears in conjunction with the ability to predict future events based on the present and memory, or mental time travel (Addis, 2008; Leffert, 2010; Schacter, Addis, & Buckner, 2008). Internal working models (Craik, 1943/1952) also play a role in these functions. In all of these last few paragraphs, we are speaking phenomenology, not theory.

Depending on life experience and exposure to trauma, anxiety will appear in a wide range of contexts. Over the course of development and into adulthood, two ontological shifts will take place in the basis of anxiety. The first is a change from the earliest physiological experiences of infancy, to intersubjective emotional experience, to a later psychological experience – the dread of a loss of being. The second and final change occurs at some later time when what is dreaded is not a loss of being but death. And this brings us into the phenomenological domains of everydayness and thrownness.

In the face of death (the approach of our own or the experience of another's we are close to), Dasein can behave in two possible ways. It can be thrown into the experience; that is to say, the reality of death is engaged, and with that engagement, the experience of life becomes more intense. Its limitations make it and the living of it more prized. In the face of death, mourning becomes possible. The alternative is to fall back into everydayness. The intensity of life is lost, and the existence of death is repudiated. In this state of everydayness, there is a global dread of an unacknowledged death, a loss of being, or there is *no feeling at all*. The impossibility of death, and of engaging its meaning, brings with it the impossibility of mourning.

Some recommendations for employing a phenomenological approach in clinical psychoanalysis

Although there has been some limited interest in phenomenology in the contemporary psychoanalytic literature, there has been little writing about what you

Psychoanalysis and Daseinanalysis **61**

actually *do* if you are attempting to apply phenomenological principles to psycho-analytic practice. Orange (2009), in a brief paper, offers an overview of a few excellent guiding principles, and Stolorow (2011) offers the only contemporary account of Heidegger that I have found in our literature, as well as a discussion of some of his own personal experiences. The strange terminologies that accompany a discussion of phenomenology would suggest to the uninitiated that we are dealing with a series of arcane procedures that are experience-distant. To the contrary, at least for many Contemporary psychoanalysts, the situation is much more akin to that of Monsieur Jourdain, in Molière's (1959) comedy *The Would-be Gentleman*, who was surprised to learn that he had been speaking prose all of his life. For clinical descriptions of the work and the clinical theory they follow from, we really have to go back to the mid-century literature on phenomenological and existential psychoanalysis that we have already discussed. We find the work of Medard Boss (Boss, 1963; Heidegger, 1987/2001) and that of Rollo May (May, 1958a, 1958b, 1964, 1966; May et al., 1958), who began with Sartre (1943/2003) and whose work was enhanced by the creative interchanges that he shared with Boss during the latter's visit to the United States in 1961–1962.

Boss (1963) immediately distinguishes the two theories of psychoanalysis, the clinical and the metapsychological; he finds metapsychology internally and externally contradictory and levels the same critiques against it as I (among many others) do. He distinguishes the phenomenological psychoanalyst from classical psychoanalysts and their orthodoxies in that the latter tend to look *behind* the immediate phenomena of the psychoanalytic situation in search of some deeper (and unverifiable) theoretical meaning, whereas the former stay with the experiences of patient and analyst. The goal is to discover their meaning for the individual patient. This involves an exploration of a patient's historical narrative and personal archaeology (Leffert, 2013). The primary tools in this phenomenological method are discourse and deconstruction (Heidegger, 1975/1982), with interpretation used judiciously and not as part of a search for depth.[18] A little interpretation goes a long way, and like seasoning, overuse may ruin the dish. If *The Interpretation of Dreams* (Freud, 1900/1953a) was essentially a phenomenological book to which Freud had added a metapsychological epilogue (Chapter 7), Boss is about removing the epilogue. A phenomenological approach to the patient – treating him as an independent subject capable of decisions – differs from the power-relations focus of a great many therapeutic relationships. In standard analytic technique, the demand for free association is, in effect, a way of bypassing the person (and their autonomy) to get to putative unconscious depths, a procedure that has never been proven to exist and has been replaced in Contemporary psychoanalysis with discourse. We are concerned with the *beingness of the patient*.

---

18 It should be clear that these are familiar tools that have been discussed in the psychoanalytic literature; phenomenology provides context for better understanding their use.

62 Psychoanalysis and Daseinanalysis

We are interested in investigating and describing the patient (as she is interested in us), not in destroying what we find through interpretation in search of some level of deeper meaning. What we do want to open and free through a constructive deconstruction are the ways in which a patient's life is constrained and limited to a few routinized, inauthentic, being-less functions and the suffering that attends it. There has been, over the long history of psychoanalysis, a tendency to posit the existence of tools, some of which, like working through,[19] seem quite dubious. What we are offering instead is a specialized form of care and healing (Chapter 6) and the goals we are seeking to accomplish, in addition to the above, are relief from pain and suffering.

Rollo May (1958a), with more than a touch of irony, asks the question: Are we seeing the patient as she really is in her own reality, as opposed to a blank screen upon which *we* project *our* theories and then act upon them? How do we further separate her own unique worldview from our own and that of our shared culture? In fact, this can be accomplished fairly simply, but it requires hard work on our parts. We have to come to know our patient, not her metapsychology, very well, to know both who she is and what symptoms she struggles with. We should try to avoid theorizing as much as we can, but must expect to be partially unsuccessful. (An analyst who can *only* think theory will be unable to think.) From my own experience, this kind of knowing requires many months of both listening and participating in order to bring it about. I have found that an indication that this knowing has begun appears when it occurs to me reflectively that this patient's being and world are very different from my own. I became aware in this way of the geographic constriction of Carol's world and Roger's angry, somewhat arrogant world. They were distant from others and, in both cases, manifested a terrible solitude. I believe that many of us practice this technique spontaneously without any notion of what we are turning to. Being also involves potentiality, a different future. It is a being-in-process. We are interested in looking into being out there (or out here), not collections of internal representations. The investigation of our patient's being in this way should be accompanied by a similar re-investigation of our own.

A phenomenologically informed psychoanalyst engages the same sorts of issues in the therapeutic encounter as one who organizes her work around some theoretical base. However, rather than listening to a patient in order to offer some theoretically based interpretation directed towards some theoretically understood psychopathology, the phenomenological analyst seeks to understand her patient's existence, how it has been shaped by life history, and observes psychopathology descriptively, organizing it around the patient's pain and suffering rather than some theoretical depth. In analyzing the structure of existence, she seeks out the reality of situations of human crisis (May, 1958a).

---

19 Working through has always seemed to me to be more of an excuse for why what we are doing with a patient doesn't work and waiting until *any* connection between our actions and what is happening with the patient is lost.

May (Schneider et al., 2009) is particularly critical of treatment or analysis aimed at the self or at changing the self. What he means is treating the self in isolation as opposed to the self as inseparably being-in-the-world. This is about internal capacities verses external gimmicks: "existentialists were always for man in the world, using his capacities.... Man is not a bunch of gimmicks.... He is *a human being who cannot make a go of his life*. And that may be a variegated problem, but it's a very profound problem" (p. 421, italics added). May is about enlarging a person's sensitivity, her capacity to feel, to love, to think.

May (Schneider et al., 2009) sees the analyst or psychotherapist as focusing on a patient's particular anxiety or suffering, descending with them into their personal hell. Using technical language of whatever sort with a patient takes him away from that hell, away from what needs to be experienced and worked with. He believed that an analyst's first task is to build a relationship with a patient, which, I think, gives him the courage to face himself. In order to do this, she has to also be able to face her own personal hell.

Roger's analysis: phenomenologically speaking

Drawing on the material in these last two chapters, we can reexamine the work I did with Roger from a phenomenological point of view.[20] When I first met Roger, the question I had in mind – the same question I have with any patient – was what it was, exactly, that he wanted from me and whatever work we might do together. I am prepared to wait for an answer, to help a patient define one, or to regard the answer I get as at best a partial one. It made things easier that Roger could actually tell me what he wanted – a relationship with a woman he could love. I asked him with great seriousness why he considered this a problem to bring to a psychoanalyst (if he felt he needed help with finding the right woman, this was not necessarily a problem for an analyst as opposed to a dating service or Match.com). Not at all put off by my question, he responded that he was not sure he was capable of it and that he was deeply unhappy. Taken together with the shambles of his work relationships, it was clear that his way of being-in-the-world was both curtailed and stereotyped. He was not truly *in* the world so much as caught in the everydayness of his heuristics (Kahneman et al., 1982) that failed him so miserably. I told him something of this (without any of the jargon); I thought his problem had to do with the very nature of his being,[21] and that this was indeed something we could deal with. It seemed[22] that these observations had a great deal to do with his concurring with my suggestion to begin an analysis.

---

20 I would suggest re-reading Roger's brief case history in Chapter 1 before proceeding.
21 This phraseology might at first glance seem hard for a patient to grasp, but in those times that it has seemed appropriate to the clinical situation, patients have appreciated it.
22 I say "seemed" because I believe that we are ignorant of much of what really is going on in a therapeutic encounter, however much we might think otherwise, and the shorter the episode under consideration, the more true this is.

64 Psychoanalysis and Daseinanalysis

Let us also consider the precipitant of Roger's referral to me by his ward attending. His behavior with the ward staff did eventually catch his *attention* in an interesting way. In a word, the way he treated these people was lacking in intentionality.[23] Intentionality gives meaning to experience and to action; it involves truly being-in-the-world and perceiving it accurately. Had I tried to draw Roger's attention directly to this problem (and it *was* a problem because it could have had a detrimental effect on his training experience and his career), he would not have been able to hear it as such or to acknowledge its existence. Problems with intentionality are not clinically uncommon.

Similarly, it was clear to me that Roger's relationship with his mother, fraught with insecurity and *her* seductive attachment to him, pre-figured his adult relations with women and his epistemic approach to them. His rules of knowledge governing relations with women had remained the rules he had developed in childhood in his relationship with his mother. He expected women to behave seductively towards him. Women would unexpectedly disappear; it was wise not to forget that and to be fearfully on guard. At the same time, a woman's feelings for him could be depended on (even if *she* could not); he didn't have to concern himself with them. He could not, however, have made any use of an etiological observation suggesting either repetition or transference. His problem and his analysis existed in the present, informed by his *history*, not by theory. Elements of either could be concealed or hidden, but they could also be explored, deconstructed, or revealed. This is the essence of a phenomenological approach to psychoanalysis.

I first pointed out to Roger that he seemed to have no idea what he was about with women. He had a purpose, it is true – but the way he framed the world and his being in it had nothing to do with what he wanted. If he knew what he intended, if his very being were involved with it, he would not have behaved with women as he did, pursuing them with such desperate anxiety. We had the discussion about anxiety: how he knew or didn't know what women were feeling, and how it was or wasn't like him.

It was at this point, a year and a half or so into the analysis, that I did raise the question of the original problem he had had with the ward staff. I called his attention to the fact that this, too, was a problem involving women and how he thought, or didn't think, about them. Roger had since left the ward and moved on to other parts of his training without a repetition of these difficulties. I was interested in revealing to him just how widespread his stereotypical experience of women was.

A few weeks later, Roger began to talk about his relationship with his mother. I thought that this move back in time to the historical narrative became possible after exploring the very limited view he had had of present-day women as human beings. But I also knew that I could not be sure that this was the case (as we can

---

23 Intentionality should not be confused with "purpose." It is not about action directed toward accomplishing a goal; it is about the *knowing* of what one intends in the world that one is in.

never be *sure* of such connections between process and change). He told me, in keeping with Slade's (1999b) observation, that although he knew his mother loved him and supported him, he didn't think that she ever really knew him or who he was. I asked him how he had been affected by her death. He told me that he had been profoundly shocked, startled really, by it – even though her health had declined significantly in the months before she died. But beyond this feeling of shock or startle, he had felt nothing. He knew that there was something wrong with this, but not why he was as he was or that this was a description of his being. And although he knew what mourning was, he did not mourn because there was nothing in his head *to* mourn.

His relationship with his mother had been ambivalent, to be sure, with her caring, her support, and her loyalty outweighing the anxiety her seductiveness and secular unreliability caused him. However, I thought that the phenomenological problem caused by her death, and the accompanying falling back into everydayness, needed to be approached first. Since there was no access to any emotion in the present about her death, the route to the everydayness had to lie in a consideration of his earlier feelings toward her.[24] So I asked him simply if he remembered anything in particular about his feelings during his mother's illnesses or hospitalizations. He described two experiences in which his mother had been hospitalized. The first was a rather fuzzy memory from about age five when she was gone for a number of weeks. He was taken to see the facility she would be going to, and corresponded with her through his father while she was there. At the time, he could not understand why she was going there or what would be done to her. The only other memory he had of this experience was that his father had left for a few days before his mother came home; he was left with a babysitter he did not know for these long days and felt anxious and helpless in his parents' absence.

A number of things happened during Roger's eighth and ninth years. His mother was hospitalized for a hemorrhoidectomy for about a week, and this time, he was told in graphic detail about the procedure and the hemorrhage that had preceded it. His mother also told him that she might have died as a result of it. (Roger could not know at the time that this was an exaggeration.) Shortly after this, his father left for a number of months to find work in another city, where the family eventually moved. During this period, the boy was figuratively buried under an avalanche of material concerning his mother's medical history, which she described to him in detail. This did much to foster his already precocious intellectual development and interest in medicine.

It also seems that when he was 6 months old, his mother had had a partial gastrectomy to remove a benign tumor. There had been a post-operative infection

---

24 That this is essentially the same route an analyst who had never heard of phenomenology would have followed should not really come as a surprise. In either case, one is seeking narrative and experience in the therapeutic situation; the therapeutic approach informed by phenomenology focuses first on being and does not seek resonance in the clinical situation with preconceived metapsychology.

66 Psychoanalysis and Daseinanalysis

and a second surgery, all of which were later described to him. Ultimately, the post-operative and convalescent pain had led to an opiate addiction that required the hospitalization in a sanitarium that the boy remembered. Although opiate-free, his mother still relied on barbiturates for insomnia. Roger *knew* all this but had not thought about it until I asked; it had been unconscious.

My therapeutic stance during this phase of the analysis was to regularly ask follow-up questions in pursuit of the narrative. It turns out that he suffered another major trauma during his eighth and ninth years. At the time, his father was out of the home looking for work in another city. It seems that his mother was in the habit of taking her sleeping meds before actually getting into bed; she hated lying there awake. Roger was awakened one night by a crash that was his sedated mother falling to the floor. She was too big for him to move; by pleading and crying he was able to rouse her sufficiently so that she could half-crawl and he could half-drag her until he got her into bed. To say he was overwhelmed would be an understatement. Every night thereafter, he would stay awake and listen "for a long time" until he heard she was safely in bed. Roger's experience was entirely consistent with Stolorow's (2002) observation that trauma imparts a crushing burden of unbearable emotions that leads to all emotions being reduced or obliterated. The experience was repeated once or twice more before his father returned. He had no one to talk to about it; his mother seemed to treat it as an Oedipal secret that he felt he must honor, and, he confessed, the whole thing had also made him feel important. But it also made him less likely to talk to anyone about anything of emotional importance to him. When I asked him what he was afraid of when his mother fell, he told me he thought she might die. Perhaps not surprisingly, Roger was also left with a kind of insomnia in which it usually took him two hours to fall asleep. Interestingly, when he first slept (as opposed to just having sex) with a woman, the insomnia disappeared permanently; he knew this particular descendent of his mother was safe.

In this context, Roger brought up a memory of a tonsillectomy he had had around age four. The anesthetic induction with ether was terrifying. He remembered the mask, the feeling of spinning, his useless struggles, and being forcibly held down. When I asked him what he now imagined it had felt like, he responded immediately, "It must have been like dying."

There is only one other piece left to Roger's story. When he was 12, his mother suffered what was a fairly serious heart attack. It was at night; an ambulance was called. Details emerged slowly. In those days, not much was available beyond supportive care, and children were not allowed to visit in hospitals. There was a history of heart disease and much lore about it in his mother's family; an uncle had already died of an MI. Roger, of course, heard it all. The first heart attack was a warning; if you survived it, you had the chance to mend your ways; what that was supposed to consist of beyond deciding not to feel stress and not eating butter, cream, and eggs was not clear. Irrespective of this regimen, Roger's mother suffered two more heart attacks during his high school years. While she became obsessed by and fearful of them, his father acted as if nothing was going on, and Roger learned to deny their potential danger. By the time he was away at college and his father called to tell him his mother had died in her sleep, he felt nothing at all.

I was the first person to hear Roger's story in its entirety, and was horrified by what he had been through. I told him so. He burst into tears; as he wept, he wailed that he wanted his mother back. I observed quietly that it must have been hard to lose her. Death and loss were both on the table for the first time. In keeping with my view that the phenomenology must precede the mourning, I asked about his feelings and ideas about death and dying. Roger told me he did not believe in God or any sort of afterlife. When you died, it was the end and you simply ceased to exist as a human being. His own eventual death did not particularly trouble him. What he dreaded, however, was the dying part of it, which he thought would be like *consciously* ceasing to exist and knowing that was what was happening. When I asked him what he thought that would feel like, he replied, "It would probably be like what I felt when I was anesthetized – frightened, struggling, and immobilized." I felt, over the hours that followed, that Roger was becoming more alive and more of a feeling person.

Roger's mourning followed from this, requiring little of me beyond my presence as a caring witness. Throughout this work my analytic stance remained one of asking questions as breaking points appeared in the narrative, and deconstructing any conclusions on his part that seemed arbitrary and unstable. For example, I noted at one point early on that he didn't seem to consider the feelings of the women he sought out. Sometime later, he was dating a woman and told me he thought she really cared for him. He had described nothing about their relationship that suggested such a thing, so I asked only how he knew this. There were many other ways to raise this question, all of which seemed potentially injurious. In his usual fashion, he took the question home and returned, telling me that indeed he had no reason to think that other than his wishes. From that point on, his relationships, although at times still rocky, were more substantial and freer of anxiety.

In this chapter, I have offered a more clinically oriented discussion of phenomenological psychoanalysis, accompanied by case material offered to illustrate what the work actually looks like. Although there is some difference in emphasis, it doesn't look all that different from any other contemporary psychoanalysis, which is implicitly phenomenological. What I have tried to show is that the thinking behind the work is different and much clearer; it serves to free it of theoretical suppositions that are often used to direct an analysis toward what the analyst already believes about the patient. Although I have alluded to the point several times, the role of unconsciousness and the therapist's thinking about it has been so far deferred. We will turn to it now in the next chapter.

4

THE PHENOMENOLOGICAL UNCONSCIOUS

Introduction

The earliest maps of exploration date perhaps from the 15th through the early 16th centuries. They contain large blank areas around their edges labeled *terra incognita* – unknown lands – that are often populated by sea monsters and other mythical creatures. They have always been the subject of fascination, interest, and an uncanny dread. It is this experience that has informed our sense of unconsciousness, or the unconscious. It owes its fascination to the consciousness of the left cerebral hemisphere beholding the processes of the right (Baars, 1988/2003a; Baars, 1993/2003b), metaphorically gazing at them across the cerebral commissures.

In a previous work (Leffert, 2010, Chapter 5), I offered a series of critiques of the psychoanalytic concept of a dynamic system unconscious held in place by repression. It has now been almost a century since Freud (1923/1961a) attempted, at least in his publications, to do away with the systemic unconscious and 50 years since Arlow and Brenner (1964) made a further attempt to eradicate it from psychoanalytic metapsychology. Although multiple critiques drawn from psychology, philosophy, and neuroscience render such a concept of a unitary unconscious unsustainable, it still remains in widespread clinical use, at least implicitly. (Its cousin, the relational unconscious, this time dyadic, has also appeared recently on the scene.) This seems to be as true for Contemporary psychoanalysts as it is for classically oriented ones. Concepts, once named, tend to continue to exist, cluttering up the ontology, regardless of what has happened to the basis of their existence.

However interesting this discussion may once have been, it will not be the focus of this chapter. Instead, I will offer an overview of it at the start because it does raise issues, particularly in the area of neuroscience, that have relevance to a much wider consideration of unconsciousness. Specifically the relationship of unconsciousness to psychopathology is a very small piece of the action. What we will be interested in here is the phenomenology of unconsciousness (not set off by the use of the definite article) as it exists in Dasein, its intersubjectivity in the therapeutic situation and the *Mitwelt*, its place in social networks, its functional neuroanatomy, and its empirical psychology. I would go on to posit that the unconscious aspects of the Self are at least as important as its conscious ones, and probably even more so. Baars (1993/2003b) posited that consciousness comprises a small, slow, serial system operating in the presence of a large, fast, parallel processing, unconscious one (*not* a system in the psychoanalytic sense but rather in the holistic sense). Nisbett and Wilson (1977), speaking from the perspective of uncertainty and prospect theory rather than a neuroscience one, found that when they studied their subjects' responses to being questioned about their ongoing mental processes, the subjects didn't have the remotest ideas about why they were thinking what they were thinking. Thus the origins of specific thoughts and behaviors must lie beyond the conscious, somewhere in a collection of multifaceted functions and processes that manifest an unconsciousness not particularly related to psychoanalysis.

This chapter will explore the nature of unconsciousness that is consistent with these critiques as well as consider how the concepts of knowability and unknowability might offer a better foundation for our clinical observations. In the original German, the terms *conscious* and *knowable* are much closer to each other than they are in English; we have *bewusst* and *unbewusst* and their root word, *wissen*, which means "to know." This chapter will also consider personal epistemology and archaeology and where they fall in the realms of consciousness and unconsciousness. We are, in other words, interested in the role of unconscious mental processes in the holistic self.

To ignore the fact that the unconscious parts of the self are both diverse and complex entities that influence each other and consciousness interreferentially is to render our understanding of the latter incomplete. This was not always the case. Prior to the mid-20th century, not enough was known about neuroscience or empirical psychology to miss their presence in general psychology, psychoanalysis, or phenomenology. In the first half of the century, it really was quite possible to think of phenomenology as having to do only with conscious experience and existence and to dismiss psychoanalysis in particular for its focus on an unconscious (Sartre, 1943/2003). The importance of the physical body and brain could similarly be dispensed with. However, as the century wore on, the weight of the neuroscience, combined with that of the empirical psychology that was building up, made it impossible to disavow it.

Although the old psychoanalytic practice of moving unconscious contents to conscious reflection via hermeneutic interpretation remains central for some of us, others have come to lessen its singular importance as a factor in therapeutic action. I have argued (Leffert, 2010, 2013) that much of what goes on in a psychoanalysis or psychotherapy takes place beyond the consciousness of either analyst or patient. It would seem that both Relational and Intersubjective authors have grasped this point, and, over the past decade, a stream of papers describing a

70 The phenomenological unconscious

"relational unconscious" (e.g., Orange, D.M., 2000; Safran, 2006; Zeddies, 2000) has appeared. The field of Network Studies (Leffert, 2013, Chapter 4) can help us gain a wider sense of this terrain.

The unconscious and unconsciousness

The nature of unconsciousness and its relations with consciousness is a problem that has troubled the sleep of psychoanalysts far less than it should. Our interest in the subject began quite honorably with the clinical observation that, over the course of a psychoanalytic treatment, patients come to remember things, usually of a painful or traumatic nature, that they couldn't remember at the start of it. This observation led to the development of a number of less satisfying metapsychological arguments. Freud's interest in unconsciousness and that of those analysts who came after him were not focused on furthering the knowledge of cognition or mental function per se; rather, so much as seeking, in the ruins of the seduction theory and the affect-trauma frame of reference, a comprehensive theory of psychopathology and cure. These various approaches have all failed to stand up in the face of a growing body of neuroscientific evidence. For their part, neuroscientists have tried to have as little as possible to do with psychoanalytic formulations of unconsciousness and the arcane language that goes with them. Be that as it may, their work requires a reformulation of *our* thinking on the subject. Let's take a look at the neuroscience and neuropsychology.

Laterality

The best place to start looking at the neuroscience of unconsciousness is in the laterality of the brain. Above the level of the cerebellum, the brain exists in duplicate. This includes the two cerebral hemispheres, right (RB) and left (LB), each with an accompanying hippocampus, amygdala, thalamus and limbic system. These two brains (or half-brains?)

> communicate with each other [mostly but not entirely] through the cerebral commissures and, independently, they communicate with the external world and the people in it. Both independently and interreferentially, they self-organize, develop higher levels of complex content as they process new incoming information, and elaborate and reprocess existing information that they already contain. (Leffert, 2010, pp. 138–139)

None of this pertains to any notion of psychological depth; everything is just what it is phenomenologically and where it is neuroanatomically, their being can be discovered, examined, and revealed through the study of things as we find them, but those things are all present as they are.

Beginning in the 1940s, commisurectomies began to be performed to treat intractable epilepsy (successfully), effectively creating anatomically "split brain" individuals. This made it possible to study the neuropsychology of each of the cerebral hemispheres, more or less in isolation (Bogen & Vogel, 1962; Hoppe, 1977; Sperry, Gazzaniga, & Bogen, 1969; Wolford, Miller, & Gazzaniga, 2004).

The most basic of observations that can be made about the functioning of the two cerebral hemispheres is that the sensory and motor nerve fibers decussate or cross over; thus the LB, dominant in right-handed individuals, has motor and sensory connections to the right side of the body and vice versa. Dominance is no longer thought to be as absolute as it once was, particularly with respect to language (Bogen, 2000). Consciousness as we experience it, although not modular (as no brain or bodily function is), resides largely in the LB. While it can be inferred (Bogen & Vogel, 1962; Hoppe, 1977; Sperry et al., 1969) that the LB knows that the RB is working and what it's up to, it cannot be verbally conscious of RB thoughts or ideas.

Bearing in mind these caveats, the LB thinks logically, verbally, uses language and syntax, and reasons and recalls linearly. Although it also possesses information organized in parallel, it is presented linearly after often ad hoc choices are made by the LB. Implicit here is that a significant amount of the information present in the LB is, at any given time, also not conscious. It *experiences* anxiety and guilt[1] while being *verbally aware* of the entire range of emotions. The LB *appears* dominant because in it resides the consciousness that we know, but in a normal brain with its hemispheres connected, much of what is going on goes on in the RB. The two have separate dissociable memory systems in which the RB is able to "keep secrets" from the left (Risse & Gazzaniga, 1978).

The RB is nonverbal and knows words only as symbols of what they represent. It is conscious of them, and one can communicate directly with it in split-brain studies (the result of either commisurectomy or unilateral sedation). It is organized in parallel with multiple emotional and cognitive processes occurring simultaneously. It is very fast, with activity taking place in the range of 2 msec, literally too fast to be aware of. The RB is capable of solving problems almost before the LB even knows they exist. It has a separate dominant, experiential emotional system; it processes emotional and "nonverbal" prosodic speech. It, like the LB, has a self-organizing life of its own (Galin, 1974; Schore, 2003a, 2003b). For our purposes here, we cannot locate unconsciousness in a single hemisphere; the unconsciousness present in each, and in other areas of the brain, all manifest different properties.

The neuropsychology of unconsciousness

Both psychoanalysis and phenomenology have a considerable interest in unconscious memory. A distinction between the two is that psychoanalysts are mostly wedded to the concept of repression, while analysts whose work is informed

---

1 This would be consistent with anxiety and guilt representing the outcome of synthetic functions.

72 The phenomenological unconscious

by phenomenology (e.g., May, Angel, & Ellenberger, 1958; Stolorow, Orange, & Atwood, 2002) and phenomenologists themselves (e.g., Askay & Farquhar, 2006; Heidegger, 1987/2001) seem to be able to abide unconsciousness only in the absence of repression. Although unconscious memory would seem to be a simple matter, neuropsychology demonstrates just how complicated and obscure it is (Holmes, 1990; Singer, 1990) and, after 60 years of research, can still find no justification for a concept of repression.

There are things that we are aware of at a given time and things of which we are unaware. Some of the latter always remain so, while other memories are capable of moving in and out of awareness, given internal and external impingements on the self. This is essentially all we know about memory systems; the rest of it, although certainly interesting, consists only of elaborations of this basic statement. A further complication is that none of the authors responsible for the major work on memory done over the past half-century make use of or discretely consider the area of mental activity described by the term *the unconscious*. This omission should not be considered to be accidental; instead, it signifies that they have found no ontical basis for recognizing such an area.

If we classify memory by descriptive types, things become clearer. There is episodic memory, the ability to recall events that have happened to us, an area that is of interest to psychoanalysts and phenomenologists. Then there is semantic memory, our knowledge base; for example, the Battle of Hastings took place in 1066. A description of the Battle of Hastings – that is, a narrative – would seem to fall somewhere in between. These can be recalled (that is, enter consciousness) or not. The limbic system, and the hippocampus in particular, serve as a retrieval catalogue and are centrally involved in the recollective process. The *information* that is assembled into each individual episodic or semantic memory is encoded in synapses whose activity is facilitated or inhibited by experience (Kandel, 2001, 2006; Kandel & Tauc, 1965). Each act of recall (retrieval) offers a unique memory different from past and future recollections of that same event. Each recollection of an event or narrative is affected by its context and subsequently becomes a part of the memory. It then affects what is remembered the next time. Episodic and semantic memories vary enormously in stability, some lasting for decades and some passing away in days or weeks. And, of course, they are all subject to distortion occurring at the time of encoding and/or retrieval (Schacter, 2001). Failure at encoding, often taking place in traumatic situations (Fonagy, 1999; Martin, Wiggs, Ungerleider, & Haxby, 1996; Schacter, 1996), can affect to a greater or lesser degree what is available for recall and may damage other memories as well.

Lastly, there are four kinds of memory that cannot be conscious: procedural memory – the stuff of bicycle riding – and three kinds of priming: visual, auditory, and conceptual. Priming is the result of previous exposure(s) that manifests itself in preferentially selecting possibilities or having ideas about them without awareness of having been previously exposed to them.

The phenomenological unconscious **73**

What is important is that each of these memory types is concentrated in a different anatomical area of the brain. However, all of them are interreferential; for example, the presence of a conflictual episodic memory could interfere with priming or procedural functions. Thus, pushing someone off a bicycle could interfere with his subsequent ability to ride. In addition, some psychological phenomena can be seen as drawing on multiple kinds of memory. A moment's thought about transference, for example, would suggest that it combines elements of episodic and semantic memory, as well as conceptual and, probably, sensory priming. The same would be true for entirely different kinds of processes like heuristics and biases (Kahneman, Slovic, & Tversky, 1982). Willingham and Preuss (1995), drawing on all this information about unconscious memory, conclude that there is no functional, anatomic, or psychological commonality that could possibly lead one to posit the existence of a single unconscious memory system.[2]

The piece we have not yet talked about is repression, in which some part of the self acts to interfere with a particular memory coming into consciousness. We began with the neuroanatomical idea of consciousness on the left (LB), unconsciousness on the right (RB), and repression as the functional severance of the two at the commissures. Galin (1974) in effect said this, as did Hoppe (1977). However, the neuroanatomy did not hold up. Some fibers in the commissures are inhibitory, and there are cross-connections in other parts of the brain as well. In addition, the Right Brain is also conscious, as the split-brain studies (Sperry et al., 1969; Wolford et al., 2004) have shown. It is only that the Left Brain is not aware of its consciousness, which is nonverbal and symbolic. The hemispheres *do* normally exchange information, albeit not information coded into language. In the best of phenomenological traditions, the right hemisphere (Risse & Gazzaniga, 1978) and the left keep secrets from each other that can be uncovered.

If we look at repression as a putative concept, we find it harder and harder to sustain. It is not qualitative; there are degrees of repression. Anatomically, there must be at least three kinds of it: that occurring between the hemispheres, that occurring within each hemisphere, and that impinging on the contributions of other unconscious processes elsewhere in the brain. Repression would thus be *associated* with many structure/functions. While it acts on them, they are not the structure/function of repression. The term must encompass many *different* processes that need have nothing in common and, in fact, don't. Some might act by inhibiting excitatory neurons, while others might act by exciting inhibitory ones. When deconstructed anatomically and functionally, no single, stable process emerges. What began as "the king of defenses" turns out to be nothing but another unstable convention. Holmes (1990) reviewed 60 years of research on repression in experimental psychology and, reluctantly, reached the same conclusion.

---

2 The memory systems of the RB similarly need not be unconscious.

74 The phenomenological unconscious

The phenomenological unconscious

Early psychoanalytic thought viewed *the* unconscious as manifesting primary process cognition characterized by displacement and condensation. Later psychoanalytic authors (Holt, 1967; Klein, 1970) viewed the unconscious as highly organized, albeit on the level of primary process. The latter was no longer seen as primitive; rather, it developed first and continued to develop and elaborate throughout the life cycle. Secondary process logical thought did the same, only it started somewhat later. (There wasn't then much evidence for these two particular characterizations.) Still later (Baars, 1993/2003b; Rumelhart & McClelland, 1986), neuroscience defined (with evidence this time!) two sorts of cognitive processing, serial and parallel, with the latter at times manifesting (but not defined by) the properties of condensation and displacement. Serial processing was seen in the Left Brain, while parallel processing is seen on the Right, although, nowadays, this distinction is not absolute and at least some of each kind of functioning is seen on both sides. Similarly, language functions (Bogen, 2000) are no longer thought to be confined to a single dominant hemisphere.

Heidegger (1987/2001) actually dealt with the problem of unconsciousness and "unconscious intention," a much more descriptive telling of repression, in the *Zollikon Seminars*. He, too, is critical of repression, even in this somewhat phenomenological form. He describes something becoming unconscious as a result of Dasein's choosing to let something "slip away." This is consistent with George Klein's later formulation that it is the self who chooses to forget something, not repression. He goes on to say, "[a] matter [attributed to] unconscious intention is an explanation opposed to a phenomenological interpretation. This explanation is a pure hypothesis that in no way advances the understanding of the phenomenon itself" (Heidegger, 1987/2001, p. 169). Forgetting something painful involves not its slipping (passive, unconscious voice) away, but our *letting* it slip away. Heidegger maintains a focus on Brentano's (1874/1995) concept of intentionality.

Heidegger (1987/2001) viewed Freud's discovery of "the" unconscious as of tremendous importance. However, Freud's wish to craft a natural science out of psychoanalysis led him to force repression into a mechanistic, Procrustean bed of putatively scientific theory rather than grasping unconsciousness as *a phenomenon of existence*. Psychoanalytically oriented clinicians, at least through the 1950s, uncritically and unanimously accepted repression. In letting some painful thought or feeling slip away, it is the self – continuously afflicted by the painful event – that is relieved. This leads to the avoidance of the painful event, which still exists, albeit in an entirely *unreflective* way.[3] From a Freudian perspective, what is required is a container in which to throw the experiences that have slipped away, and no such container can exist.

---

3 We would consider this a *fallen* state.

The phenomenological unconscious **75**

Forgetting involves concealment, veiling, and making hidden. In the German, forgetting (*Vergessen*) is related to the English "to get," to keep together; the prefix *ver-* turns it into the negative, "not keeping." Recalling a thing is not remembering a thing; it is only a making-present. It becomes a remembering when it is made present as an experience from the past (this is the same distinction that Tulving, 2003, makes between noetic and autonoetic remembering).

The goal of the phenomenological analyst is "to get," to help the patient to remember and to make known rather than just to recollect. One inquires into the present and past being of the patient; the inquiry is aimed at recollection that leads to the re-emergence of narrative. For example, a sibling had recently told Louise, a woman in her 40s, that their father had sexually abused him during his early teen-age years. Louise had mentioned this to me in passing the second or third time I saw her. She did not attach any particular significance to this; it had not happened to her, and she was surprised to hear about it. I asked her if anything came to mind from that period in her life. She now remembered that the house had seemed creepy to her in those years, with a sense of secrets. She felt much more comfort-able at school. She also had a sense of not *ever* allowing herself to be alone with her father. What had begun as a recollection had become a fragmentary remembrance, a piece of narrative for future work. The creepiness and secrets were a part of her personal archaeology, the episteme of that period in her life. The one thing I did not do was to offer any sort of reconstruction. To do so is to take the patient out of being and into the everydayness of an outside "explanation" that she has neither connection with nor understanding of. Reconstructions only grow from theoreti-cal foundations; they cannot reliably reach unconscious experience. Even if histori-cally "correct,"[4] a reconstruction is not about the patient and cannot be claimed by her; it is instead about the *therapist's* being.

Techniques other than reconstruction *are* available to help a patient to pull together his personal narrative (held in autonoetic memory) and the feelings that accompany it. Questions and discourse are most likely to stir up unconscious mem-ories and nudge them into the discussion.

Contemporaneously, Stolorow, Atwood, and Orange (2002) offered an alterna-tive to Freud's view of *the* unconscious that more or less still persists in classical psychoanalytic circles. They offered what amounts to a critique of the Cartesian construct of the self-as-conscious-subject and the unconscious as inhabiting a sealed off chamber whose walls were constructed of repression. For Freud, the concept of repression is inseparable from that of unconsciousness. However, what these authors fail to note (as do most all Anglophone psychoanalysts) is that, in the original German, as opposed to Strachey's translation, repression is also inseparable from regression (Leffert, 2013); "the" unconscious tends towards the infantile. They

---

4 There is, of course, no single historically correct narrative of anything; each calling into consciousness of an event-memory is a new and unique event.

76 The phenomenological unconscious

see, as I do, Freud's position as essentially a pessimistic one in which we are all victims of our unconscious impulses and instincts for which we need expert (i.e., psychoanalytic) help to decode.

They (Stolorow et al., 2002) go on to posit "instead of a container . . . an experiential system of expectations, interpretative patterns, and meanings, especially those formed in the contexts of psychological trauma – losses, deprivations, shocks, injuries, violations, and the like" (p. 45). This, like Freud's, is also a pessimistic view; what cannot be felt or known simply slips out of awareness; repression is not required. Psychoanalysis is thus a mutual dialogic exploration or discursive practice rather than an archaeological excavation.

A further problem with stocking unconsciousness exclusively with psychopathology that got there in a developmental way is that this formulation also ignores the fact that there is all sorts of good stuff in there that we sometimes just don't happen to be thinking of in the present momentary world of experience. Askay and Farquhar (2006) describe Heidegger's position on unconsciousness in the *Zollikon Seminars* as involving shifts in attention and awareness akin to Stolorow et al.'s (2002) fluidity of consciousness. Unconsciousness characterizes vast reaches of the self that are very different, interreferential, and offer no basis for separating out one particular kind from all the others as psychoanalysts have always done. A particular problem here is that there are unconscious connections between individuals. We can talk about them today as intersubjective connections or as making up a relational unconscious, but Freud (1915/1957) knew about them long ago, long before we had this language. We still know very little about how these linkages take place. Although they deposit information in a psychoanalytically posited unconsciousness of whatever sort, they must involve other as yet undescribed processes, including (but not limited to) the Mirror Neuron System. However much we don't know about them, their actions and outcomes have become the subject of Network Studies (Christakis & Fowler, 2009) that we have discussed. Network Studies, too, lies outside the ken of most psychoanalysts.

What we can say is that a phenomenology of unconsciousness necessarily exists and is in no way a contradiction in terms, however much Sartre (1943/2003) might have thought so. Although some unconscious phenomena (procedural memory and priming are but two examples) *stay* unconscious, they are neither secret nor hidden, and we can find out *about* them through phenomenological inquiry (examining their manifestations; for example, riding a bicycle). There is much work still to be done in understanding the expanded place of unconsciousness in psychoanalysis.

The relational unconscious

As accounts of the birth of a Relational psychoanalysis began to appear in the psychoanalytic literature of the late 1980s, it very much appeared that this new paradigm most essentially involved a clinical discourse of mutual enactments and disclosures taking place within a two-person frame. Spezzano (1998) made note

The phenomenological unconscious **77**

of this and observed, reassuringly, that between such activities, Relational analysts carried on their clinical work in much the same manner as the rest of us – that is, they listened and interpreted. At the same time, not much was made of the place of *the* unconscious in such therapy, and this in turn led a number of authors (Gerson, 2004; Orange, D.M., 2000; Safran, 2006; Zeddies, 2000) to posit and describe a relational unconscious. But before we can go on to talk about what these authors have to say about the relational unconscious, there is one caveat: None of them consider the neuroscience of unconsciousness.

If one is to include the neuroscience, it seems best to think in terms of different mental elements having the property of unconsciousness, some of which, through the interaction of some number of processes, do come into consciousness. However, there is a problem – the right cerebral hemisphere. There is an understandable wish to be done with all of this and just locate the Freudian unconscious in the Right Brain (Bogen, 2000; Galin, 1974) and get on with it. But this just won't do.

Allan Schore (1994, 2003a, 2003b, 2005, 2009, 2011) has been arguing repeatedly and ever more convincingly for a very different sort of Right Brain. Drawing on a wide range of neuroscience research carried out by many investigators, he has posited that the early maturing Right Brain has a central role in the development of attachment paradigms and affect regulation through the mother-child relationship. During that process, autonomic functions are "burnt in" for good or ill. We have tended to prize left-brain serial cognition that is logically organized over a depreciated Right Brain – depreciated because of its apparent isolation and "primitive" organization. Nothing could be farther from the truth. Conscious cognition in the Left Brain lumbers along in its logical way, taking seconds or minutes to process information. Surprisingly, it frequently makes mistakes, offering a kind of best guess accuracy. In contrast, the right brain operates as a parallel distributed processing network (McClelland & Rumelhart, 1986; Rumelhart & McClelland, 1986) that processes information in as little time as 2 msec and is spot-on accurate. The presence of unconscious parallel processing in the Left Brain, and its relationship to consciousness, is not well understood. Schore, along with many other investigators, views the Right Brain as the cognitive and emotional processing center of the brain. He also posits (Schore, 2011) two forms of communication in the psychoanalytic situation: explicit verbal communication (Left Brain), and implicit Right-Brain-to-Right-Brain, nonverbal communication between patient and analyst that comprises a relational unconscious. He leaves no room for doubt concerning which of the two he considers more important in this eponymously titled paper, "The Right Brain Implicit Self Lies at the Core of Psychoanalysis."

There are two refinements necessary in Schore's (2011) position. The first is that he continues to make use of the concepts of primary and secondary process cognition, where they refer to the actual neurocognitive concepts of serial and parallel processing. The latter is less about a looser, more emotive form of cognition functioning via condensation and displacement than it is about multiple simultaneous interreferential threads of unfolding mental process including cognitive *and*

78 The phenomenological unconscious

emotional elements. The second issue, as was discussed, is that the Right Brain is neither implicit nor unconscious. It *is* conscious; rather, it is that the Left Brain is not conscious *of* it. Information passes from the Right Brain to the left across the cerebral commissures in symbolic non-language form. That passage of information can be inhibited or disinhibited to varying degrees. The corpus callosum, comprised anatomically of a number of commissures (Zaidel & Iacoboni, 2003), is not just wiring between the hemispheres but is a complex cortical structure in its own right.[5] If we are going to talk about a relational unconscious in an analysis or psychotherapy that makes any sense at all, it is necessary to consider the neuroscience behind it. It includes communication between the Right Brains of the participants but must involve their perceptual, memory, and mirror neuron systems as well; each of these operates in its own kind of unconsciousness. And since the Right Brain is only unconscious *from the perspective of the Left*, we are forced to conclude that the relational unconscious also includes *right brain conscious elements*. Other necessary components will be discussed, with a good deal of speculation, below. With these refinements in place, what Schore is offering is a part of a phenomenological account of unconsciousness. He describes what is, not what relates to metatheory.

Gerson (2004) "propose[s] that [the] reciprocal and mutual influence of unconscious minds upon one another creates a *relational unconscious*" (p. 73). He sees it as a fundamental property of interpersonal relations. Following Ogden (1994), he posits that it involves thirdness (which he wants to conserve) as the best way of capturing the implications of intersubjectivity. It is one of many "unique relations of twos, of the permitted and the prohibited, that transcends the individual conscious and unconscious elements of each partner" (p. 71). (It is not at all clear why only couples are permitted here.) He wants a "theoretical framework" (p. 72) where we want a phenomenological one. Following Spezzano (1995), he sees an object of therapy, perhaps *the* object of therapy, as bringing the relational unconscious into the left-brain consciousness of the patient and analyst. He does also posit that "if we postulate that all human groupings are characterized by both conscious and unconscious domains of experience and belief, then we may describe each individual's unconscious life as existing in a continuous relation with the unconscious life of all other persons and groupings in which his or her life is lived" (p. 74).

With the exception of the old goal of making unconscious things conscious that Gerson (2004) wants to conserve, these are important points. This last observation concerning the fact that we are all unconsciously connected to each other as parts of larger groups is especially so, although Gerson, along with other analysts, does not quite know what to do with it. Christakis and Fowler (2009) tell us what to expect from the behavior of such groups. Unconscious information (feelings are

---

5 The neuroscience of the corpus callosum and the condition of callosal agenesis (split-brain studies, nature's way) has burst on the scene in recent years. Zaidel and Iacoboni (2003), in an edited volume, offer a summary of current research in these areas.

The phenomenological unconscious **79**

also a form of information) spreads across social networks, facilitated or impeded by the geography of its membership and the presence of other social factors that act upon them. Each self in the world is connected to all the others, the results of which being determined only be the degree of separation.[6] A relational unconscious begins to form with the patient and therapist's first contact, but their individual connectedness to their own larger social networks influences this formation from these very first beginnings. The result of all this is that our seemingly most private and intimate thoughts are communicated to and shared with others – sometimes others that we don't even know.

Zeddies (2000) continues with a fairly conservative view of the relational unconscious. He relies on four premises in his arguments: that meaning and understanding are co-constructed and intersubjective rather than objective and absolute; that the boundary between consciousness and unconsciousness is fluid and intersubjectively mediated;[7] that language is fundamental to human experience in general and conscious verbal experience in particular; and that the therapist acts on the patient's unconscious experience to bring it into awareness. The latter two premises are the most conservative ones; we will develop an alternative to them. He sees the relational unconscious as not a replacement but a complement to the earlier formulation of an unconscious defined by repression, a position similar to Grotstein's (1979).

Consciousness and unconsciousness are inseparable, lacking a static boundary. Zeddies (2000) tries to posit this while still hanging onto a separate unconscious defined by repression. Unconsciousness, like consciousness, is a manifestation of intersubjective states and the product of a relational context. Neither exists entirely within a given individual (e.g., a patient or a therapist). Unconsciousness manifests the same atmosphere of unknowability and uncertainty as does conscious cognition. Both inside and outside of the therapeutic situation, there are only subjects; there are no objects or uninvolved witnesses. The therapeutic situation is rooted in discursive contexts where unconscious elements must be included in what has been described as discursive and implicitly conscious, even if they are not explicitly known.

If what is central to an analysis is the co-creation of meaning, this would seem, at first glance, to critique Heidegger's (1927/2008, 1927/2010) view that phenomenological inquiry involves reaching for something that is hidden or secret. This distinction is more apparent than real. If we put aside the contemporary language that was unavailable to Heidegger, the therapeutic reaching involves the co-creation of meaning, of new meaning, of new understandings, of things that are already there

---

6 Our ability to study or measure these connections fails at three degrees of separation, which is not to say that meaningful transmission of information doesn't take place across longer interpersonal and geographic distances.

7 As opposed to being mediated by a mind in isolation.

80 The phenomenological unconscious

that are waiting to be understood and assembled *not* waiting to be discovered (*terra incognita*). In this way, something new is always appearing intersubjectively.

What remains a source of considerable uncertainty in the literature on the relational unconscious is how the therapeutic process ought to act on it. Zeddies (2000) insists that in a supportive, encouraging, therapeutic relationship, what was unconscious and disassociated can be brought into awareness and discussed verbally, but "conversely, if certain meanings, experiences, and understandings cannot be explicitly acknowledged and explored by patient and therapist, then the therapeutic relationship is unconscious [and limited] in one way or another" (p. 473). Stern (1991) takes this position even further: "It is language, *and language only*, that defines meaning, and the limits of possible meanings are precisely the same as the limits of language. If a meaning cannot yet be spoken, it does not yet exist; and if it is not within the capacity of language to represent, it is not meaning at all" (p. 58, italics added). But is this true? It is perhaps unfair to be overly critical of positions dating from the 1990s, as there has been much thought and writing on these subjects since, but do we really want to assert that material outside of consciousness and language, particularly when the boundary between the two is now understood to be so volatile, lacks meaning for or influence on an individual? If language is the motive force that moves the circle of consciousness, what happens to the stuff that falls out of the circle? A further concern about consciousness and meaning is that the neuroscience now tells us that, at best, conscious thought is only an approximation of the scope, affective content, accuracy, and speed of unconsciousness.

Orange (Orange, D., 2000; Stolorow et al., 2002) shares some of these same concerns. She views the creation of a dichotomy between consciousness and unconsciousness as an aspect of the formulation of minds in isolation and prefers emergence to co-construction. What emerges is the product of the organizing systems of patient and therapist. The therapy bumbles along in as phenomenological, experience-near a way as possible. The process is fallible and must be accepted as such, but it also operates beyond awareness. She takes the position, in contrast to that of Zeddies (2000) and Stern (1991), that language and consciousness are not co-extensive, "whether we consider the wordless terror of the shattered worlds of trauma or what Kant called the sublime and Wittgenstein the mystical, we must not fall into the temptation to idolize or idealize linguistic expression" (p. 492). We have a phenomenological unconscious that is, well, unconscious, and this does not make it any less phenomenological.

Safran (2006) offers a perspective on the relational unconscious that is much less wedded to older metapsychologies than either Gerson's (2004) or Zeddies' (2000). He draws on three observations that actually date back to the work of the radical ego psychologists and that of Carl Jung. They move beyond traditional psychoanalytic categories: "The" unconscious, rather than being the seething contents of a cauldron held in a container constructed of repression, is both generative and creative. It also manifests its own organization. Unconsciousness encompasses the mystical and the spiritual. Lastly, it infuses life with vitality; it does not need to be

The phenomenological unconscious **81**

tamed or modulated (or, necessarily, brought into consciousness?) by the self for protection. Drawing on a number of authors, particularly Newirth (2003), Safran describes a developmental failure of an individual's ability to experience herself as a subject. Safran sees this as the result of an inability to access unconscious experience. However, it is not simply limited access, it is rather the failure to access unconsciousness as a manifestation of a very large system of experience and relatedness being rapidly processed in parallel. As such, it stabilizes the self and bestows subjecthood. It is these properties of unconsciousness that allow it to apprehend aspects of existence that cannot otherwise be grasped (and are lost without it).

Safran (2006) proceeds to describe a relational unconscious that is spiritual and enchanted in its interiority. Drawing on American culture prior to the appearance of European psychoanalysis on our shores a century ago, the unconscious was a source of wisdom and a channel to some kind of "Universal Spirit." We would want to note that the experience of subjectness or selfhood in its discreteness is very much a left-brain sort of business, while the experience of embeddedness that we have been discussing is much more a phenomenon of the Right Brain. It brings with it a sense of connectedness.

I want to offer a more radical formulation of the relational unconscious and its place in psychoanalytic therapy than these authors have so far succeeded in doing. Contemporary psychoanalysts have, by and large, described psychotherapy or psychoanalysis as modes of discursive practice, where such practice is dialogic and language is a fundamental part of evolving ever more nuanced states of meaning for both participants. This practice has, in turn, focused on bringing unconscious elements of thought and feeling into the empathic, conscious resonance of both discursive partners. Contemporary psychoanalysts mostly recognize that each such occurrence is a unique event; things are not sitting around in a dormant state waiting to be discovered but are newly formulated or reformulated as discourse proceeds.

What I want to posit is that a major part of any psychoanalytic therapy takes place *in* the relational unconscious without its necessarily entering or having recourse to consciousness for therapeutic action to occur (although we would expect that it would eventually influence or find its way into conscious thought, without, however, *any* temporal relationship to those unconscious events). Therapeutic process would thus be taking place in two different ways, one of which, almost by definition, is very difficult to get ahold of. We don't currently have any basis for hypothesizing that one is more important than the other; we would expect that, if a therapy is proceeding optimally, both processes would be operating more or less in parallel. The discursive conscious stream of the Left Brain would also be taking seconds or minutes to process information that the relational unconscious is processing in milliseconds, before one could consciously even be aware of its existence. This is a complex and difficult position to take, but I feel we have little choice.

We do know a number of things about this state of affairs, some of which extend far beyond the limited world of psychoanalysis. We know that unconscious

82 The phenomenological unconscious

cognition occurs, and that it merges into an array of different unconscious processes or activities. We know that unconscious communication regularly occurs between individuals. We acknowledge that nonverbal communication takes place through exchanging visual and auditory cues. We do not generally consider that this communication could also be telepathic but there is a small literature on the subject. We know that material, some of which originates in the external world, finds its way into dreams without going through consciousness at all, and that information is unconsciously passed between individuals via the Mirror Neuron System.

If we accept the hypothesis that an analysis is taking place simultaneously in two different ways (as is any cognition or communication), we would have to acknowledge that there is some ongoing communication between the two. We would also have to wonder about its implications. Bernard Baars (1993/2003b), in a paper on consciousness and its origins, explored the questions of how and why consciousness – a small, slow, serial, and limited system – emerged out of a nervous system comprised of large bioprocessors that is mostly unconscious, distributed and parallel rather than serial, and of enormous capacity. More interesting still is that, while the parallel system is highly efficient in terms of computing power and requirements for glucose and oxygen, serial consciousness is highly inefficient, requiring a great deal of capacity and energy to get relatively little done. Consciousness can only orient itself to one information stream at a time. So why do it this way at all? What evolutionary benefits could be derived from such an arrangement of processes? Baars asked himself these questions as well. As it turns out, there is a class of information processing architectures that has just this property; it combines a slow serial system with a fast parallel one. These architectures were *not* derived to model human cognitive function (so that if they do, they provide outside corroboration), but rather to solve very difficult problems involving multiple knowledge sources. They are expensive in terms of processing resources, but the cost can be justified because they can combine the activities of many different specialist systems to solve problems that cannot be solved by any one of them.[8] As a whole, they are referred to as global workspace architectures that contain paired conscious and unconscious processes. The intelligence of the problem solving is contained in the unconscious specialist elements, with the final results entering the conscious serial stream.

I believe that this process is a way of describing some of what takes place for both analyst and patient in the psychoanalytic situation. Such a system accounts for many complex mental functions and describes a kind of problem-solving that is one of the ways unconscious and conscious processes operate together in a psychoanalysis.

If we accept this view of clinical psychoanalysis, what is it like, then, to participate in an analysis? First, it is a lot different than we thought it was. As we sit with

---

8 In the face of a complex, novel problem, the global workspace processors, integrated by memory, "publicize" it to all of the distributed specialist systems of the self. The specialist(s) capable of addressing the problem do so, are prioritized, and convey the result to the global workspace and to consciousness.

The phenomenological unconscious **83**

a patient, we consciously experience listening to him, reflecting on what we are hearing, and on our own thoughts and feelings, and speaking to the patient. We are often so caught up in the moment of our experiencing our own thoughts or the patient's that we are without reflection and can lose awareness of the analysis as a discrete entity. *It is possible that at those times what we are actually experiencing is right-brain consciousness.* We also think about what the patient might be thinking. I believe that most of us would agree that these activities pretty much sum up what we think goes on in an analysis. We could add some more elements, like thinking about what we are going to say, but this is still pretty much it. But if we add unconscious-to-unconscious communication and global workspace activity (which is a neurocognitive model), the latter description falls apart. It falls apart because even though the conscious serial thread is important to the process, most of what is going on, as well as the intelligence of the system, is and remains unconscious. Confirmatory evidence for this latter point comes from an entirely different source that we have already mentioned. Nisbett and Wilson (1977), in a now-seminal paper, "Telling More than We Know: Verbal Reports on Mental Processes," studied subjects' descriptions of how they reached conclusions and how they described the mental processes that led them to reach those conclusions (as analysands *and* analysts could also be asked about why things happen in an analysis). Upon close study, these authors concluded that their subjects had no idea how they reached conclusions and often left out key and necessary elements from their descriptions. What they had instead was a series of "a priori implicit causal theories" (p. 231) about the plausibility of their conclusions in the absence of actual introspection. On some occasions, there was a close enough fit between subjects' judgments and the kinds of processes that, by inference, would seem to have had to be going on, so that they were more or less in the ballpark. Unfortunately, the work of these authors speaks to the stringent limitations on the meaningfulness of our own and our patients' thinking about what is going on in an analysis and whatever theories we might harbor about it.

When we add the realization that unconscious-to-unconscious communication is a major part of any analysis, we must also accept that we neither know nor understand what is taking place on a moment-by-moment basis or, for that matter, how what we say is influencing the process. Furthermore, if much of this work *stays unconscious*, as I am positing, we will know nothing of it directly. One way of following an analysis under these circumstances is by following how a patient is living her life. We can also think *very imperfectly* about the ongoing quality of the analytic relationship and the behavior of the patient in the sessions.[9]

---

9 The latter is a rather iffy proposition. Some years ago, Yalom (Yalom & Elkin, 1974) brought out a book comprised of his and his patient Ginny's side-by-side narratives of their individual psychotherapy sessions. In keeping with what the above would lead us to expect, their descriptions had little in common.

84 The phenomenological unconscious

There is another conclusion that follows from the unconscious analysis hypothesis that is potentially problematic. Orthodox classical psychoanalysts have always operated in what they imagined to be an atmosphere of clinical neutrality. This psychoanalytic stance was based on the hypothesis (or belief, really) that if one said little and said it with no apparent emotion, then the analyst could remain anonymous and whatever the patient thought the analyst was thinking or feeling was entirely a projection. Such an hypothesis is blatantly false. After all, there was only one person in the room. Contemporary analysts have abandoned this position. Whether of a Relational or an Intersubjective ilk, they solidly root psychoanalysis in a two-person psychology in which much is inevitably communicated by both participants. These analysts go even further and, to a greater or lesser extent, choose to talk to their patients about what they themselves are feeling. However, unconscious analysis posits so much more.

We have tended to operate clinically as if we have control over what we communicate to our patients about ourselves and what they come to know about us. I think that, at best, this is true for serially organized, logical statements we choose to make or not make about ourselves. As psychoanalysts and psychotherapists, however relational and self-disclosing we may be, we are accustomed to thinking of our thoughts as our own. Yet this is, at best, only true to a degree. Although the concept of a relational unconscious has gained, and continues to gain, traction among Contemporary clinicians, it has not brought with it the realization that the privacy we in part rely upon does not really exist. To be sure, it remains true that the action of a therapeutic unconscious does not mean that our patients are conscious of our most closely held thoughts (as we are not conscious of theirs), but it does mean that they must possess some unconscious awareness[10] of them. This is another disturbing revelation concerning the therapeutic situation that we will have to become accustomed to. But we are not there yet. A recent issue of *Psychoanalytic Dialogues* (Bass, Ipp, & Seligman, 2013) contains an exchange of papers (Brody, 2013a, 2013b; Frommer, 2013; Murphy, 2013) on the topic of forced self-disclosure, in this case of a serious illness. The authors talk about comments about themselves they might have made or physical changes that they have begun to manifest that understandably require that some explanation be offered to the patient. What's interesting about this is that, even at this late date, none of the authors consider or deal with the possibility that their patients could have some unconscious awareness of the situation. The choice is one of being prepared to begin a conscious discourse on the subject and thereby explore and modulate the patient's fantasies, decide for clinical reasons that it is best not to make the issue explicit, or not consider the issue as these authors have failed to do.

Beyond relationality, unconsciousness has still other relevant properties that fall under the rubric of the uncanny.

---

10 If you have been following my arguments, it should be clear that this is not an oxymoron.

Unconsciousness and the uncanny

There has been only limited interest on the part of psychoanalysts in a number of psychological phenomena that may be grouped around the concept of the uncanny or parapsychology. They include, in order of decreasing numbers of publications: the spiritual experience of god, the uncanny itself, thought transference, telepathy, and the collective unconscious (for non-Jungian analysts). All of these phenomena, to the extent that their existence is accepted, are normative manifestations of psychological functioning that offer additional insights into the unconscious aspects of the self. Attempts to explain uncanniness in the small literature on the subject generally refer to psychoanalytic modes of understanding. Telepathy and thought transference have been described psychoanalytically, beginning with Freud (1915/1957), but without any hypotheses being offered to explain them, and a belief in god has been thought about as a function of metapsychologically described processes, without any consideration of what it might be referring to in reality. The comment "you read my mind" offers a folkloric definition of telepathy. According to Allik (2003), Freud commented to Jones that he was reluctant to say very much about the etiology of some of these phenomena lest psychoanalysis be seen as involving itself in the supernatural or with parapsychology. I believe that trend has continued, but I will posit that the supernatural is not and need not be involved in any of them. I would suggest instead that social networks, both the smaller ones and very large networks, whose numbers can reach the millions and have not yet been at all studied, play a role in these areas.

The uncanny

The term *uncanny* has mostly resided in a kind of psychoanalytic backwater of limited clinical or theoretical interest. Freud (1919/1955d), writing in German, used the term *Unheimlich*, which does not translate well into English. It literally means "un-home-like," to which Freud added that it referred to something frightening that arouses dread or horror. *Merriam-Webster's Collegiate Dictionary* (*Merriam-Webster's Dictionary*, 2004) defines uncanny quite differently, as eerie, mysterious, perhaps supernatural or superhuman in origin, certainly not normal or expected. Freud's definition signifies one class of uncanny events, but there are others that we find interesting or fascinating, sometimes surprising or shocking. The experience of uncanniness can be pleasant, with a kind of *frisson* accompanied by a response of the sympathetic nervous system, bodily hair standing up, etc.

Freud noted that uncanniness related to disruptions in what seemed dead or alive, animate or inanimate. But he also identified uncanniness as a process, which I would term mysterious, whereby the familiar is rendered strange. He wanted to connect it to the repression of elements of infantile sexuality, particularly castration anxiety, and to the return of the repressed.

The uncanny is of considerable importance to Heidegger (1927/2008, 1927/2010) as well. He stays closer to *Unheimlich* in the sense of not being at home.

86 The phenomenological unconscious

He puts a positive gloss on it; although accompanied by anxiety, it is part of the experience of thrownness. In it, Dasein is aware of itself and its being as distinct and authentic. For Heidegger, the fundamental character of Dasein's being-in-the-world is *Unheimlich*. He would speculate that the primordial state of development is filled with thrownness and the uncanny. That certainly rings true empathically for the first year of life. We have no evidence for that, of course, but we do know that (developmental) failures during this early time tend to lead to states of being that we could describe as both fallen and everyday.

Why be concerned with the uncanny at all? If not repression, it does offer a point of entry into certain properties of unconsciousness and its relations with consciousness that we have not had before. We are used to a consciousness-centered experience of self, informed by conscious or consciously sought perceptions and in verbal communication with others. However, at least as important are the unconscious areas of the self, informed by unconscious perceptions and in unconscious communication with others, either singly or in groups. Both are phenomenological. We are further interested in the normal functioning of these unconscious processes, not their psychopathology (although they may have dysfunctional contents) and not simply as a justification for the concept of repression. Speculatively, these areas can function to change the self through their connections to social networks or as a part of a collective unconscious (Jung, 1933/1968). Uncanniness would seem to refer to a class of experiences that occur when conscious and unconscious forms of cognitive-emotional activity brush up against each other.

In examining any of these topics, the neuroscience adds to our understanding. As an example, Freud (1919/1955d) describes a kind of uncanny experience that occurs when what appears inanimate, an automaton, is suddenly found to be alive. The experience is compelling and pleasurable to such a degree that it is sought out. Bach (1975) describes in detail an exhibit widely found in French country fairs called *The Fabulous Automate*. A figure in street clothes with chalk-white face and hands, fixed, unblinking gaze, and stiff gait gives, for all the world, the appearance of being an automaton. The initial reaction is one of fascination at how lifelike the *automate* appears. After a time, one suddenly realizes that the automaton is, in fact, a living man, and the realization is accompanied by the frisson of the strange, eerie, and uncanny. What has happened is that the Left Brain, privileging its synthetic function, is taken in by the ruse that this is a *very* lifelike illusion, but the Right Brain gets it right from the start; this is a person pretending to be an automaton. It takes a few moments for the Left Brain to get this information from the Right.

If, for the moment, we put aside Freud's ideas that this has to do with some hypothetical castration anxiety or death instinct but consider instead that we have all kinds of existential reasons and methods for discerning whether someone is living or dead, a different answer emerges, resting not on metapsychology but rather on neuroscience. You will recall that left-brain conscious cognition, while logical, is imprecise and somewhat slow (its priority is continuity rather than accuracy), at least by right-brain standards. The latter operates in parallel, and, although it does

The phenomenological unconscious **87**

not use symbolic logic, is precise and operates in milliseconds. What happens with the *automate* is that the Left Brain, relying on visual cues (the chalk, the gait, and the eyes), concluded in seconds that the figure is inanimate. Meanwhile, the right brain has spatially identified the figure as human in milliseconds. The conflicting experiences are in great discord (dead or alive or inanimate or animate is an important distinction for us), which is resolved by the Left Brain becoming suddenly aware of its error through its experience of this discord, hence the uncanniness that we feel. This awareness grows out of the Right Brain's being somehow/eventually able to communicate its findings to the Left Brain (we use words like *repression*, but in point of fact, we haven't a clue how this happens and why it takes a period of time measured in seconds to occur). The feeling that accompanies the communication is something of strangeness and weirdness. These observations support the hypothesis that the right brain acts in support of the left's phenomenological engagement with the world.

The concept of the uncanny has occupied a position of importance in disciplines other than psychoanalysis, among them literary theory, cultural studies, and philosophy (Kearney, 2003; Masschelein, 2011; Royle, 2003). Whereas the term *uncanny* has retained a fairly circumscribed meaning within psychoanalysis, it has blossomed in these other disciplines (Masschelein), offering a genealogy (Foucault, 1969 & 1971/1972, 1966/1994) of its own, and has most recently become associated with the formation of particular kinds of narratives and readings. This can bring us back to clinical psychoanalysis and the quest to assist the patient in the development and reading of personal narrative. In particular, uncanniness is found in the defects in narrative structure that we uncover as the psychoanalytic process proceeds.

A patient, Bill, describes a conversation he had the day before with a friend in the small town in which we all live. Over the course of the conversation, Bill commented that two distant acquaintances with the same surname were married. His friend did not think so, but Bill was certain that he knew it to be the case. He nevertheless felt troubled by the inconsistency and thought about it on and off for several hours. It was with an uncanny feeling that he remembered that, when he first heard of these people with the same name, *he* had assumed they were married; he had *not* heard it. The left brain takes events and experiences and knits them together so that we have a continuous, seamless, narrative experience of life, in which continuity is prized over accuracy and validity. In Bill's case, it was the discovery of a hole in the narrative that he had himself synthetically filled which gave rise to the uncanny feeling. For a moment, *reality wasn't real.*[11] The genealogy of this uncanny experience grew out of a particular episode of not-thinking, a questioning of the text, so to speak, and its correction.

---

11 We did not ever discover anything about his reactions to these people that either produced conflict or merited defense.

88 The phenomenological unconscious

The uncanniness of dreams can lie as much in their interpretation by an *autre* (in this case, the analyst) as it can as a sensation felt in the dream. (I use *interpretation* here not in the sense of addressing some deeper meaning, but rather in the phenomenological sense of revealing what is present but hidden in a text.) A patient tells me a dream in which the cloth wrapping of a mummy is being unwound. There is no feeling in the dream. She is Jewish. I observe that the *unveiling* of her father's gravestone (customarily on the first anniversary of someone's death) will take place the following week. She is shocked in an eerie but pleasant way (she smiles) by her ability to create such a dream and wonders whether there is something about her father that she has not seen before. The question is not really whether psychoanalysis reaches the uncanny so much as: Does this happen often for our patients, but they don't know to tell us about the feeling? And then, recently, a patient told me that she found the way that she or her patients changed as a therapy progressed to be surprising and magical. I took her to mean that it was uncanny, with which she agreed.

Uncanny feelings are also very much a part of the functioning of larger social networks. Being a part of a human wave can feel positively uncanny, whereas being part of a mob offers a very dark kind of uncanniness.

The collective unconscious or the superorganism of social networks

If we are to consider other properties of the uncanny, we will first have to look at the manner in which an individual's unconsciousness functions as part of a group. In speaking of a collective unconscious or social networks, we do not know anything about which sorts of unconsciousness are involved other than that they in part must include the Mirror Neuron System (Iacoboni, 2007; Iacoboni et al., 2005; Iacoboni et al., 1999), cortical midline structures (Uddin, Iacoboni, Lange, & Keenan, 2007), and the right cerebral hemisphere.

However, what we do have is Christakis and Fowler's (2009) social network theory, and that *is* accompanied by evidence. These authors have mostly studied smaller social networks, but have commented on larger networks as well. They look at information (called contagion) being transferred across one to three degrees of separation. They coin the term "superorganism" to describe these networks and posit that they have a life of their own beyond that of, and unknown by, their members. Social networks represent true complex structures, and complexity theory dictates that the properties of such systems are greater than those of the sum of their individual members. I believe that it is to these superorganisms that we can turn to understand something about telepathy, thought transference, and where we might ultimately find god. In doing so, I am in no way meaning to forsake the natural for the supernatural and whatever purely speculative manifestations it may tend to evoke.

Telepathy and thought transference

What is perhaps most interesting about telepathy and thought transference is not the notion that a misplaced belief in their existence grows out of the paranormal,

The phenomenological unconscious **89**

remnants and fantasies of infantile omnipotence, or the projections of a paranoid schizophrenic (Ehrenwald, 1974), but rather just how everyday and matter-of-fact such phenomena are treated as being. If we reflect on works of literature, narrative fiction (Royle, 2003), and even biography, one of the features that is most striking is how we take for granted that we can know the thoughts, feelings, and perceptions of another person. Indeed, to encounter a work lacking in these features is to strike us that something is seriously amiss. The field of biography is based on our interest in the biographer's ability to get inside the head of her subject. We must go back to antiquity – to *The Iliad* (Homer, 1998), for example – to routinely find texts where other people may only have feelings that are given to them by the gods. The knowledge of another person's interiority, present in contemporary narrative, can only grow out of a functioning theory of mind (Baron-Cohen, Tager-Flusberg, & Cohen, 2000), but an element of *accessibility* must be added to it.

The term *telepathy* itself was first introduced (Royle, 2003) in 1883 in the proceedings of the Society for Psychical Research as referencing "all cases of impression received at a distance without the normal operation of the recognized [sic] sense organs" (p. 261). The definition serves as well now as it did then. As Freud (1941 [1922]/1955a) is at pains to declare at the very beginning of his short work "Dreams and Telepathy," he is reluctant to embrace telepathy because of its perceived connection to the occult.

In this work, Freud (1941 [1922]/1955a) is clearly intensely ambivalent about telepathy and its occurrence in dreams or other modalities. He denies ever having heard a telepathic dream in 27 years of practice, describes himself as "occult-poor," and goes on to describe a number of instances of prophecy from his practice that were either not borne out or could be explained in other ways. If telepathic dreams *were* to exist, he posits, they would not in any way affect the manner of working with dreams psychoanalytically. A further measure of Freud's distaste for the subject lies in his withholding the paper from publication while he was alive. However, he does offer an observation on telepathy that is, for our purposes, important: "If the phenomenon of telepathy is only an activity of the unconscious mind, then, of course, no fresh problem lies before us. The laws of unconscious mental life may then be taken for granted as applying of telepathy" (p. 220).

By 1925, Freud (1925/1961b) was much more receptive to the idea of telepathy or thought transference in general and telepathic dreams in particular. He still dismisses prophecy, but talks about experiments with thought transference in his circle of acquaintances and notes that strongly emotional recollections are more commonly transferred. He also posits that telepathic dreams may reflect unconscious thought transference occurring during waking hours that then later reach consciousness in this manner. In addition, there is the moot point that, since we dream an average of five times a night and forget most of them, many telepathic dreams may go unnoted, but are unconsciously active nonetheless.

What is perhaps most shocking is the relative dearth of articles in the psychoanalytic literature exploring either telepathy or its relationship to clinical psychoanalysis. A PEP-Web search yielded only 28 results (e.g., Anonymous, 1969; Ehrenwald,

90 The phenomenological unconscious

1974; Eisenbud, 1946, 1948; Freud, 1941 [1922]/1955a; Major & Miller, 1981), beginning with Freud's 1922 paper on dreams and telepathy that he was embarrassed to publish in his lifetime through Major and Miller's "Empathy, Antipathy, and Telepathy in the Analytic Process." The authors largely content themselves with describing instances of telepathy or thought transference usually occurring through the medium of dreams. They do so in a respectful manner; some of the instances they are able to explain away psychoanalytically, while others they accept, albeit with a little discomfort. There are no speculations concerning a mechanism by which telepathy takes place, but, when mentioned, there is general agreement that it occurs unconsciously. Telepathy does not, then, take the form of my looking at another person and it coming to me that he is thinking about having a steak dinner this evening. Telepathy would seem to involve an unconscious process that then may or may not make its way into consciousness in some fashion that we *can* speculate about analytically. Telepathic material may appear in consciousness through dreams or through waking thoughts. Its appearance does not signal itself; we may or may not notice its telepathic nature. There is also no reason to believe that all, or even most, products of telepathy are directed to consciousness even in a distorted form, but rather simply remain a part of the unconscious parts of the self. Whether or not any of these outcomes occur, telepathic results go on, probably quite rapidly (in the manner of the right brain), to interact with existing unconscious content and process, and would need to be reckoned with as a possible contributor to the content of an analysis.

If the literature on telepathy and thought transference is quite limited in psychoanalysis, it is vast outside of it. Books too numerous to count, ranging from the scientific to the popular and sensational, exist on telepathy and the paranormal. Belief in its existence as a piece of folkloric wisdom is widespread. A limited search on my part revealed four reputable scientific journals on the subject: *Journal of Parapsychology*, the *International Journal of Parapsychology*, the *Proceedings of the Society for Psychical Research*, and the *Journal of the American Society for Psychical Research*. There are also many articles in the extra-psychoanalytic psychological, psychiatric, and medical literature. This material is beyond the scope of this small chapter section. However, it is of concern that, with all that is available, we psychoanalysts have succeeding in doing so little with it.

If we are not to consider all this literature on telepathy, what do we have to say about it? None of the authors of the works mentioned above offer any descriptions of the *mechanism* by which telepathy occurs. There is a sense that some people are more facile at it than others, but there is no understanding of why. I believe that we do have something to say about the *where* and the nature of the *how* of it and that they are consistent with a phenomenological approach to clinical psychoanalysis.

The answer to the *where* is that telepathy represents one variety of contagion present in social networks. This would be consistent with such networks functioning at up to three degrees of separation, but must take into account first that researchers in Network Studies as yet know nothing of *how* information transfer takes place or about network functioning over long geographic distances. The functioning of very large networks has been studied (Cacioppo, Christakis, & Fowler, 2009), but to a lesser extent. For our purposes, it is important to note (Christakis & Fowler, 2008) that geographic distance between nodes did not lessen network effects so that, to the extent that telepathy is a property of social networks, it would be unaffected by distance. The nature (if not the specifics) of the *how* rests on a line of reasoning I have referred to previously. The argument against the occult origins of telepathy and in favor of the scientific[12] is based on physicalism (Freeman, 2006; Strawson, 2006), the hypothesis that extant phenomena can be explained in terms of physical properties *even if we have not yet learned to identify or measure them*. Certainly, elements of contemporary science were thought of as occult a century or two in the past. Network Studies has so far looked at contagion, the progression of information from node to node through a social network, in terms of the general (Cacioppo et al., 2009; Christakis, 2004; Christakis & Fowler, 2007, 2008) rather than the individual. Telepathy and thought transference could be explored in an interdisciplinary effort involving Network Studies and telepathy researchers.

An unsatisfying look at god and spirituality

Many will be surprised, as I was, to find out that there is a rapidly growing psychoanalytic literature (exclusive of the Jungian literature, which has been there from the beginning), already numbering in the thousands of papers, that discusses god and spirituality in one form or another. As Grotstein (2004) observes, psychoanalysts seem to write on these subjects with some discomfort (Anonymous, 1969; Balint, 1955; Ehrenwald, 1974; Eisenbud, 1946, 1948; Freud, 1941 [1922]/1955a; Lazar, 2001'; Major & Miller, 1981). They write from the perspective of anthropologists studying primitive peoples. Grotstein pretty well summarized the classical psychoanalytic views of god and religion as matters of psychic topography and structure residing in a positivist world. They are seen as myths of the superego and the ego ideal in which reside the descendants of pre-Oedipal idealized parental imagos and ideals. Gods and religious worship date to prehistoric times, when magic was an integral part of the self's subjective experience of reality. Until the last few centuries, meta-knowledges of the physical world, separate from magic and the paranormal, hardly existed at all. If this is an archaeology of knowledge (Foucault, 1969 & 1971/1972) of our species, the personal archaeology of the contemporaneous self similarly begins with developmental periods in which knowledge and magic are indistinguishable. It is all too easy to attribute any of Dasein's experiences of the uncanny or the paranormal as nothing more than continuations of these early ways

---

12 Not Newtonian positivist science (something of a contradiction in terms since Newton was also an alchemist), but the science of contemporary Science Studies (Latour, 1991/1993, 1999; Latour & Woolgar, 1986)

92 The phenomenological unconscious

of thinking and feeling. It does make sense that these early memories (memories encoded in many possible forms) and the self's reactions to them can inform the *experience* of uncanniness. However, to claim such exclusive origins of these feelings and their current manifestations is to return once more to the Cartesian mind-in-isolation along with all the ills that such a conceptualization is heir to. It is the more-than-hypothesized interreferential role of social networks in these experiences that render such a conclusion unsustainable.

These various papers share an approach to god as a descriptive term that is applied to elements of psychic structure, various mental functions, development, and mythological elaboration. Along these lines, god is variously the unborn infant in the womb, the result of an external group projection of the superego, a construct of early helpless humans, the source of dreams, or the subject of myths. All of these possibilities involve possible aspects of a god *concept*. There are two questions that are germane to our inquiry into unconsciousness and the uncanny. The first is: What if there really *is* something out there? By this, I do not mean a gentleman with a white beard, a white robe, and sandals, and I don't claim to know anything about how the universe was created.[13] I am simply referring to what people who have some experience of god or the spiritual are experiencing and whether we can say anything about its location.

The second involves how the idea of gods may have arisen. I have previously (Leffert, 2010, Chapter 6) discussed Julian Jaynes's work, *The Origins of Consciousness in the Breakdown of the Bicameral Mind* (1977). Without claiming to do him justice here, Jaynes hypothesized that the kind of consciousness that we have today did not always exist; rather, it first appeared in Mediterranean cultures around 1300–1000 BCE. Prior to that, consciousness consisted of intermittently heard, hallucinatory voices that, as I then put it, the Left Brain heard over the cerebral commissures coming from the Right. These were taken to be the voices of gods. When contemporary consciousness appeared, the voices and the gods they emanated from were no longer tangibly present, although, as we know, they have persisted in various hallucinatory states. For much of its existence, the bicameral mind was present when human beings lived in social groups numbering 160 or less. This is Dunbar's number (Dunbar, 1993), which has been researched back to prehistoric times; it represents the number of individuals in a medium-sized independent social network and is the building block of larger networks. It appears that the hallucinatory gods were first shared at least among these medium-sized groups and later among larger ones. Historically, great social dislocations occurred around the time that these gods clashed or disappeared.

My hypothesis is that what replaced our "relationships" with these gods can be referred back to the human superorganism of Christakis and Fowler (2009), and

---

13 However, the noted biochemist and science fiction writer Isaac Asimov offers a delightful short story, "The Last Question" (1956/1974), that provides a rather satisfying explanation of the latter.

that what those of us who sense god are experiencing is an aspect of the unconscious connections that we have with our exceedingly large social networks. This connection to god is a connection to an emergent property of superorganisms. Not all of us are capable of or willing to engage in this particular sort of god-connection. I would also speculate that there is not a single worldwide superorganism – the degree of social differences we manifest would seem to mitigate against it – but rather that some small number (3? 5? 7?) of these super-networks exist.

My purpose here is not to offer a complete, brand-new theory of religion but rather to suggest that our relations with our social networks are multiple and complex. For us as psychoanalysts and psychotherapists to ignore or discard them, privileging *only* the therapist-patient relationship and *its* manifestations, is to step out on very thin ice indeed. In doing that, we should not really be surprised if the therapeutic results do not turn out as expected. However, in many ways, our unconsciousnesses are smarter than we are in this respect, and we may sometimes succeed in our therapeutic endeavors in spite of rather than because of our efforts.

We have taken a very far-reaching look at unconsciousness and its many different manifestations, all of which are phenomenological. They bring with them a high degree of uncertainty, a subject that I have been hinting at in the preceding chapters, to which we will now turn. It is a subject that is at once more difficult and more complex that we might at first imagine.

5

THE ROLE OF DECISIONS MADE UNDER UNCERTAINTY IN CLINICAL PSYCHOANALYSIS

Introduction

This chapter started out life as an eight-page essay, "A Plea for Uncertainty," in the final, forward-looking chapter of my last book, *The Therapeutic Situation in the 21st Century* (Leffert, 2013). I thought at the time that I had made the case that applying the study of uncertainty to clinical psychoanalysis was a new way of thinking about the problems with knowability and certainty that some of us have been struggling with for at least a couple of decades.[1] A number of readers were critical of this, observing that contemporary psychoanalysts had written at length about uncertainty and that I was not covering new psychoanalytic ground. Perhaps, then, the best place to begin this chapter is with a review of what we, as contemporary psychoanalysts, think about uncertainty and unknowability before progressing to a discussion of what the study of judgments made under uncertainty has to offer us.

The terms *unknowability* and *uncertainty* have quite distinct domains; they involve Dasein in very different ways. Unknowability involves the nature of a thing in the world. For whatever reasons, the thing has some properties that cannot be ascertained, sometimes because the very attempt to know them changes and thus obscures them. In contrast, uncertainty is a property of Dasein, the subject who is in the world, trying to know something about it or other subjects who are in it and deciding how to act on that knowledge. It refers to a particular subject at a particular moment in time. A different subject possessing a different knowledge base or the same subject who, at a different time, possesses different knowledges, might not have any reason to be uncertain about something. For example, Robert

---

1 The same critique cannot be made about those working towards psychoanalysis from the opposite direction. Decades ago, both Paul Meehl (1991, 1983/1991) and Richard Nisbett and Lee Ross (1980) had begun considering how their disciplines bore on psychoanalysis.

did not appear for a session. I inevitably thought of reasons for his not coming to his hour. These were based on what I know about Robert (they were not based on the metapsychological concept of resistance). I arrived at what I thought was the reason for his not being there, but it was a conclusion reached under uncertainty. When Robert showed up a bit disheveled, a half-hour into the session, and told me he had a flat and changed the tire, the uncertainty disappeared.

I mean here to offer first a philosophical and then a procedural critique of certainty. If they do not offer up sufficient reasons for adopting a position of epistemological uncertainty in the therapeutic situation, there are secular reasons for doing so as well. If the arguments in the last chapter dealing with unconsciousness are at all convincing, then the very nature of the therapeutic enterprise should demand great respect for approaching it with uncertainty.

Uncertainty in contemporary psychoanalysis

Laced throughout Freud's writings are his often-repeated observations on the provisional nature of his conclusions and the limits to certainty and knowability to be found in both clinical and theoretical psychoanalysis. What now, in retrospect, seems quite strange is that such judicious modesty more or less then disappeared from the psychoanalytic literature, not to reappear in earnest until the contemporary period beginning in the 1980s.[2] Prior to this time (and to a significant degree extending into the present), clinical and theoretical writing presented ideas with a degree of implicit certainty. The fact that psychoanalysis is not known for *any* sort of theoretical consensus or agreement has not in any way lessened the certainty with which acolytes of any of the various theoretical schools went into combat, either in print or at conferences, in defense of their particular beliefs. In recent years, these battles have mostly (but not entirely) morphed into more civil, if only sometimes less certain, discourses.

Of even more concern, however, is the manner in which generations of analysts and therapists have brought certainty to their clinical discourse with patients and their writing for the psychoanalytic literature.[3] The problem then is what happens when the analyst presents his patient with a statement or interpretation that the patient considers inaccurate or false. The patient may verbally disagree, in which case a therapist has a number of choices: to dismiss this as denial; or, worse, interpret the denial; or, in recent times, to actually discuss the mistake or at least acknowledge it. All too often, a patient who has been well-schooled in the power relations of the

---

2 Rapaport's (1960, [1957]/1967) theoretical writings, which include the idea of limits on knowability, are an exception.

3 I have no way of assessing just how common this certainty is in current psychoanalytic practice. I do hear about it occurring on a case-by-case basis and, for myself, always phrase any declarative statements I might make to a patient in at least a slightly tentative fashion. My own experience with three different analysts and a handful of supervisors in the 1970s and early 1980s was that I never encountered doubt or uncertainty in anything they said to me.

96 Decisions made under uncertainty

therapeutic situation (Leffert, 2013, Chapter 1) disagrees but says nothing about it. The result of this is that the treatment has been seriously and – if this occurs frequently – fatally compromised.

Eisler, as far back as 1968, understood that the analyst's knowing was at best a temporary and conditional thing, requiring periodic updating. In the meantime, the best course of action for an analyst to take was to simply tolerate his uncertainty for as long as he could bear it.[4] When uncertainty did come to psychoanalysis, it showed up, somewhat surprisingly, clad in the *metaphor*[5] of the Heisenberg Uncertainty Principle (Wheeler & Zurek, 1983). A number of papers (e.g., Coltrera, 1962; Leshan, 1965; Scott, 1962; Waelder, 1963) appearing in the early 1960s referenced to the Uncertainty Principle mostly in the context of arguments leveled against psychic determinism.[6] We would probably best designate this period as Pre-Contemporary, in which the first cracks in theoretical orthodoxy were beginning to appear. Coltrera, in particular, in a discussion of uncertainty, existentialism, and phenomenology unusual for the times, offered up existentialism as a critique of Freudian psychoanalytic psychology. He saw this as an approach limited to a degree by its dismissal of the dual concepts of cathexis and psychic energy that he still considered important.

Heisenberg had posited in 1927 that you could not determine the position of a subatomic particle in space because the act of measuring its position could not be accomplished without putting energy into the system. That energy would displace the particle by some unknown amount; hence, you could never perform such a measurement and the location would always remain uncertain. Of less concern to Heisenberg (but not to us) was the fact that by trying to perform the measurement, the *system itself was changed*. As a metaphor, the uncertainty principle had two things to say about the psychoanalytic situation. The first is that any attempt to try to know a patient also changes the patient and results in aspects of the patient remaining unknowable. The second is that, unlike in particle physics, the act of measuring also changes the measurement device – that is, the analyst. What was included in this metaphor for us was the necessity of seeing the therapeutic situation as a two-person rather than a one-person psychology, the irreducible subjectivity of both participants, and the stringent limits on knowability that faces both participants.

What appeared in the Relational literature of the later 1980s and 1990s was a profound epistemological critique – drawn from often-uncited postmodern sources – of psychoanalytic theory and knowledge. The critique focused on

---

4 This is somewhat surprising, in that Eisler was otherwise a very orthodox, mid-century psychoanalyst.
5 It remains unclear how well-understood it was that this *was* about metaphor rather than a wish to bring psychoanalysis into the physical sciences.
6 A critique of this position today would be based on complexity theory and postmodernism (Leffert, 2008).

uncertainty, unknowability, and their ramifications in the clinical setting. Although mentioned, uncertainty has been much less of a focus in Intersubjective writing and, where mentioned, is descriptive rather than epistemological.

A number of Relational authors have taken roughly similar positions concerning uncertainty and unknowability at roughly the same time. In a 1987 paper and a discussion following it, Wittenberg (1987) and Hoffman (1987) laid out much of the then-innovative thinking about psychoanalytic uncertainty as it stood 25 years ago. This thinking particularly involved a critique of the utility of psychoanalytic theory in the clinical setting. Wittenberg observed that "We know that we help people who come to us. We are only on the verge of knowing how this help works" (p. 183). Unfortunately, psychoanalysis has remained on the verge, still attempting to understand therapeutic action and cure in theoretical ways. People have only just begun to ask entirely new sorts of questions about what we are trying to accomplish with patients. Wittenberg described the paradox of needing to know, and that the more we know, the more we realize what we don't know and have to live with the uncertainty. He dealt with this in two ways. One was to posit that, as clinicians, we both need to know and need to believe. The other is to take a pluralistic approach to theory. Theories reside in our analytic toolbox, to be taken up and used as they fit a particular clinical situation at hand. (He was not ready to abandon theory altogether and replace it with clinical phenomenology.) Inherent in this is the position that there is not and never can be a single theory that can do the whole job. Skolnikoff (2004) later wrote about integrating theories as a way of dealing with uncertainty, and Shevrin (2003), perhaps surprisingly for this late date, still argued for a comprehensive metapsychological theory awaiting us somewhere in the future that would free us of our uncertainty. It should be noted that they were addressing inevitable *theoretical* uncertainties rather than struggling with *clinical* uncertainty.

Hoffman (1987, 1998) and Renik (1993) located uncertainty in the analyst's irreducible subjectivity. "What is not possible in this point of view is a total transcendence by analytic therapists of their own subjectivity" (Hoffman, 1998, p. 168). Hoffman saw this as a good thing, freeing the analyst to "be himself," allowing him to make mistakes, and requiring of him regular critical reflection on the positions he has taken in a therapy. He saw this uncertainty as an important component of the wider analytic shift from a positivist to a social-constructivist model of the therapeutic situation.

A brief case illustration shows how, at least for me, no such solution seems likely. Joe, a lawyer in his 40s, consulted me a few years ago. He had two related problems: periodic hypochondriasis and insomnia, with his fear of the latter becoming a self-fulfilling prophecy. He came to me because he had been told by the psychologist he had been seeing that medication (an SSRI) could help with this, but then said that he would take it only as a last resort. On the face of it, this seemed a problem tailor-made for an analysis, but Joe had neither the money nor the interest

98 Decisions made under uncertainty

to pursue such a course. I never mentioned analysis to him[7] but rather suggested that we meet once a week. This was in keeping with his wishes. So, for about a year and a half, we met and talked once a week, and his symptoms gradually lessened and then disappeared. It was clear to me that issues remained that could have been dealt with, but there were practical reasons for not pursuing further therapy (his wish to buy a house and the financial commitment it would entail). It was also clear that this was not a transference cure; the therapy had not endowed me with any of the properties that would have made such a cure possible. I was left uncertainly wondering what I had actually done for Joe. As I thought about it (over some years), I came to understand that what my question was really about was that I had no *theory*, or even a partial theory, to hang my results on. Instead, I had conducted a phenomenologically based psychotherapy in which the cure resided in the relationship – the whole relationship, not just a part of it like transference or working alliance that was only separable for heuristic purposes. In particular, I think it had to do with how I approached his symptoms. I had not treated them head on as the object of the treatment, nor did I offer genetic interpretations of them. I had, instead, been respectful of them and treated his concerns about his health as genuine and worthy of medical evaluation, while at the same time empathizing with the emotional misery he suffered as a result of them. We spoke as well of other issues in his life involving things he had to do or decisions he had to make. My interest in him and my lack of any personal agenda, including that of shoving him into some Procrustean bed[8] of theory, were, I think, important supporting factors that set the tone of the relationship.

I realize that this is not a particularly satisfying package. It is not that I didn't understand him but rather that I understood him conditionally, contextually, and phenomenologically. I have had, and still have, patients who I understood, like Wittenberg (1987), in connection with one or another theory. I am no longer at all sure, however, that such understanding has very much to do with what actually matters: our discourse and our right-brain-to-right-brain communications. We can spin an entire analysis out of some theoretical "understanding" of a patient, but do we necessarily know that this is why the patient got better? Is this rather just some kind of psychoanalytic pastime? When students are asked, for didactic purposes, to formulate a case in a number of different theoretical ways, isn't that really saying the same thing?

Hoffman (1987) observed that all psychoanalytic knowing is provisional, dependent on perspective and subjective states, and, I would add, contextual and

---

7 This statement might well precipitate the reaction that this was a resistance on my part and a collusion with Joe's resistance, that analytic cases are made, not found, etc. I can only say that much of my practice consists of doing psychoanalysis and, in Joe's case, an insistence on analysis would simply represent an exercise in power relations.
8 Unfortunately, the situation is more complicated still. It is possible, even probable, that what I said to Joe was governed by theories or other ideas of which I was quite unaware.

Decisions made under uncertainty **99**

phenomenological rather than theoretical. This is essentially the position taken by Contemporary psychoanalysts in the 1990s and stands in marked contrast to that maintained by orthodox Freudians and Kleinians. He criticized Wittenberg (1987) for bemoaning the failures of current theories to tell us enough, forcing us instead to rely on our imaginations and biases (not the worst of things, I would suggest). Hoffman also observed that there is more comfort to be had in what he calls "general principles of theory" rather than theory that posits what to do in some particular therapeutic situation. Such general principles might include that the analyst is always a participant in the analytic process or that there is always more going on in the therapeutic situation than either the patient or the analyst can know.

In a somewhat later discussion of the utility of the social-constructivist point of view, Hoffman (1992) observed (as should have been obvious to all of us but wasn't) that, "it is simply impossible to keep up, with the stream of what Stern has called 'unformulated experience'" (p. 291). Only a very small percentage of what is going on in the therapeutic situation can be observed or commented on, with the choices often made for unconscious reasons. In the past, we have viewed such inevitability as a kind of filtering process that can be trusted to lead us in the right direction. Perhaps. But it is more likely that we have identified an element of procedural uncertainty that we must simply learn to live with. This does not mean that we need be doubt-ridden and therefore reluctant to speak. It does mean, in an analysis in which it is made clear that our observations are not to be taken as pronouncements carrying the full weight of truth and certainty, that we can operate with a certain freedom and spontaneity. We don't have to worry about being "right" about "the Truth" or about trying to convince patients to accept something about themselves that they do not agree with. Conclusions that are both tentative and conditional invite a patient to also be more spontaneous in the therapeutic discourse. Analysis is not about the discovery of a preformed "truth" but about the co-construction of new meaning.[9]

All of these authors essentially lay the blame for our uncertainty at the feet of irreducible and interreferential subjectivity. Instead of analytic uncertainty, Cooper (1993) cast the problem in terms of the analyst's fallibility. In the process of doing so, he wished to leave metapsychological pluralism in possession of the field by arguing that the concept can be applied across the differing theoretical orientations or orthodoxies held by the members of our acrimonious profession. By fallibility,

---

9 It is important to ask the question: What sort of meaning are you talking about? If we are attempting to ascertain context (historical and contemporaneous), or to explore the archaeology of some event or experience, then we are doing something that makes phenomenological sense. If, however, meaning is deployed in the sense of seeking some *deeper truth*, something that ties a patient's utterances or behavior to some extant *theory*, I would have to argue that this is not meaning at all, but rather an attempt by the analyst to make *himself* more comfortable and certain. This should not in any way be taken as a position grounded in therapeutic nihilism; it addresses the *kinds* of knowledge that are available rather than positing a *lack* of knowledge.

100 Decisions made under uncertainty

he meant to signify the limitations that anyone faces in trying to determine either objective or psychic reality. He described a number of tensions facing the analyst in the therapeutic situation. One of the more problematic is between constructing meaning and borrowing from whatever theoretical predilections we may have as a way of combating rather than engaging the wider problem of judgment under uncertainty.

With the exception of this last paper, what these authors were about was a fundamental change in how the discourse of the therapeutic situation is understood.[10] It is a shift away from the orthodox metatheories of the Freudian, Kleinian and Self-psychological schools (all still active today), in which the analyst follows her patient's associations, compares them to her particular metapsychological belief system, offers an interpretation based on some component of that comparison, and listens for confirmation in subsequent associations. Analysts working in this manner are usually sufficiently comfortable with their conclusions to label a patient's disagreement as a sign of resistance.

As a result a shift occurred more or less in the later 1980s and 1990s from a modern to a postmodern episteme in which the rules concerning the accumulation and deployment of knowledge changed fundamentally. The analytic process became one of mutual textual analysis and deconstruction of an affect-rich therapeutic discourse in which both therapeutic partners have standing but no one has the last word. Knowledge, absent errors in reasoning, was no longer seen as a manifestation of certainty, but rather as always conditional and contextual. This was particularly true for knowledge of the other, as becomes so glaringly obvious when comparing therapist and patient accounts of a therapeutic session. So what do Contemporary analysts do with this awareness? An affectively rich discourse that gropes toward meaning replaces a largely one-sided search for information. Meaning is always new and co-created; following the *metaphor* of the Heisenberg Uncertainty Principle, it is best if we put as little information into the system as is consistent with a true therapeutic discourse. If we are wrong, for reasons of content, tact, or timing, we run the risk of introducing extraneous material and altering memory (Schacter, 1996), obliterating some aspects of meaning.

Of the various interpretive interventions available to us, the one with the greatest potential for introducing distortion is reconstruction. What this involves is providing a patient with an entirely new narrative accounting for a series of experiences or memories that, heretofore, were only thought of separately. Even if "correct," they do not establish contact with these experiences except in a serial conscious way. Reconstructions remain separate, but drawing for a moment on Complexity Theory (e.g., Palumbo, 1999), they can function as strange attractors, distorting ever-larger fields of affect and memory. I think it best to not venture forth beyond

---

10 That change was well-summarized in the edited volume *Bringing the Plague: Toward a Postmodern Psychoanalysis* (Fairfield, Layton, & Stack, 2002).

what might be called crypto-reconstructions: words or phrases that might at most *hint* at a direction that might or might not lead somewhere.

Beyond these admittedly major accomplishments and technical suggestions gleaned over the past 25 years, Contemporary psychoanalysts have not gotten much further in their attempts to either more fully understand the ontology of uncertainty or to know quite what to do with it. For myself (as, I suspect, for many of us), I have come to think and speak to my patients less declaratively and more conditionally. As is all too often the case, what we have *not* done is to try to inform our understanding of uncertainty by looking beyond the boundaries of psychoanalysis in order to see how other related disciplines treat it. Let's turn to them now.

Decision-making under uncertainty

During the 1960s and '70s, a sea change was occurring in the ways the disciplines of psychology, economics, and sociology regarded human decision-making. Previously, human decision-making had been understood solely in terms of logical, machine-made choices (general utility theory), rendered a bit less accurately as a result of the human condition. The seminal work of a number of empirical psychologists has progressively shown to what extent this is simply not the case.

Paul Meehl (1991, 1983/1991b) approached psychoanalytic theory-building from within the field with the greatest of skepticism. He first commented (1991) on the methodological difficulties of psychoanalytic research, noting that, given the depth and breadth of its footprint on Western thought for most of a century, it is decidedly strange that "its fundamental concepts still remain a matter of controversy." He went on to note, "this fact in itself should lead us to suspect that there is something methodologically peculiar about the relation of psychoanalytic concepts to their evidential base" (p. 272). He then asked the fundamentally damning question that can only lead us to subjectivity and uncertainty: "How do we get the advantages of having a skilled observer, who knows what to listen for and how to classify it, without having the methodological disadvantage that anyone who is skilled (in this sense) has been theoretically brainwashed in the course of his training?" (p. 280). He then confounds what he has just asserted with:

> On a personal note, I may say that, as is true of most psychologists seriously interested in psychoanalysis, I have found my own experience on the couch, and my clinical experience listening to the free associations of patients, far more persuasive than any published research purporting to test psychoanalytic theory. (p. 274)

Meehl (1983/1991b) continued to amplify his concerns about the subjectivity of psychoanalytic inference. He observed – correctly, I believe – that orthodox psychoanalysts felt at the time that they had the answers. However, non-Freudian psychologists also felt that they had the answers, and these were different, non-Freudian

102 Decisions made under uncertainty

answers. Meehl was prefiguring the debates over psychoanalytic uncertainty and irreducible subjectivity that would shortly appear within psychoanalysis. In those times, circa 1980, most psychoanalysts spent much of their time interpreting and constructing, preferably focusing on the transference. Meehl found transcripts of such sessions generally boring (a telltale sign) to read and, drawing on other authors, observed that such single-minded, moment-by-moment attention to the transference in isolation did not work. "Non-Freudian therapists like Joseph Wolpe, Albert Ellis, and Carl Rogers have argued plausibly that psychoanalytic efficacy (marginal as it is) *is an incidental byproduct of something other than what the analyst and the patient think they are mainly doing*" (p. 288, italics added). He frames the problem rather baldly: "When you listen to a person talk, you can cook up all sorts of plausible explanations for why he says what he says . . . what credentials does this kind of alleged knowledge bring?" (p. 288).

But Meehl had been struggling with other, even more serious aspects of this problem for some time. In a now classic monograph, *Clinical Versus Statistical Prediction* (1954), he compared predictions made by expert clinicians with those arrived at actuarially. He noted that the principle difference between the two is that actuarial models assign particular weights to the various facts going into solving a problem based on actuarial tables or regression equations. The clinician, however, in drawing her conclusions, is free to assign greater or lesser weights to one fact or another *based on her clinical judgment and past experience*. This is usually not done in any formal way but is rather the result of often-implicit, immediate, impressionistic responses to the clinical situation that are subject to change – that is to say, *clinical intuition*. While we would wish for something more, and in contemporary times we clinicians are reluctant to admit this, it nevertheless has the advantage of honesty to recommend it.

The area Meehl (1954) found best-suited to comparisons of actuarial and clinical predictions involved data collected from psychometric testing, and from projective testing in particular. By turning to psychometrics, he was able to avoid the methodological problems of collecting actuarial data from treatment hours, whereas the predictions of expert clinicians could be obtained in either case. Meehl found two things. The first was that the actuarial predictions made from the psychometric data turned out to be more accurate than those made by expert clinicians. The second was that, when the clinicians were told of the disparity, they still insisted that their predictions were more accurate than those made actuarially. These findings led over the years to the development of an area of psychological study dealing with decision-making by individuals in complex real-world situations when only a part of the data is knowable. These are judgments made under uncertainty, and the field of study is Heuristics and Biases (H&B).[11]

---

11 Simon (1956) had suggested that modeling the problem in terms of intuitive judgments versus actuarial rationality imposed an impossibly high standard on human judgment and suggested instead what he termed "bounded rationality" as a lesser standard that we humans ought to be capable of. Although a sensible revision of the standard, it in no way solved the problem posed by Meehl's (1954) two findings.

Decisions made under uncertainty **103**

Nisbett and Ross (1980) continued this inquiry into human inference and human error. They observed gifted and intuitive scientists "whose attempts to understand, predict, and control events in the social sphere [were] seriously compromised by specific inferential shortcomings" (p. 3). This resulted, as they put it, from "both underutilization of normatively appropriate strategies and overutilization of more *primitive* intuitive strategies" (p. 3, italics added). Thus, "the seeds of inferential failure are sown with the same implements that produce the intuitive scientist's more typical successes" (p. 6).

By judgments made under uncertainty, we mean just that – we are confronted with a situation in which no rule or axiom can guarantee a correct result. For example, solving the equation 2 + 2 = ? does not require a judgment made under uncertainty; the rules of addition can be counted on to produce a reliable and replicable result. On the other hand, "tell me about the next four people who are going to walk through this doorway here" is a judgment that must be made under uncertainty. We have two different kinds of tools to approach this question: the cognitive procedural knowledge[12] that we have accumulated over a lifetime, and a group of shortcuts called *heuristics* that allow us to reduce complex problems to a few simple judgments. However, the problem with these tools is twofold: that we may choose (for our own biased reasons) to apply the wrong chunk of knowledge to the problem, and that heuristics, which are indeed shortcuts, can sometimes turn out to be shortcuts that take us down the wrong path.

I will argue for two clinical positions here: that a study of our manner of making judgments under uncertainty (Tversky & Kahneman, 1974/1982b) and risk (Kahneman & Tversky, 1979/2000) can inform our performance[13] in the therapeutic situation, and that the mutual and systematic study of a patient's consistent errors in decision-making can lead to therapeutic change that may not have occurred in its absence.

Risk

Risk is of importance to psychoanalysis on both macro and micro levels. On the macro level, there is the risk that the process could go awry and harm a patient due to failings on the part of the analyst or improper case selection. One sometimes sees patients who have been injured in a previous analysis due to failings of knowledge, countertransference, or character on the part of the prior analyst. We can find out something about selecting patients for analysis from the case selection committees

---

12 The "how to's" of figuring things out: theories, memories, beliefs, and algorithms.

13 When thinking about the therapeutic situation relationally, we are often neglectful of the phenomenologically diverse roles of therapist and patient. The therapist is there as a subject, to care for, heal, and cure, hence her performance *is* ultimately at issue, while the patient is there to be cared for, healed, and treated. In this sense, the patient is an object of the therapeutic process, whereas he is otherwise a subject participating in an analytic discourse.

104 Decisions made under uncertainty

in psychoanalytic institutes. Generally, a candidate evaluates and writes up a case and presents it to a number of faculty members, who then consider analyzability and suitability. Sounds good – so far. Unfortunately, these committees usually seem to approve almost all of the cases that are presented to them. As a supervisor, an instructor, or a training analyst, one then hears about patients being selected who are obviously unanalyzable. How has this happened?[14] Typically, these cases limp on (whether or not they are ultimately really an analysis is a subject of conjecture) or the patient drops out, and clinical associate and patient are each left to make of it what they can. Certainly there is outcome risk here for both. On the micro level, uncertainty entails risk whether we say something to a patient or remain silent. To say it or not to say it? Have we got it right? There is ample reason to hang on to such doubt. As Gilovich and Griffin (2002) put it, "the juxtaposition of modest performance and robust confidence [inspires] research on faulty processes of reasoning that yield compelling but mistaken inferences" (p. 2).

Kahneman and Tversky (1979/2000), in a groundbreaking paper, offered an analysis of decision-making under risk. Prior to this work, expected utility, or its successor, bounded rationality (Simon, 1956), dominated the study of decision-making under risk. It was thought that all rational people would want to make decisions based on the likelihood of success and would do so much of the time. They found, to the contrary, that in making choices among outcomes involving risk, subject preferences systematically violated the axioms of expected utility theory. As an alternative to utility theory, Kahneman and Tversky offered Prospect Theory, which accounts for these behaviors and their resulting effects. Prospect Theory distinguishes two phases in the choice process (Tversky & Kahneman, 1992/2000a): framing and valuation.[15] In the framing phase, the subject constructs a representation of "the acts, contingencies, and outcomes that are relevant to the decision" (p. 46). Although a rational theory of choice would assume invariance in the framing process, what we get in the real world has considerable variance among framing options, which often lead to very different preferences. Put in a way that we are more familiar with, framing involves the construction of internal working models, on a trial basis, that embody many things, including the subject's memories of past experiences. These models remain and influence the construction of new models that shape subsequent choices. What we have here is a way of formulating the *clinical* experience of our patients making choices that seem to be strange or illogical. In the valuation phase, the decision-maker assesses the value of each framed prospect (recall that framing is an individual process) and chooses the one that she values most. Due to the idiosyncrasies of the framing process, the choice

---

14 I suspect that, given the difficulty that clinical associates have in finding patients for analysis, the committees feel under enormous pressure to do so.

15 Again, this work has a dual relevance to the therapeutic process: It suggests a constant reevaluation of how we make micro clinic decisions with a given patient and an additional line of inquiry when we observe a patient's decision-making to be consistently askew.

can often turn out not to be what the decision-maker truly wants or expects. Alternate ways of framing a choice will give rise to different preferences (Tversky & Kahneman, 1986/2000b).

In our struggles to understand a patient's life and the choices that predominate in it, we intuitively make use of Prospect Theory. By learning about it and using it explicitly, we can improve therapeutic results. We have spoken about Roger, the psychiatric resident, twice already: once in Chapter 1 and again in Chapter 3. In Chapter 3, I offered a phenomenological rather than a metapsychological formulation of his dilemmas with the women in his life and with his ward staff (also mostly women). However useful our mutual study (with overtones of secondary intersubjectivity, Bråten & Trevarthen, 2007) of these formulations may have been, they did not in themselves lead to any change in his relationships. Let us consider how he made his choices about women and how they turned out.

Roger framed his choice of women in terms of their attractiveness and, more importantly, the degree of romantic interest in him that they showed (or appeared to him to show) at a first meeting or date. The valuation phase was largely aborted and replaced by his almost immediate declaration of feelings for the particular woman. We had talked about the dysfunction of his attachments, their relation to his mother, and the dependence and disautonomy he felt with any woman who had caught his eye. What began to shift things was my observation that he wasn't making choices at all. He would thus find himself "committed" to a woman when he had no idea who she was or how he felt about her as a distinct human being rather than a rough match with the template he carried around for such purposes. He also knew nothing about *her* feelings, as I observed to him, when he was busy declaring his. It seemed clear that any woman who responded to this approach (such as his ex-wife) would have her own agendas and fairly serious problems, while any well-functioning person would flee the situation, as many women did. When he was able to take stock of their responses, he became deeply embarrassed about what he must have looked like to them. At this point, he began to think about these prospects, and his relationships began to manifest actual depth. We were both struck by the fact that he had been unable to reflect at all on his real world experiences with women and that his behavior towards them had always travelled the same path and produced the same negative, painful results.

Before going on to the foundations of decision-making under uncertainty, we need to consider something that is both an offshoot of Prospect Theory and a kind of prequel to Heuristics and Biases. It is the "law of small numbers."

The law of small numbers

In order to avoid any confusion, let me say that the law of small numbers, as an accurate description of real events, *does not exist*. However, *belief* in the law of small numbers as a way of understanding events in the external world does exist and is widespread. The law of *large* numbers (which *does* exist), simply put, is that in large

106 Decisions made under uncertainty

or very large samples drawn from some population, the frequency of the appearance of some property or quality will be exactly the same (or very, very close to the same) as that of the population as a whole. The law of small numbers is the belief that small samples drawn from the population will *also* manifest that frequency. Or, in other words, *frequency of appearance is independent of sample size.*

Tversky and Kahneman (1971/1982) hypothesized "that people have strong intuitions about random sampling; that these intuitions are wrong in fundamental respects; that these intuitions are shared by naïve subjects and by trained scientists; and that they are applied with unfortunate consequences in the course of scientific inquiry" (p. 24). People, they say, view *any* randomly drawn sample as highly representative of a population. I would add that psychoanalysts and psychotherapists, in the course of their clinical work and, more dangerously, in their theory writing, behave in just the same way.[16] An example of this kind of thinking can be found in what is referred to as the gambler's fallacy and the accompanying myth of the "fair coin." The gambler's fallacy grows out of a widespread tendency on the part of people to erroneously intuit a self-corrective property to probability. It goes something like this. You plan to toss a coin 100 times. The results should be pretty close to 50 heads and 50 tails. Let's say the first ten tosses come up heads. What will the results now be for the 100 tosses? The answer is close to 55 heads and 45 tails. However, most of us *want* to think it will be 50/50. Herein lies the myth of the fair coin. The idea is that after the first ten tosses, the probabilities of the coin will change and it will subsequently come up tails more often than heads to get back to 50/50. Anyone who plays roulette or dice knows this feeling; it is the affective component that is common to all intuitions concerning decisions made under uncertainty. The two intuitions we have here are that all samples, regardless of size, are very similar to each other (a representation hypothesis), and the belief that sampling is a self-correcting process.

As practicing psychoanalysts and psychotherapists, our clinical experience perforce involves dealing with small samples of the population at large or of the population of people in therapy.[17] During the long years in practice after formal training, we continue to educate ourselves through reading and attending conferences, but by far the major source of our continuing education hopefully comes from our informed reflections on our clinical work. If we trust the significance of our conclusions and have confidence in our work (most of us do), then we are demonstrating that we believe in the law of small numbers. Interestingly, if we go about our work staying on the level of the individual patient and limit our explorations and

---

16 In a psychoanalytic paper in which an author believes that the presentation of clinical vignettes provides proof, not just an illustration, of his hypothesis, he seems to think that two or three of these vignettes are enough to do the trick.

17 If one's practice is limited to intensive psychoanalytic psychotherapy and psychoanalysis, then a career's worth of experience can be limited to 200 patients, with the number probably being somewhat lower.

observations to the *phenomenological* rather than the metapsychological, we mitigate much of this risk.

I had a naïve experience with the law of small numbers involving psychophar-macology in the early 2000s. Citalopram, then a new, much-touted SSRI, made its debut at about that time. Over the next six months, several patients came to see me for a consultation; all were experiencing severe anxiety and mild thought dis-orders after being given citalopram for depression. I concluded that citalopram was a terrible, problematic drug. I discontinued it and watched these patients for two to three weeks, referred out those patients wanting only medication, and started the remainder, who also wanted therapy or analysis and who needed pharmaco-therapy,[18] on venlafaxine, an SNRI that I had been prescribing for several years and felt comfortable with. These patients all responded well to the regimen of psycho-therapy or psychoanalysis and venlafaxine. Some years later, I saw a patient who seemed to need an antidepressant but had had significant side effects with several of the drugs we tried. Citalopram was reputed to have a minimal side-effect profile, so, after cautioning the patient to be on the lookout for anxiety (which should have effectively removed any placebo effect), I prescribed it, initially at a low dose. It worked like a charm (as it has for a number of patients since)! I was well aware of what I was seeing but had no idea why. Same drug, same kinds of patients, oppo-site result. I continued to wonder over this until I began looking into uncertainty around 2009. I realized that I had fallen victim to the law of small numbers and that I could conclude absolutely nothing about either of these medications from the small samples I was working with. I also had missed the point that my sample wasn't even a random one; no conclusion about citalopram per se could be drawn when the sample came from the population that had had adverse reactions to the drug. And yet, and yet, this is how we work: Both in and out of psychoanalysis, we try something out, a kind of interpretation or a drug, see how it works, see how we *like* it, hopefully how our patients like it, and, if we do, continue to use it. If it works, we treat this as proof we are correct and, on those occasions where it doesn't, we often attribute the failure to something else and dismiss it (shades of *Clinical Versus Statistical Prediction*, Meehl, 1954). Much of our implicit procedural learning about how we go about our work does, unfortunately, take place in this fashion.

In working with small numbers of patients in situations in which we are "study-ing" the relatively small effects of our actions or interventions, it may well prove impossible to distinguish between them and the background noise in the system. (The "noise" can include something else that might in fact be what is causing the

---

18 After some period of preliminary work and evaluation, I fairly routinely start patients with Major Depressive Disorder (MDD) on an antidepressant, particularly if they also are experiencing cog-nitive slowing. (After all, how can someone participate in therapy if they are unable to think?) Psychoanalysis is the *only* discipline in which many of its practitioners would find such treatment controversial or misguided.

108 Decisions made under uncertainty

effect.) We have to *at least* set this rather dismal view of human inference beside that of the intuitive analyst using his or her "unconscious" to successfully scout the clinical landscape of a therapeutic discourse. If we are prepared to recognize our reliance on the law of small numbers, we can instead hold onto our clinical uncertainty now for statistical as well as intuitive reasons. If the law of small numbers offers a general theory of uncertainty in the therapeutic situation, Heuristics and Biases gets us into the specifics of it.

Heuristics and Biases

I must begin this section with a number of caveats. Heuristics and Biases (H&B) are *good*. Much of the time, they serve as very useful tools with which to make judgments under uncertainty in the moment. H&B offer what Gilovich and Savitsky (2002) termed "quick and dirty" results. These are right-brain processes (they are right-brain conscious and left-brain unconscious), only the outcomes of which appear consciously in the Left Brain. They do so, however, through the action of highly sophisticated neurocognitive processes that represent the outcome of a lifetime of priming, procedural learning, and narrative and semantic memory. When these judgments fail, they offer additional tools with which to investigate their failures. People make use of many heuristics to navigate life, but they fall into relatively few categories. They offer a subjective assessment of probability that is quite similar to our subjective assessments of physical properties like size or distance and demonstrate similar accuracy. Although heuristics can function as quite reasonable estimation procedures, their use is sometimes confounded by individual patterns of biases in the way we collect information. I have taken the concept of Heuristics and Biases out of the realm of probabilities and prospects and, following Nisbett and Ross (Nisbett & Ross, 1980), have applied it to the therapeutic situation to inform the search for meaning in how both patients and psychoanalysts think. Heuristics and Biases is not a theory. It *replaced* a theory, general utility theory (and later bounded rationality), because the latter did not account for the way people made decisions under uncertainty. As such, H&B are descriptive of how people behave; they are phenomenological and serve to reveal what is hidden. Studying clinically the H&Bs that we and our patients have developed, how we deploy them, and the systematic errors in being and doing that may follow from them offers a new dimension to therapeutic action and the nature of healing and cure. What Tversky and Kahneman (1974/1982) did was to study how people assessed probabilities and made decisions. Although these were very individual solutions, gleaned from a lifetime of conceptual and procedural learning or priming (Schacter, 1996), they nevertheless fell into a number of basic categories that were the same across individuals. In this first, groundbreaking paper, Tversky and Kahneman (1974/1982) defined three (more would come later) sorts of shortcuts or heuristics: Representativeness, Availability, and Adjustment and Anchoring.

Representativeness

In navigating the world, we are confronted with all kinds of events and behaviors. For example, John, an inhibited young man, suddenly falls into a deep but transient depression. Probably the best course of action is to initially do nothing except to follow the process phenomenologically, accompanied, perhaps, by an expression of concern. What we are more *likely* to do is to move to identify some process or theory – say, for example, narcissistic injury in the theoretical framework of self-psychology – that will account for John's behavior. What we as analysts are interested in is the probability that his behavior is representative of a class of responses to narcissistic injury (Tversky & Kahneman, 1974/1982). However, we don't think in terms of probabilities; we "simplify" probability into Yes/No decisions.

The representativeness heuristic is first and foremost about pattern recognition. Nisbett and Ross (1980), who were interested in psychoanalysis, observed that "the cornerstone, the chief contribution, and the Achilles heel of psychoanalytic thought all are one – [is] Freud's discovery, for it was his, of the enormous importance to mental life of the representativeness heuristic [sic]" (p. 242). They also posited that much of mental life as well as the process of making judgments under uncertainty is not available for introspection; that is to say, it is unconscious. *This* in turn means, as Nisbett and Wilson (1977) also posited, that any attempt by a person to verbally report is also a matter of judgments made under uncertainty. There are two ways that Representativeness can fail; the pattern that is ostensibly being recognized doesn't actually exist, or it exists, but the particular event being judged does not actually fit that pattern.

The Representativeness Heuristic appears in the therapeutic situation in two different ways and can be potentiality problematic in both. Let's return to Roger for a moment. Roger was seeking a woman he could love and be close to and who would love and care for him. He had developed a maladaptive representativeness based on his mother and the combination of her seductiveness and unreliability. The pattern that he recognized was not, as he thought, a pattern of closeness and constancy. His use of it led him to women who did not offer what he wanted. His subsequent disturbed relationships with them served to round out this heuristic. He was unable to question it and thought that perseverance would save the day. It in fact led him to Janet, his borderline ex-wife.

The other way that the Representativeness Heuristic appears (and has always appeared in an unnamed fashion) in the therapeutic situation is as a tool that an analyst or psychotherapist uses in her attempts to comprehend her patient. At its best, it involves wielding past understandings of patients, and at worst, past explanations of their behavior that may easily lack validity. The process occurs as the therapist listens to her patient, not without memory or desire, but rather trying to reach some understanding of what the patient is telling her.[19] At its best, it is a search for

---

19 This is *listening* in the autocentric mode as opposed to *being* in the allocentric mode.

110 Decisions made under uncertainty

meaning, for representativeness, through listening to a patient's associations and a review of clinical experience. It takes place with varying degrees of consciousness. At its worst, it involves a review of whatever flavor of metapsychology pleases the analyst. If one's thinking can instead remain phenomenological, a particular Representativeness Heuristic is employed first to decide whether this particular instance is a member of a category of instances that one has defined over the course of clinical experience and then to assign cause and effect to different parts of the current instance. Through listening and reflection, a connection is recognized between what has just appeared in the therapeutic discourse and past clinical experience. Over the course of a successful treatment, these processes take place in a growing atmosphere of mutuality and collaboration on the part of both participants.

As Nisbett and Ross (1980) described it, the analyst does follow his patient's stream of associations. The difficulty here – and it is a central problem in the whole of clinical psychoanalysis – "is the uncertainty of criteria for determining when it is the patient's associative networks that have been laid bare and when it is the analyst's" (p. 243). We are, in effect, continuing to explore the very real limitations of clinical inference. The first of these is that in using representativeness to then uncover supposed meaning, we are involved in a circular process in which representation is used to validate the original pattern – the inevitable problem with hermeneutics. In keeping with this problem is that, in my example, the hidden premise is that, in psychoanalysis, we tend to take for granted a parental heuristic within representativeness and even argue that doing so constitutes psychoanalytic science.

The second limitation is that, in using heuristics, we are relying on our own associative links that relate to the patient. Okay so far. But the danger lies in our inability to determine whether or not what's in our heads is also what is going on in our patient's, irrespective of what they tell us verbally (Nisbett & Wilson, 1977; Yalom & Elkin, 1974). In practice, the process is often based on the analyst's guesses, and these guesses are elevated to the level of causality: "Once this epistemological error is committed the guesses are [then] used to dictate subsequent guesses with subsequent patients" (Leffert, 2013, p. 243).

Availability

Another heuristic is used to assess the likelihood of an event taking place or a person's thinking of something or performing some action. The Availability Heuristic assesses the frequency of such an event coming to pass in terms of the ease with which past instances of the event's occurring can be recalled (Tversky & Kahneman, 1974/1982). Lest it be thought that the operation of the Availability Heuristic is of little use in psychoanalysis or psychotherapy, consider the situation when a new patient appears for a session and describes having suicidal ideation; we face the urgent task of making what we can of it. Availability is a tool used to access frequency and probability. Unfortunately, things other than frequency and probability affect availability, and overreliance upon it can lead to certain expectable biases. For

Decisions made under uncertainty **111**

example, a middle-aged patient is reminiscing about a lost love. He notices that he is much more able to remember some of the many highpoints in the relationship than he is the negative things, of which he knows there were many, that ultimately led to its ending.

When the size of a class or the likelihood of an event taking place are judged with the Availability Heuristic, cases or events that are easily retrievable (more recent or more intense) appear more numerous to the subject than those that are less easy to retrieve *even though the frequencies of both are equal*. Things that are more *familiar* are also seen as more likely than less familiar things occurring at the same frequency. *Saliency* is thus also a factor. Having a patient commit suicide is much more likely to influence a therapist's subjective estimates of probability than attending a continuing education class on suicidality, and such a class is more likely to influence subjective probability estimates than reading a newspaper article about a suicide that mentions that the person had been in some kind of therapy.

Egocentric biases (Ross & Sicoly, 1979/1982) have been shown to be operative in the Availability Heuristic, especially in the area of attribution. A number of factors are responsible for these biases. Selective encoding and storage of personal narratives and procedural memories increase the availability of self-generated meta-narratives of self and world. Our own ideas, for good or ill, fit more easily into the schemas we use to define self and navigate the world. We are more likely to retrieve our own material from memory than that of others. Motivational factors, such as narcissistic vulnerabilities, may require privileging one's own thoughts about oneself over the observations of us made by others. All these factors are active in the therapeutic situation as they play out in the individual thoughts of patient and analyst alike.

There are particular risks that accompany the action of availability in the way we think about our patients. Things like experiences with other patients earlier in the day or week, papers read or written (as I write, I make myself keep in mind the unsurprising tendency to apply it to my work), conferences, supervision received but also given – all of these possible events, singly or in combination, affect availability.

Another source of availability that operates on both patient and therapist, and not explicitly considered in the Uncertainty literature, is the role played by the social networks they are each members of. These networks provide a steady stream of information via the process of *contagion*. We receive this information unconsciously; it is a right-brain function of the Mirror Neuron System and of Cortical Midline Structures that can appear in *left-brain* consciousness, often as something intuited in circumstances of uncertainty. The fashion industry, for example, is blessed by contagion. In the therapeutic situation, contagion effects on ease of recall constitutes a factor in availability. The unconsciousness of the input makes this process very hard to track. As an example, the attempted World Trade Center bombing in the early 1990s did not greatly influence anyone and was not taken up by social networks. In contrast, of course, 9/11 influenced everyone; I noticed afterwards that my thinking

112 Decisions made under uncertainty

with specific patients was going in the direction of PTSD, which I had not considered as relevant in the past.

Adjustment and anchoring

We often attempt to solve problems by starting from a trial solution (an anchor) that we then adjust as we attempt to move towards a final solution (Tversky & Kahneman, 1974/1982). The initial anchoring solution may suggest itself in the way the problem is formulated, may be explicitly given to a subject, or it may be the result of an initial partial or coarse attempt at a solution. Subsequent adjustments unfortunately tend to demonstrate a bias toward the initial trial solution. It should be obvious at this point that although many different variables can influence the choice of anchoring points, some of these choices could be influenced by other heuristics. Representativeness or availability can bias a subject's choice of anchoring point. This is not the result of some active conscious left-brain choice but rather the outcome of parallel distributed processing in the right brain in which multiple heuristics can be tried simultaneously, with those found to be effective in making a choice carried forward while those deemed not useful being put aside. Anchoring turns out to define a significant portion of therapeutic discourse, employed by both patient and therapist.

Recent studies in clinical medicine (Bornstein & Emler, 2001; Klein, 2005) have shown that clinicians too often rely on the Representativeness and Availability Heuristics. Meeting with a patient for the first time, they rapidly focus on an initial idea of what is wrong with him and quickly ask follow-on questions to bring the diagnosis home. Although most of us in our left-brain conscious processing of the ongoing therapeutic discourse make a largely successful effort *not* to operate in this fashion, what is going on for us in our *Right* Brains is another matter entirely. What is going on there is right-brain business as usual. That is to say, my Right Brain is first in communication with that of my patient unbeknownst to my Left Brain. It sizes up the situation and the clinical choices available to me in 100 msec, give or take. I can consciously decide not to ask a series of questions, but, over time, my therapeutic actions are likely to move in that direction. I also have lots of other Right-Brain-to-Right-Brain ways of pursuing my right-brain agenda. By waiting (to the extent I am able), I get to be exposed to more and different therapeutic information that leads to a more effective adjustment process.

The Heuristic and Biases argument for judgments made under uncertainty, if taken seriously (as it is by multiple disciplines), raises significant issues for psychoanalysis. We make the Relational argument, with a considerable sense of certainty, that central to therapeutic discourse is the intuitive, affective connection that we and our patients form with each other over time. Psychoanalysts and psychotherapists encountering H&B for the first time are likely to dismiss it, claiming that clinical intuition trumps H&B and we do not make the kinds of mistakes that it describes. This argument is not dissimilar from the old Intersubjective position that sustained

Decisions made under uncertainty **113**

empathic inquiry is able to cut through subjectivity and get to some version of the truth. We should not forget Meehl's (1954) cautionary tale: When he showed his experts the data demonstrating that results gleaned from actuarial data surpassed those based on intuition, *the experts simply refused to believe him.* Anyone attending a clinical case conference at some point encounters this recalcitrance from one or another member of the audience who believes that he, and he alone, has divined the truth. The evidence suggests that we do make mistakes – lots of them – but, if we are able to process them with the patient, the results can be beneficial.

That said, there is an even greater problem awaiting us if we allow ourselves to be overly influenced by Representativeness and Availability. Daniel Schacter (1996, 2001), one of the foremost contemporary memory researchers (see Leffert, 2010, Chapter 4 for a further discussion of his work), has studied witness testimony and examination. What he and his colleagues have found is that questioning witnesses about remembered events can actually *change* their memories, depending on the questions asked and the follow-on questions posed. The effect is even more pronounced in children. Schacter found that this distortion of memory could be eliminated if questions were asked in such a way as not to predispose the witness to answer and a range of different questions were asked. The same effect can inadvertently be produced in the therapeutic situation when the analyst asks a question or follow-on questions and offers interpretations consistently about some things and not others. The transference and the therapist's implicit or explicit authority heighten the effect.

Inherent in all of these arguments is the rather unhappy and at times narcissistically injurious re-affirmation of the conclusion we reached earlier – that much of what goes on in the therapeutic situation does so beyond our awareness or control. We then have to rely on the rather general premise that, with respect to the patient, our head is in the right place (as opposed to other possible places) and, if not, that we remain flexible enough to eventually be able to figure that out and revise what we are trying to do.

The simulation heuristic

Tversky and Kahneman (1974/1982), in their original treatment of availability, described two different processes: recall of instances and the construction of scenarios. These are, in fact, very different processes, and, although much research has since been done on the former, they observed that relatively little has been done with the latter. To further study availability for construction, Kahneman and Tversky (1982a) described a mental operation they termed the Simulation Heuristic. Their starting point was the observation that there are many situations in which questions about events and outcomes are best answered by the construction and running of a simulation model. Mental simulation does not seek a model that leads to one right answer. Simulation looks at the proclivity of a constructed model to return the various possible outcomes that are most probable, potentially accompanied by

114 Decisions made under uncertainty

a prediction of their likelihood.[20] Simulation, then, offers assessments of proclivity and probability.

Kahneman and Tversky (1982a) looked at counterfactual assessments: the process by which people judge that some event (that didn't occur) was close to happening or nearly happened. They viewed them spatially as the distance between what happened and what might have happened. They offered an example of such a counterfactual model. Two men, Mr. Crane and Mr. Tees, are taking the same limousine to the airport where they are scheduled to take different flights departing at the same time. They are caught in a traffic jam and arrive at the airport 30 minutes after their scheduled departures. Mr. Crane is told that his flight had departed on time, while Mr. Tees is told that his flight was delayed and left just five minutes ago. Who is more upset? It will come as no surprise to anyone having just read this vignette that 96% of subjects asked about it answered that it was Mr. Tees. Note that *the objective situation is the same for both men*, and, since they both expected to miss their planes, the difference cannot be attributed to disappointment. It is rather that, somehow, Mr. Tees catching his flight seems more possible. He is more disappointed because he can more easily *imagine* arriving five minutes earlier than Mr. Crane can imagine avoiding the 30-minute delay. That is to say, he (or we) can more easily construct a simulation that has spaces or turning points that could allow for differing events that would result in making the flight. The imaginings are counterfactual constructions that are structured as scenarios.

Simulations are somewhat magical. They mix elements of reality with *bounded fantasy*. Elements that are too fantastical and too distant from reality are rejected during the process of building a simulation. Thus, the idea "if the limousine driver had just driven faster before the traffic jam" can find its way into the simulation, but "a wooly mammoth walked onto the runway and delayed the flight for another 10 minutes" does not.

Simulation is a subcategory of the wider search for meaning through the organization of past experience that allows it to be taken into the future. It involves an assessment of future possibility making use of both conscious left-brain memory and reasoning and unconscious (probably) right-brain priming and conceptual procedural memory. In recent years, the role of episodic or narrative memory in the simulation of future events has become an area of great interest in the cognitive neurosciences (Schacter, Addis, & Buckner, 2008). Schacter and colleagues located simulation among the functions they group under the concept of the "'prospective brain' which proposes that a crucial function of the brain is to use stored information to allow us to imagine, plan for and predict possible future events" (p. 39).

Taylor and Schneider (1989) went on to discuss the role of simulation in the maintenance of coping strategies and affect regulation. Taylor and colleagues (Taylor, Pham, Rivkin, & Armor, 1998) then considered the role of simulations both in

---

20 The similarity to Craik's (1943/1952) concept of internal working models should be apparent.

coping and self-regulation. Active components of cognition and affect-processing necessary for simulation include capacities for mentalization and Theory of Mind (Baron-Cohen, 2000; Baron-Cohen, Tager-Flusberg, & Cohen, 2000; Fonagy & Bateman, 2013).

What is perhaps most striking about this large interdisciplinary literature that describes and defines simulation, a process phenomenologically fundamental to Being-in-the-World, is that it is quite unknown to psychoanalysis. The fact that this important area of executive function, subsumed by the prospective brain hypothesis, cannot then become a subject of analysis may be one of the reasons that what otherwise appears to be good analytic work does not translate into changes in behavior, affect, or ongoing experience. Of particular relevance to clinical psychoanalysis is the way simulations go astray when they are informed by distorted or overwhelming experiences, producing maladaptive behavior and emotional suffering.

The closest the psychoanalytic literature comes to the topic are a few recent articles (Gaensbauer, 2011; Gallese, 2009; Gallese & Goldman, 1998) on a related concept, that of *embodied simulation*. Implicit in this concept is Gallese's contention that simulation is a thing of the entire body that is pre-rational, non-introspectivist, and does not involve thought out cognitive statements.

A different research thread (Holmes & Mathews, 2010; Raune, MacLeod, & Holmes, 2005) explores visual imagery, anxiety, and emotion as they relate to simulation. Raune and colleagues noted that anxiety and its disorders are increased in the presence of a subjective probability judgment of negative events coming to pass in the near future (such appraisal can draw on all of the Heuristics for good or ill). These imaginary events take place in simulations and are often linked to visual imagery. They suggested that improving access to simulations in which negative events do *not* happen would be helpful in the treatment of anxiety disorders. As clinicians, we are well-placed to explore the reasons that a patient systematically formulates negative simulations that could otherwise persist in the face of more usual psychoanalytic explorations.

Holmes and Mathews (2010) noted how mental imagery plays a central role in Post-Traumatic Stress Disorder (PTSD) and flashbacks. Such imagery is evocative of intense emotional states. Panic attacks and phobias are only somewhat less intense examples of the same phenomena. Imagery has much stronger connections to emotion than do verbal descriptions of events. Directed imagery and modification of the disturbing images have been used by non-psychoanalytic therapists in treating these conditions for decades.[21] Imagining an event outcome increases our belief that this outcome will occur (the Availability Heuristic). This suggests a mechanism whereby traumatic re-experiencing would serve to strengthen and maintain the trauma. Repeatedly going over traumatic events and memories in

---

21 This is entirely consistent with Freud's recommendations for the psychoanalytic treatment of phobias.

116 Decisions made under uncertainty

therapy or analysis would thus seem to be an at best questionable therapeutic technique.

To make this theoretical material more relevant and accessible in a clinical setting, I offer the following case illustration. Peter was a 34-year-old pediatrician who came to see me suffering from depression after the breakup of his 10-year marriage to Margaret, also a pediatrician, whom he had met and married in medical school. I found him to be moderately depressed but without any cognitive slowing. As a result of the latter, I did not think antidepressants were called for and recommended twice-weekly psychotherapy with the possibility of an analysis in the back of my mind. Much of the first year of therapy was taken up with the divorce, which he blamed on his inability to be emotionally intimate with his wife or anyone else (I got a sense from him that Margaret had repeatedly tried to reach him emotionally and had finally left in desperation). Uncovering his defensive identification with his cold, distant mother was both relieving for him and led to his thinking about taking tentative steps to connect with people. When I asked him why he didn't take those steps, he answered as if it were obvious that new social situations made him desperately anxious. When I then asked – in some confusion, I have to say – why he had never, in the 18 months we had been working together, mentioned this to me, he replied that he had assumed everyone pretty much felt that way and wondered how *I* could have seemed so at ease when I first met him.

In past years, I might have first addressed the characterological nature of this social phobia and his idea that it was just a normal part of his social landscape. As I have become more cognizant of the role of internal working models and simulation heuristics in adult psychological function, my clinical approach has changed, and I first inquired about the nature of the events that led to anxiety and the specific thoughts he had around the experiences. Peter, after I had told him that his reactions were *not* what was only to be expected but that he could hope to be free of them, talked easily about the anxiety. It seemed to be a variety of stranger anxiety. He felt it dealing with new people when there were no friends or acquaintances present, when he had to telephone someone he didn't know (*receiving* calls from strangers was okay), and when he had to go to a strange place, even if people he knew would be there. If any of these things were truly optional, he just avoided them. If they were things he *wanted* to do, he also avoided them but felt anxious and very sad and left out. If they were things he had to do, he did them, but with a great deal of anxiety.

I asked him to take us through the mental events that preceded a couple of these experiences. He told of an instance when he was a senior in medical school and had to contact a faculty physician, Dr. Schwartz, whom he had not seen for two years, in order to ask for a letter of recommendation he needed in applying for an internship. There was no question of not doing it (for many, perhaps most people with such an anxiety disorder, this would not be the case). He was first aware of the anxiety as a kind of psychological lump that came and went in his head. When the day he decided to make the call came (he had no thought of delaying it), he experienced several fast, condensed simulations that included a cartoon-like sketch of

Dr. Schwartz's face and an experience without words of Dr. Schwartz telling Peter he had no idea who he was.[22] The anxiety built up as each simulation played out and ended with his feeling completely alone and embarrassed. When he actually made the call, the anxiety seemed to have been lessened somewhat. As it turned out, Dr. Schwartz *did* (of course?) remember Peter and seemed happy to write him a recommendation. What happened after the call was also interesting. There was no feeling of relief but the anxiety did disappear. It did not occur to Peter, as it never did, to use the positive outcome to question or challenge his anxiety then or in the future (that is, to make its way into Representativeness).

In a different sort of event, an intern who Peter and a group of other students had worked with, Dr. Teitlebaum, invited them all to a little party to celebrate the end of their internal medicine studies. Peter liked the intern and his group of students and very much wanted to go. However, the party was to be at the intern's apartment, and the idea of going there frightened him. The simulations this time also included an image of Dr. Teitlebaum's face and then two thoughts: being lost in the building and not being able to find the apartment, or showing up at the apartment only to find that he was there on the wrong day or that there simply was no party. Peter did not actually believe these things, but he also knew he wasn't going to that party. On the evening it was to take place, he walked by the apartment building feeling alone and sad.

After only telling me about these anxious episodes over a period of months and understanding that they were symptoms of something, the anxiety became much reduced; it never again led Peter not to do something he wanted to. Clinically, we came to recognize these episodes as post-traumatic repetitions of what had been an insecure attachment to a mother who chronically left him alone in many different physical or psychological contexts. My recognizing the simulations for what they were was an important part of the healing process. By then, the anxiety had long since disappeared.

Cognitive heuristics: similarity and contagion

Rozin and Nemeroff (2002) have posited what they call the *laws of sympathetic magic*. A subset of magical thinking, they describe forms of human beliefs about the world that are contrary to perceived scientific knowledge. They offer a discussion of two heuristics, contagion and similarity, that are manifestations of magical thinking. These differ from other heuristics in two ways: They are often associated with affect, and, strangely, it can be relatively easy or virtually impossible to make someone aware that they are irrational. Descriptively, they are manifestations of what psychoanalysts are used to describing as primary process cognition.

---

22 These were the *conscious* elements of the simulation. In all likelihood there also were unconscious elements that I had no direct access to but may well have been unconsciously monitoring.

118 Decisions made under uncertainty

The Similarity Heuristic states that like causes like (two similar things will have the same effects) or that appearance equals reality (Rozin & Nemeroff, 2002). Put another way, causes resemble their effects. Appearance equaling reality is more about categorization than it is about cause and effect inference; it is *not* about phenomenology. Similarity can frequently piggyback onto the Representativeness, Availability, and Adjustment Heuristics. It goes something like this. A thought about chronic refractory depression comes to mind. I saw a patient this week (availability) who came in with a refractory depression. He is Mexican-American. He has responded well to a combination of intensive psychotherapy and a novel regimen of medication. I think of a depressed man I know socially. He is also Mexican-American. Their shared ethnic background has *nothing to do with their presenting problems*. Yet, when a couple of weeks later another Mexican-American man calls for an appointment, my implicit sense, over the phone, is that he is depressed. When he comes for his first appointment, I quickly realize that he is not depressed at all. It is only then that I become aware of how I came to think he was depressed – appearance equals reality. I believe we make similar mistakes in our clinical thinking as they occur within a particular analysis or across analyses, but that they are very hard to become aware of.

Phobias are, in effect, a magical statement that appearance equals reality. The same is true for obsessional thoughts or rituals large or small. Again, these are phenomenological observations not associated with any particular metapsychological interpretation. A powerful example of appearance controlling reality is drawn from outside psychoanalysis. Rozin and colleagues (Rozin, Millman, & Nemeroff, 1986) studied a group of undergraduate subjects who first watched sugar being poured into two identical bottles. The *students* then prepared labels for the bottles, one saying "Sugar" and the other saying "Sodium Cyanide Poison." They then arbitrarily affixed a label to each bottle. Even though the students had participated in the whole project, *they were reluctant to consume sugar from the bottle labeled poison*. In a follow-on experiment, the students were also reluctant to consume sugar from a bottle labeled "Not Sodium Cyanide." This is entirely consistent with the action of the Similarity Heuristic and with the right-brain parallel process cognition upon which heuristics operate. It should again be stressed that similarity represents a phylogenetically ancient, fairly primitive mode of cognitive evaluation (it is used by animals as well as people) that is often a highly useful way of navigating the world both physically and emotionally.

The Contagion Heuristic states that once two things are in some kind of contact, they remain in contact. It is richer and more complex than similarity (Rozin & Nemeroff, 2002), involving a number of different elements. An object, usually animate, is a *source*; a second object, usually human, is the *target* or recipient. The law of [magical] contagion states that *physical contact* between the two, or through an intermediary called a *vehicle*, results in the transfer of some quality or essence from source to target. Common vehicles for transfer are food, clothing, and the possessions of source or target.[23] There may also be an exchange of properties and, in any event, the connection once made is permanent. Contagion has a negative bias in that negative effects are very much stronger than positive ones. It also holds, in opposition to similarity, that appearance is not equal to reality. Thus, wholesome or delicious food can be seen as contaminated and beautiful pieces of clothing can seem disgusting. It is scientifically true that some diseases *are* contagious. That is not what we are talking about. The Ebola epidemic we have been living does manifest contagion through exposure to the bodily fluids of symptomatic individuals. The now widely held belief that proximity to a not yet symptomatic Ebola patient will result in infection is scientifically false, but it is a manifestation of psychological contagion. The belief that vaccinations cause children to contract autism is another example of psychological contagion.

Contagion related to disease, like other heuristics, serves both useful and dysfunctional purposes. Over the centuries, magical contagion provided some protection prior to the discovery of the germ theory of infectious disease. AIDS is a recent negative example in North America. Reinforced by homophobia, people have been reluctant to touch an AIDS victim, his clothes, his food, or his possessions. This all occurs in the face of scientific knowledge that AIDS (unlike, for example, the anthrax bacillus that can exist for centuries as spores) is a weak virus that can exist outside of a human host for only very short periods of time.

Clinically, it is doubtful that a single human being is without some experience of magical contagion. Roger only pursued rail-thin women. Women of normal weight (like his mother) seemed smelly and contagious to him, and he avoided them accordingly. Although little is known about the development of contagion (Rozin & Nemeroff, 2002) or of the child's mental models of it, we are drawn to use the Representativeness Heuristic to locate it somewhere in the reaction formations of the anal phase of infantile sexual development (Freud, 1905/1953b). However, it is important to recognize that we have no *non-circular* reasons for doing so and no way of proving that its presence is other than coincident (hence Available and Similar). Meanwhile, research in cognitive development *outside* of the therapeutic situation (Flavell, 1986, 1993) has shown that the appearance-reality distinction and an understanding of false belief appear between the ages of 3 and 4 or 5. Prior to that, young children evidence a confusion of appearance and reality that would be a requirement for the initial development of the Similarity and Contagion Heuristics.

The affect heuristic

The idea that affect, here defined as the specific "goodness" or "badness" associated with a course of action (Slovic, Finucane, Peters, & MacGregor, 2002), should be

---

23 A moment's thought immediately suggests that transference is a variation of the Contagion Heuristic.

120 Decisions made under uncertainty

a significant factor in guiding judgments and decisions would seem to be obvious, but, in fact, it has not been much studied. Indeed, such decision-making has instead been considered in cognitive rather than affective terms. Affective responses to choosing or deciding are virtually instantaneous, identifying them as right-brain responses. These authors argue that reliance on these sorts of feelings in decision-making or choosing is evidence for the existence of an Affect Heuristic. They posit that images marked by positive or negative feelings guide judgment and decision-making. Such decision-making is usually reliable and requires less time and is more efficient than cognitively weighing memories and pros and cons to reach a decision. The Affect Heuristic also piggybacks on to Representativeness and Availability.

In arguing for the importance of affect in decision-making, Slovic and colleagues (2002) cited Zajonc's (1980) earlier work in which he argued that affective responses to a prospective decision are the first on the scene. Zajonc also posited that the belief in a rational cognitive approach, weighing all possibilities, is illusory. (Such post facto reasoning implies a level of knowledge of our decision-making that we do not actually have.)

The Affect Heuristic speaks procedurally for the importance of expressed emotion by both members of the analytic couple. (This shared emotional information is then encoded by the right pre-orbital frontal cortex acting in conjunction with the mirror neuron system.) It fits into the wider conceptual shift in the therapeutic process from cognition to emotion that is currently a center of interest and controversy. Recent neuroscience research (Panksepp, 1998; Panksepp & Biven, 2012; Porges, 1998, 2009; Schore, 2009) has confirmed both the importance and the validity of this shift.

Slovic and colleagues (2002) summed up the Affect Heuristic and their excitement about it: It "appears at once both wondrous and frightening: wondrous in its speed, and subtlety, and sophistication, and its ability to '*lubricate reason*'; frightening in its dependency upon context and experience, allowing us to be led astray or manipulated – inadvertently or intentionally – silently and invisibly" (pp. 419–420). Study of the Affect Heuristic is still in its infancy.

Variants of uncertainty

The study of uncertainty across the disciplines of philosophy, sociology, economics, and the physical sciences have all tended to treat whatever form of uncertainty that is under consideration as unidimensional (Kahneman & Tversky, 1982b). It is as if it involves a single ontological thread of probability or belief. What we find in the study of uncertainty is the operation of a multiplicity of factors ranging from the micro (the behaviors of the synapses of individual neurons) to the macro (the way the behaviors of whole societies can surprisingly change in response to the interplay of individual heuristics).

We exist in a sea of uncertainty. Secure attachment provides a foundation for dealing with it, and the peek-a-boo game already signifies some degree of mastery over it.[24] We are frequently required to act before the uncertainty has been resolved (if it is resolvable at all), and we must be prepared to do so; systematic failures in these capacities can lead to dysfunction or overwhelming collapse.

We approach the world of unfolding events with explicit or implicit expectations; surprise can occur afterwards in the face of discrepancies. We construct our lives around *stable* expectancies, the failure of which may be psychologically or physically catastrophic (e.g., the Kennedy assassination, Hurricane Sandy). The frequency of specific past events prepares us to face the uncertainties of what happens next. This, too, exemplifies the representativeness heuristic.[25] Confidence is a way we describe the subjective probability, the likelihood as we imagine it, that something we imagine happening will happen.

Uncertainty can arise in two ways. It can occur as a measure of the behavior of the external world or as a result of limitations of our knowledge of the world. Internal ignorance is not always easily distinguishable from external uncertainty: We and our patients are capable of systematic errors in making this distinction. As therapists, the situation is further complicated by the problem of false knowledge – thinking we know when we don't know. Patients are subject to similar distortions. Roger, for example, thought that his failures with women grew out of the impossibility of knowing who they were, when in fact he simply had not done the internal psychological work necessary to prepare himself to find out. My observation of this struck him as a kind of revelation.

Why psychoanalysts need to study uncertainty

So what's the point of this? One of the fundamental aspects of psychoanalysis is the search for meaning. This privileges the Eriksonian dyad (Erikson, 1950/1963) of meaning versus meaninglessness through the life cycle, which is the same dyad as the phenomenologically authentic versus inauthentic and thrown versus fallen. It does not mean that we are searching for some deeper meaning whose existence lies in one or another metapsychology but rather phenomenological meaning (simply discovering what is) that is hidden, secret, or heretofore unformulated. This chapter

---

24 We visited our then 8-month-old granddaughter, Sarah, who we had been seeing every six weeks or so. On this three-day visit, when Sarah first saw me (bearded, unlike her father), her mouth turned down and she burst into tears. It seemed clear to me that stranger anxiety had appeared. Her response moderated and, by the third day, she consented to sit on my lap. She began to whirl her head around, look piercingly into my eyes with a facial expression that was half-smile and half-laugh. Over the three days, my strangeness had become a good joke.

25 After Hurricane Sandy, nearly all the residents of homes that were destroyed elected to rebuild. Should a number of such storms occur annually, we would expect that frequency to decline.

122 Decisions made under uncertainty

has been taken up with a major problem with that search – that it must take place under uncertainty.[26]

The tool for carrying out this search is therapeutic discourse. It encompasses both conscious and unconscious elements. Among other things we are about is an explication of narrative. The process by which this takes place is Dialectical Constructivism. But the great risk in employing this process is that the meaning may *not* in fact be co-constructed – that, due to the operation of the various heuristics and particularly the Representativeness Heuristic, the meaning that is being constructed resides in the analyst's head. It is then conveyed to the patient's with no evidence that it actually refers to anything actually residing therein.

Two new psychoanalytic tasks follow from this caveat. The first is that the analyst's own heuristics and biases need to be the subject of ongoing self-analysis, along with its other, more familiar, components.[27] The second is that the analysis of a patient's H&Bs should be a part of *any* analytic therapy. There is no particular requirement, indeed quite the contrary, to make use of this terminology as part of the analysis (just as other technical language would usually not find its way into the discourse).

In this chapter and the four that precede it, I have offered a series of building blocks that are at once familiar and novel. They at once offer both searching critiques of how we have been carrying on business as usual and more effective ways of viewing the therapeutic situation. The next two chapters continue these discussions on into what we are trying to accomplish clinically with our patients.

---

26 At a recent presentation of these ideas, I was asked whether uncertainty indeed left me caught somewhere between pragmatism and nihilism. This is an important question, but the answer is "no." The argument I have been making is only problematic to someone who demands a metatheory to cleave to. Otherwise, Uncertainty is not nihilistic; it is an ontological fact that demands of us more flexible thinking. Although I see nothing wrong with pragmatism, what I am arguing for is not pragmatism but contextual phenomenalism.

27 Metapsychologies really comprise only a particular series of heuristics developed and taught over the decades.

6

CARE AND SUFFERING IN THERAPEUTIC SITUATIONS

Introduction

This chapter has the ambitious goal of suggesting a fundamental shift in the therapeutic identities of psychoanalysts and psychotherapists as well as an alternative ontology of the therapeutic situation. Beginning with Freud, the therapist had claimed an entirely new identity as "one who analyses" (along with the depreciated identity of "one who supports"). A major shift in therapeutic *praxis* has taken place in the contemporary period, roughly defined as beginning in the mid1980s, under the auspices of the Relational and Intersubjective schools of psychoanalysis. However, this shift has not gone so far as to suggest any change in the professional identity of its practitioners, only a change in the therapeutic toolbox they carry.

By therapeutic identity, I mean something very different from the name of some founding mother or father or some treatment modality with which many therapists and analysts display an unfortunate tendency to brand themselves. What I am speaking of is a change from "one who analyses" to "one who cares for and heals." I am *not* suggesting that we do away with analyzing or analysis, but rather suggesting that analyzing and analysis must be considered as necessary *sub-categories* of care and healing. I would also posit that analysis not employed in the service of care and healing is not analysis at all, not really. Rather, it is an intellectual exercise or game (Wittgenstein, 1953) at which both partners may develop at least some degree of proficiency. These are powerful claims that require substantiation.

There is almost no psychoanalytic literature on the nature and role of care of the patient in psychoanalysis or psychotherapy beyond a handful of papers we will discuss shortly. Boss (1963) and Winnicott (1972), in their work with more disturbed patients, stand out as marked exceptions. A search of PEP-Web returns only 14 psychoanalytic papers with the much-depreciated term *palliation* in their titles between 1871 and the present. As I have had to observe on many different occasions, there is

124 Care and suffering

a robust interdisciplinary literature on the subject, in this case dating back at least to the medieval period in Europe, but as analysts and therapists, we have hardly availed ourselves of it. This literature includes a multiplicity of terms, among them *pain*, *suffering*, and *unhappiness* on the one hand and *care, cure, healing, palliation, placebo*, and *hospitality* on the other. Just as psychoanalysis is only one of many disciplines offering talk and feeling therapy for broadly defined psychological problems, so it is only one of many offering care explicitly or implicitly for these problems. The overlapping relations among these signifiers, so foreign to the language of psychoanalysis, are not at all simple. They will, however, much concern us.

Prior to the advent of the relational schools of psychoanalysis in the 1980s, clinical theory had made little attempt to address any of these issues. As I observed in 2013 (Leffert):

> Training in psychoanalysis or psychoanalytic psychotherapy privileges insight/interpretation and depreciates support or palliation as a sort of necessary evil. Such valuing or privileging has no basis in fact, it amounts to no more than arbitrary practice that dates from Freud's (1919 [1918]/1955b) original comments on the subject, comments that are inconsistent with how he actually worked (Blanton, 1971; Freud, 1909/1955c; Kardiner, 1977). This bias has not been rethought in the contemporary literature in the light of relational (small *r*) or interpersonal ideas and the evolution in thought about therapeutic action that has taken place. (p. 246)

It is important to note that when talking about care of the patient, we are talking about two different kinds of care that may overlap to a significant extent. The first refers to a series of procedures performed on or for someone. They are independent of any relationship per se and do not involve emotion. These range from the performance of tasks like therapeutic housekeeping to the actions of a surgeon in the operating room, to much of how medical care is delivered by the contemporary healthcare system, to the behaviors of mental health works governed by adherence to some theory of technique like the newest big thing, Dialectical Behavioral Therapy (DBT), or, for that matter, making interpretations.

The second kind of care involves the emotional and language elements present in a particular caregiving relationship. In most caregiving relationships, there is, ideally, a *blending* of both kinds of care, the procedural and the emotional.[1] This answers those psychoanalytic critiques that attempt to portray the providers of such care as offering a relationship without content as curative in its own right. Attempts can also be mistakenly made to render the therapeutic relationship as equal as possible. While

---

1 A colleague of mine who practices orthopedic surgery will not operate on a patient (emergencies excluded) until he has seen them over some months. He deems it necessary to establish a physicianly, human relationship *with* a patient before performing *on* them.

social equality is a necessity (and an unwillingness to strive for it is always an implicit power tactic on the part of the therapist), epistemological equality is impossible. The fact cannot be avoided that patient and therapist are about very different things in the therapeutic situation and only one of them, the therapist, is an expert in it.

Cooper's (2002) observation that "palliation, the *wish* for the patient to feel better, to be less anxious, *whatever*, or the analyst's *wish* to be more attentive are both goal directed and have little to do with what is going on and emotionally real at the moment" (p. 110, italics added) certainly speaks for psychoanalysis past, perhaps present, but hopefully not future. Palliation is neither a wish nor is it a whatever; to call it such is to contemptuously dismiss it and, by extension, anyone who is trying to bring it about. To palliate is to alleviate the symptoms of a disease without curing it; to mitigate the sufferings of; to ease (*Oxford English Dictionary,*1989). Nor is there any requirement that palliation become the *focus* of an analyst's endeavors towards her patient, as Cooper claims it to be in these circumstances. What I am talking about is the hypothesis that the identities of being a healer and being an analyst or psychotherapist are closely related. So long as these issues around healing go unmentioned and these questions go unasked or remain implicit, there is no clinical problem with them. However, once they are made explicit, psychoanalysis can never really be the same again.

Palliation and support have been thought to suggest a lesser therapy, a dilution of the "pure gold" of analysis. Older models view psychological pain as an essential factor in motivating the patient to do the hard work of analysis; procedures that lessen pain (verbal, emotional, or pharmacological) are disparaged as counter-productive and even anti-analytic. I have never observed this clinically; quite to the contrary, the formation of a healing bond is likely to make a patient braver about pursuing this work. I have, however, seen many patients who simply don't want an analysis (and many who do) whether I make the offer or not. This is not necessarily a resistance (a term I have also critiqued); it can simply be the wish of an autonomous human being at odds with her therapist.

If an analyst or therapist is asked if he considers himself a healer, he can answer either "yes" or "no." If no, patients, prospective patients, members of the general public, and, yes, the health insurance industry are going to be deeply troubled, and we will find that the market for insight and therapeutic discourse for their own sakes is really quite limited. However, if the answer is yes, then much of the thinking that we call psychoanalytic is going to have to be re-thought, for even the relational schools have not gone far enough in their consideration of relational healing.

It should by now be apparent that this is exactly the project that we have taken up. (Yet, if one approaches psychoanalysis phenomenologically, as we have been doing, then there *is* an important place for both kinds of practices, as parts of everydayness and of thrownness.) For the sake of convenience, I'm going to subsume these various practices and the ills that they address under the general term *care* and break out its individual elements as needed.

126 Care and suffering

Care and hospitality have, in recent years,[2] become topics of great interest in the academy. Curiously, care encompasses practices of the most poorly paid and societally negligible care workers (Boris & Klein, 2012), such as cooks, housekeepers, and baby-sitters, as well as care provided by highly paid professionals such as nurses, physicians, and psychologists. Care studies have involved a fruitful integration of the medieval, early modern, and postmodern literature. Sadly, the traditional roles of health caregivers have been usurped, at least in America, by an alliance of the medical insurance industry, government, for-profit hospitals, day surgery clinics, and procedure-wielding surgical sub-specialists. The result has been the dawning of the age of the healthcare provider (who often provides neither health nor care). Ironically, the last person left standing in the field of care is then the mental health worker, who can choose to make the time to provide care in the context of a healing relationship. The examination of care in psychoanalysis could never be timelier.

I have written (Leffert, 2013, Chapter 3) about the role of the therapist's mature love for his patients in the therapeutic situation. Such love is a variably present part of the therapeutic relationship. None of these discussions would be complete without considering the neuroscience of love and care; a coming together of hard wiring, neuro-hormonal elements, and development. Introducing these considerations leads to the questions of what, exactly, care and healing look like in the therapeutic situation and how they are carried out both explicitly and implicitly in the patient-therapist relationship.

The nature of care

Care, as a transitive verb, has proved difficult – slippery, if you will – to define. Such an effort must begin with a consideration of the neurobiology of care. In 2013, as part of a discussion of the existence and role of a therapist's love for his or her patients, I raised three questions from a neuroscience perspective concerning it. First, is a distinction between this love and romantic, sexual, or erotic love valid? Second, if the distinction is valid, what did this love entail? Finally, how important a part of therapeutic action is this love? I raised these questions because love in the therapeutic situation was and remains such a controversial subject, one that has even provoked ad hominem attacks against those positing a necessary role for it. I would argue that the same sorts of questions must, of necessity, be raised about care.

Neuroscience foundations in human and vertebrate emotions: the phylogeny of care

In the field of affective neuroscience, Jaak Panksepp (2009) describes what he calls primary process emotions[3] "that are initially unconditioned, 'objectless,'

---

2 UCSB, for example, is about to begin its second yearlong series of workshops on these subjects.

3 Panksepp (2009) does not mean primary process in the psychoanalytic sense but rather in the sense of first present, followed by a secondary process (development) and a tertiary process (social learning).

neuroevolutionary, affect-laden response tendencies arising from [phylogenetically] very ancient lower regions of the brain, whereas all human cognitions are thoroughly conditioned by life experiences and language processes located within higher neocortical brain regions" (p. 2). The latter part of this observation, remarkable in its relevance to contemporary clinical psychoanalysis, says a great deal about how these tendencies are manifest in adult social interactions. This is *not* a hypothesis. Panksepp went on to state, "it is a scientific fact, *and not just conjecture*, that a series of cross-mammalian emotional systems has been revealed through animal brain research" (p. 7). There are seven such systems (Panksepp & Biven, 2012): "SEEKING (expectancy), FEAR (anxiety), RAGE (anger), LUST (sexual excitement), CARE (nurturance), PANIC/GRIEF (sadness), and PLAY (social joy)" (p. 2). Distinct entities can of course combine or act in sync, but this in no way compromises their distinctness or locates them on the same developmental line.[4] *This* is the 21st-century biological reality behind Freud's 19th-century drive theory.

The class *Mammalia* would not exist and we would not exist phylogenetically without the massive complementary investment of maternal care necessary to nurture and educate our offspring through a protracted immaturity into adulthood. So necessary is maternal care that it is neurally and hormonally hardwired into us. Cross-mammalian studies (de Jong, Measor, Chauke, Harris, & Saltzman, 2010) have also shown that in some species (including us) the potential for similar paternal behaviors in environmentally necessary situations is also hardwired. Other mammalian studies (Panksepp & Biven, 2012) demonstrate maternal behaviors actuated by the young of other species. Whereas some maternal bonds with their offspring are exclusive, physical, pharmacological, and social interventions can re-open what is otherwise a bonding "window."

The CARE system has an interreferential relationship with the PANIC/GRIEF system that develops into adulthood and serves as a foundation for the caring bond between individuals found in nurturing and healing relationships. Panksepp and Biven (2012) speculate on the importance of this foundation for the development of empathy, and Watt (2007) posits a role for social contagion in its development. It requires only a moment's thought to realize that contagion must play an important role in the learned ability to reliably perform acts of care.

The process that develops out of a subset of the interactions between mother and infant in general and the special case of the interactions of their respective CARE and PANIC/GRIEF systems is of course attachment (Bowlby, 1969, 1988). Secure attachment is the desired outcome of this process, and mothers who suffered deficient experiences in their own childhoods have demonstrated failings in their capacities as attachment figures for their own children (Cicchetti & Toth, 1995). Bowlby also posited that the caregiving behaviors of the primary attachment

---

4 The CARE and LUST systems *do* share phylogenic neurochemical roots in the peptide predecessors of oxytocin, suggesting that, evolutionarily at least, CARE developed out of reptilian LUST. To paraphrase the old psychoanalytic canard, phylogeny is not destiny.

128 Care and suffering

figures are organized into a behavioral system that includes the young child's reciprocal attachment behaviors. Four decades of further research have supported this systems concept (George & Solomon, 2008) as "a biologically based motivational control system that governs the rules and behaviors associated with a specific *proximate* goal" (p. 834, italics added). It is thought that caregiving became a behavioral system through "the transmission of the mother's attachment to the next generation" (p. 837). The ethological function of the system is protection of the young and increasing reproductive fitness. In a successful caregiving behavioral system, the caregiver will have made or will make a successful intergenerational transition from being the recipient to being the provider of care. Also a part of the system is the formation of mental representations of the caring relationship on the part of both members of the attachment pair. Such representations (successful or otherwise) take the form of internal working models (Bowlby, 1988; Craik, 1943/1952).

There is nothing in this macro-level description of attachment that goes beyond research findings in child development that have stood for decades. Regrettably, although attachment researchers have begun to reach out to the neurosciences (see, for example, Coan, 2008), not much complementary work has been done in the other direction. Panksepp (1998) can only cite some beginning ethological work in the vocal crying, distress vocalizations, or isolation calls made by young mammals in social isolation. For our purposes, tantalizing questions are left unanswered. The attachment histories of people in the helping professions as they pertain to their experiences as young children or adult parents have never been studied, nor have they been correlated with their performance as adults. For that matter, functions specifically related to care have never been evaluated by any of these professions. At *best*, outcomes and failures in clinical work are looked at. One would expect that attachment experiences and the capacity to form affectional bonds do play a part in adult, professional caregiving, but we as yet know nothing of this.[5]

It is now known (Freeman, 1995; Panksepp & Biven, 2012) that oxytocin, a neuropeptide secreted by the posterior pituitary and active in the CARE system, functions to strengthen social memories and bonding; both functions are impaired if it is blocked. It is known from mammalian research and human reports, anecdotal and otherwise, that a first mothering experience permanently raises maternal abilities. How this information is coded remains unclear, but it would be expected that it produces permanent changes in the underlying CARE system. Panksepp and Biven do, however, posit that the giving and receiving of parental care and devotion are linked to the development of altruism, compassion, and empathy. There is evidence drawn from mammalian research (Kinsley et al., 2008; Kinsley & Lambert,

---

5 A study of the administration of the Adult Attachment Interview to a group of healthcare professionals, psychoanalysts, or psychotherapists, while of obvious interest, has not, to my knowledge, been carried out.

2008) that motherhood confers increased neuroplasticity and benefits to brain and behavior across the life cycle. (Does motherhood make for more empathic psychotherapists and analysts?) There also is beginning evidence of a role for intranasal oxytocin in psychotherapy (Feifel et al., 2010).

Radke-Yarrow (1991, 1998), in her studies of children of depressed mothers, found that chronically sad or anxious mothers suffering from severe affect dysregulation were least able to provide a secure base (Bowlby, 1988) for their young children. Although her complex, highly nuanced results are difficult to summarize, children of unipolar depressed and bipolar mothers tended to exhibit much more anxiety, disruptive behavior, and depression than those of well mothers. Attachment status did not materially affect these results with regard to negative moods and emotions; however, secure attachment, regardless of maternal diagnosis, did correlate with the presence of positive emotions and neutral moods.

Interesting correlations are beginning to appear between attachment and neuropeptide research. If we fast forward 15 years or so, we find growing research interest in the oxytocin levels present in mothers and children. Oxytocin, along with vasopressin and endogenous opioids, runs the CARE system. It is known that maternal depression disrupts oxytocin and social synchrony in the mother (Hollander, 2013) and that the developing infant is exquisitely sensitive to such disruptions that can result in permanent impairment of the child's oxytocin and CARE system. Variations in an oxytocin receptor gene can confer either resilience or increased risk to early maternal deprivation following from maternal depression. At age 6, 61% of the children of depressed mothers showed Axis 1 psychopathology (Apter-Levy, Feldman, Valcart, Ebstein, & Feldman, 2013), mostly anxiety and oppositional defiant disorders. More telling still was the fact that, at that time, all family members showed decreased salivary oxytocin levels, and the children also showed decreased levels of empathy and social engagement. The implications for the capacity of the adult children of these families to assume vocational caregiving roles cannot be underestimated.

If motherhood confers neuroplasticity, the good enough response by mothers and loving others to separation distress makes possible the mammalian capacity for GRIEF (Panksepp & Biven, 2012). Distress cries at social separation do not occur in human infants until the second half of the first year of life. Ainsworth and colleagues (Ainsworth, Blehar, Waters, & Wall, 1978) quantified separation distress and distress vocalizations in the Strange Situation, which made it possible to distinguish and characterize healthy (secure) and pathological patterns of attachment.

There is now excellent functional neuroanatomical evidence for the existence of a GRIEF/PANIC circuit combining higher cortical (Freed, Yanagihara, Hirsch, & Mann, 2009) and phylogenetically ancient, subcortical (Panksepp, 2003) anatomical circuits. The system functions bimodally: Its activation produces pain and misery, while the activation of the CARE system in present attachment figures results in its inactivation and the operation of the care chemistries of endogenous opioids and oxytocin. Is it unreasonable to expect that something very like this process takes

130 Care and suffering

place in the presence of suitably attuned, good enough caregivers in healthcare and psychotherapy settings.

It is highly likely that the GRIEF system evolved from the phylogenetically ancient, pre-mammalian brainstem pain system. Both distress vocalizations (DVs) and the affective response to physical pain respond to opioids, and both involve ancient subcortical areas sharing the dorsal part of the periaqueductal gray (PAG) and surrounding midbrain areas (Panksepp & Biven, 2012). We should not lose sight of this intimacy between physical pain and GRIEF and the importance of CARE in both the medical and psychological treatments of pain and suffering.

GRIEF/PANIC *feels* terrible. The presence of endogenous opioids, oxytocin, and prolactin or the external supply of medications quiets the system and replaces the grief and sadness with feelings of well-being and security (Panksepp & Biven, 2012). The former appear as a result of the actions of attachment figures and adult caregivers. GRIEF/PANIC functions in effect as a social bonding demand system. If these needs are not met, the self becomes defensively closed off and all cognitive and emotional functions are impaired. Again, the implications of these cognitive and neurochemical realities for medical care, psychotherapy, and psychoanalysis cannot be underestimated.

Care of the medical patient

This section will focus on care primarily of the medical patient, where care is comprised of relief of suffering and healing or cure. These terms are more complex than they appear at first glance. A not unreasonable question might well be: What does this have to do with what we do in psychoanalysis or psychotherapy? Our work is certainly not much thought about in these ways, and there are some of us who go so far as to think of them as antithetical. What I am arguing for in this chapter and the next is twofold: that indeed this is precisely what we do, and the success or failure of our endeavors hinges on how well we do it; and that the only difference lies in the nature of the physical and psychological procedures that we perform.

Let me start by recounting a vignette from a care narrative of my own. In the summer of 2013, I was found to have a benign parathyroid tumor in my neck that needed to be surgically removed. I was reassured that the surgery would take about two hours, that I would be discharged that afternoon, could go swimming if I wished, and needed, at most, a day off from work. However, events took a different course. A serious medical error was made that replaced the swim with a five-day stay in the ICU. All of my *vital* signs (a term that henceforth took on new meaning) – pulse, blood pressure, oxygen saturation – were displayed on a screen above my bed. On the day in question, I had experienced some mild difficulty in breathing. All of a sudden, I panicked – I was absolutely terrified that I would be unable to breathe (certainly one of our primal fears). I began gasping for breath; my respiratory plumbing was not up to the job, and I could both hear and feel its protests. I hoarsely cried out that I couldn't breathe. It took only seconds to turn me from being a physician and psychoanalyst into a mindless, suffering animal. Fortunately, a nurse who had *taken care of me* the previous day and whom I trusted was there at my bedside. She did two things simultaneously: She spoke to me quietly, but with great earnestness, "You're all right, your blood is 100% saturated with oxygen," and she put her arm around my shoulder and held it. I am quite certain that neither of these two actions, if undertaken alone, would have had any effect. Together (physical touch and a cognitive appeal), they gave me the courage to first look at the screen and see that, in fact, my blood was fully saturated with oxygen and I was in no danger of suffocating. I was then able to do the horribly right, counter-intuitive thing: I simply stopped breathing. In another five seconds I was myself again, relaxed and, because I was relaxed, able to breath easily. *I* was aware that something momentous had happened to me; my nurse, however, was entirely matter-of-fact about it and saw nothing out of the ordinary in this piece of hospital life. I have since given considerable thought to her care of me. I recognized her matter-of-factness in myself, experienced as I have gone about caring for my own patients.

Let me offer another vignette of care. There is a popular BBC television series called *Doc Martin*, which is comedic rather than a comedy. The protagonist is a seemingly rude general practitioner who expertly if unempathically cares for the denizens of a picture-book seaside town in Cornwall. It turns out that he was once a noted vascular surgeon who had to stop operating because he became frightened and repulsed by the sight, smell, and feel of blood. In an early episode, he describes how this came about. One day, he was performing an entirely routine surgery on a middle-aged woman whom he found utterly unremarkable, when it struck him for the first time that what he was operating on was not some thing, some collection of blood vessels, but a *person*. (Such an epiphany is by no means universal.) As a result of this realization, he found himself unable to continue the procedure or consider operating on anyone again. It seemed, then, that he was unable to function in a setting in which care coincided with committing violence, however well-meaning.

Taken together, these stories tell rather a lot about care. Least obvious perhaps is that the sometimes distinction between care and cure, between "carative" and curative, often made in nursing (see, for example, Watson, 1979/1985), is artificial. Care is intimately related to cure and is, in itself, often curative. Helping to heal is perhaps the most effective way to relieve suffering, and *sometimes* (so long as it is truly kept to the absolute minimum), the production of a degree of suffering is an unavoidable byproduct of the most effective way to both relieve suffering and to heal a particular condition. There is, in fact, a perfectly respectable term for care that relieves suffering but does not lead to healing or cure – it is palliation.

Care is much more than the affectless performance of a series of routinized tasks for some ill individual;[6] rather, it evolves in the context of a developing relationship

---

6 It must be admitted that the formation of the health insurance-hospital-pharmaceutical industrial complex in recent decades has negatively impacted care but has by no means destroyed it.

132 Care and suffering

between caregiver and patient, built around healing and relief of suffering. Based on these observations, we are in a position to offer a working definition of care. We can say that it is a procedure, or a series of procedures, that results in some combination of the relief of pain and suffering that may also promote or bring about healing or cure. It (or they) is performed by a caregiver on or for the benefit of a patient or sufferer *in the context of a relationship*. Furthermore, the relationship *itself*, over and above the physical or verbal acts performed in it, is a fundamental component of the process. It draws on ancient roots in the CARE system and is expressed in words and often, but not necessarily, physical touch.

At the center of care is this therapeutic relationship. I see no reason to singularly focus on the doctor-patient relationship or, in order to best understand the nature of care, to separate it from the nurse-patient relationship, or the nurse practitioner-patient relationship, or the physician's assistant-patient relationship. However, for heuristic purposes, it *is* useful to treat the relationship between a psychotherapist, of whatever background or ilk, and his or her patient as a special case that will be discussed below.

Mayerhoff (1971/1990) sees caring for others as centering and ordering life. As it becomes primary, other activities become secondary and of lesser importance. It harmonizes the self, it offers an ordering in a way that is reminiscent of Heidegger's thrownness, of being-in-the-world (1975/1982, 1927/2010).[7] Mayerhoff refers to this as being "in-place." It offers autonomy, not in the sense of isolation, but of lived meaning. He also defines care as an ongoing, process concept rather than something that is about product. This formulation is not meant to lessen the importance of goals, but rather to assert that attaining goals is not about reaching endings. To care for another is to hold oneself out as offering continuity and dependability; it is a being-with. In being-with, neither the caregiver nor the recipient of care is alone. None of this requires perfection in order to be actualized; mistakes and failings are to be expected so long as the total experience is good enough.

Care has its paranormal components as well. Balint (1955) and Lazar (2001) have described how a therapist's positive feelings for her patients and optimism concerning successful therapeutic outcomes render the treatment process more successful. In keeping with the power of such effects, Lazar has also noted that prayer circles formed to physically surround critically ill patients have facilitated healing to a degree beyond what might otherwise have been expected.

Looked at from a different direction, in order to appropriately care for another, one must also determine what is the matter with her. This involves an act of diagnosis and many small, ongoing acts of diagnosis. As Montgomery (2006) observes, however, a "diagnosis is a plot summary of a *socially constructed* pathophysiological sequence of events" (p. 13, italics added). In other words, the social circumstances

---

7 However, Heidegger considered care a manifestation of everydayness; I would say that in doing so he failed to understand it.

under which a diagnosis is made – in what country or region, in the city or in rural areas, in the clinic of which psychoanalytic institute – all profoundly influence the care that follows. In trying to ascertain just what to do, we find ourselves confronting a postmodern (post-structural, actually) epistemology involving the same sorts of issues that societies have always addressed, issues that are difficult to separate from those of power relations (Foucault, 1969 & 1971/1972, 1973/1994, 1961/2006a; Lukes, 2005).

Diagnosis and care are fraught with ambiguity and uncertainty. They are best rendered as a part of a simultaneous therapeutic discourse. Multiple external factors (an office, an emergency room, a hospital bed) combine with the interreferentiality of any discourse that defeats objectivism and imposes limits on knowability. As Montgomery (2006) observed, the setting, the respective appearances of caregiver (be it physician or nurse) and patient, and the first sentence exchanged by them all act to shape what follows to a significant degree. As we discussed in the previous chapter, judgments made under uncertainty inevitably lead to the application of different sorts of heuristics, the process best characterized both as a blessing and a curse. They can lead either to an effective course of care or to therapeutic actions that are ineffective at best and dangerous at worst.

If care involves relief of suffering, the satisfaction of needs, and, to whatever extent possible, cure, then it behooves us to say more about the nature of suffering and its relief. Cassell (2004) asserted that suffering is both underdiagnosed and undertreated in medical care, and I believe that the same is true for psychotherapy and psychoanalysis. This is true for physical pain as it approaches agony and emotional pain as it approaches anguish and dread. It is partly, but not entirely, the result of the inevitable clash between the private, even secret, subjective suffering of the patient and the objective (as we know from Science Studies, not really so objective) assessment performed by a treating other. *This* part of the problem is perhaps the one best addressed in contemporary psychoanalysis through relational and intersubjective thinking. The concept that the physician has a duty to relieve suffering has existed since the dawn of antiquity, even if it is often more honored in the breech. Unfortunately, this concept has been less fully embraced by mental health professionals; I have certainly never heard it discussed as such.

If we consider, say, a patient suffering (we can't avoid this verb) from some significant form of cancer, we encounter suffering (now the noun) in myriad forms.[8] There are two forms of physical suffering connected with the illness. One is the pain that the tumor (or tumors) is causing by its presence in the body, stimulating pain receptors directly or through interfering with individual organ or systemic function. The second sort of physical suffering results from painful or debilitating

---

8 Although at first glance what follows may seem irrelevant to psychoanalysis, it is not at all difficult to find parallels in the suffering that our patients come in with, let alone those who also bring a physical illness to the office.

134 Care and suffering

attempts to treat the underlying condition: surgery, chemotherapy, and or radiation. There is also plenty of room for different sorts of mental anguish. There is anguish over the often-irreversible damage to the body that ensues from any serious illness and the changes and diminutions that take place in the patient's very life as a result of the illness. The shortening of life and the need to confront one's own, sometimes imminent death bring with them their own special anguish.

Cassell (2004) noted, and my own experience as a physician, a medical educator, and a patient confirms, that patients and their physicians share the goal of eliminating suffering through cure or control of some disease process. However, although patients consider the relief of pain and suffering as one of the highest goals of medical care (second only, perhaps, to a total cure), neither physicians nor nurses, by and large, share this view. The control of pain remains somewhat haphazard, often driven by the double message of medical licensing boards: You must adequately manage a patient's pain or sometimes face disciplinary action; however, the overprescribing of opiates is scandalous and also a subject for board action. The notion that to require or ask for pain medication (or worse, to, à la Dickens, ask for *more*) reflects a weak moral fiber has not entirely vanished with the advent of the new century.[9]

Cassell (2004) defined suffering as occurring "when an impending destruction of the person is perceived; it continues until the threat of disintegration has passed or until the integrity of the person can be restored in some other manner" (p. 32). Although it can be triggered by extreme pain, shortness of breath, or other symptoms, it is not about the physical but rather the mental, and it is personal rather than objective. This definition touches on much that we have been talking about. To rephrase what Cassell has to say only a bit, it is that suffering is both subjective and existential; it is about the threatened destruction of the self, all familiar territory to contemporary psychoanalysts. What he fails to note is that suffering is often intersubjectively determined as well. It may be a response to how a loved one behaves towards us, how a caregiver responds to us medically, or how a therapist responds to us verbally. A patient told me a story of having been hospitalized with a presumed heart attack. His symptoms had been hypotension and mild chest pain. After three or four hours in the ICU, his chest pain became excruciating. His nurse promptly treated the pain by applying nitroglycerine cream, a coronary vasodilator, to his chest, but this only made things worse. The nurse offered nothing more and my patient had felt that his "heart was dying" for lack of care. (As a metaphor, that phrase echoed throughout his analysis.) This was interpersonal suffering at its worst. The story has a happy ending. He had somehow kept his cellphone and was able to reach his doctor, who was still in the hospital and understood the problem. On the way to the cardiac catheterization lab, the pain remained but the suffering was

---

9 A neurosurgeon of my acquaintance sends his spinal fusion patients home from surgery with extra-strength Tylenol as the only medication he deems necessary for the control of their post-operative pain.

much reduced, and he could calm himself. When the blood clot totally blocking a major coronary artery was dissolved with enzymes, the pain instantly vanished and was replaced by a feeling of well-being.

I have had to stay with Cassell (2004) because there is little medical writing on the subject of suffering. There is a genre of physician narratives that deals with the autocentric experience of medical training and practice and the treatment narratives that attend it, but this is not helpful. Boss's (1963) case report of his analytic work with a deeply suffering, highly regressed patient that we discussed earlier is one of the best examples of empathic inquiry and care in the literature. It is ironic that in looking for descriptions and portrayals of suffering there is little to be had of it from the hands of healthcare professionals of whatever ilk, and we can only turn instead to art, literature, and poetry for such accounts.

The degree of suffering which individuals bear is subjective and phenomenological. We cannot generalize about why some people slip from pain and loss into suffering and others do not, why some people grow as a result of their suffering[10] while others are destroyed by it, or why some people in pain do not lapse into suffering and others who suffer recover from it. There has been a tendency to invoke the attachment-based concept of *resiliency* to explain these differences, but when you ask about the definition of this seemingly useful term, you find yourself back where you started. None of this should be taken to mean that our job is anything but trying to discover the sources and meaning of suffering in our patients and to address it.

As Cassell (2004) observed, "recovery from suffering often involves borrowing the strength of others as though persons who have lost parts of themselves can be sustained by the personhood of others until their own returns" (p. 43). We do this as healers and therapists; sometimes groups or teams serve this function. I do not, as Cassell did, consider this a latent part of what we do, but it must, at least initially, be left implicit if it is to work. Later, it can and, arguably, must be approached relationally. Although we have access to the procedures of medical treatment, the techniques of discourse, and the prescription of psychotropic medications where indicated, they by no means replace the search for meaning and transcendence in suffering that allows the ill to regain control of their selves. Transcendence places an individual's suffering in a wider phenomenological context that can sometimes lead to facing pain and death. Such a state of being-in-the-world is entirely consistent with Heidegger's (1927/2008, 1927/2010) ideas about authenticity and thrownness.

A final thought about suffering concerns Cassell's (2004) distinction between chronic disease and chronic illness, which I would amplify a bit and see as relevant to psychoanalysis as it is to internal medicine. Disease involves damage to some part of the self, occurring in response to things like injury, infection, or

---

10 The mistaken notion of the virtue of suffering devolves from this observation and has had a place in the world's religions throughout history and perhaps before.

136 Care and suffering

psychological trauma. I have argued (and still do) that the self is a holistic entity (Laszlo, 1972/1996) and, strictly speaking, cannot be divided into parts. However, for heuristic purposes, we can speak of disease as relating to or being about some particular system or organ. Chronic illness, on the other hand, is a condition of the self. It modifies the entire self and alters its experience of itself and of the world. The very experience of reality is changed. Illness profoundly alters the self's relations with itself and with its world (*Umwelt*, *Mitwelt*, and *Eigenwelt*). It also alters the way in which the social world relates to the self. It is around treating these alterations that care and caregiving enter the picture, again with respect to either the medical or the psychological.

Care and suffering in psychoanalysis and psychotherapy

As psychoanalysts and therapists, we are not much used to writing or thinking about care and suffering and tend to sometimes see healing and cure as presumptuous notions. We often focus instead on the application of metapsychologically based procedures to our patients to further, so it is posited, their understanding of themselves, provide them with emotional authenticity, and increase their psychological degrees of freedom (or some such). We are always in the process of inventing new procedures, finding reasons for why we need them, and polishing or discarding the ones we already have. Not that those *goals* aren't good things to want our patients to have or to help them to find, but, over the decades, these various *procedures* become somewhat shopworn and have less to tell us than they once did.

Some general observations are in order first. The psychoanalytic literature on these topics is very small and, with occasional notable exceptions, appears outside of first line journals and is not the work of mainstream authors. (Both of these observations are atheoretical and are unrelated to the metapsychological orientations of particular journals or authors.) There is essentially no psychoanalytic literature on care per se. This observation has already met with some degree of outrage accompanied by the observation that of course contemporary psychoanalysts care about their patients, and their writing demonstrates it. Alas, the problem here does not concern the absence of writing concerning caring *about* patients; it is the absence of discourse regarding caring *for* the patient in the therapeutic relationship.

In his discovery of the psychoanalytic method, Freud brought together two divergent traditions: the "new science" that was attempting to explain the functioning of the mind in both health and disease, and the much older traditions of the *iatroi* (healers in Greece circa 400 BCE and beyond) and the "spa culture" that had existed for millennia to offer care and ministration to ameliorate, if not to cure, the more affluent emotionally and psychologically unwell. It would be hard to find two more diverse threads formed into a sheaf of *différance* (Derrida, 1972/1982). At least until 1889, Freud did both; his treatment of Frau Emmy von N would include his massaging her "whole body twice a day" (Breuer & Freud, (1893–1895)/1955, p. 50): "The treatment [in a nursing home] by warm baths, massage twice a day and hypnotic suggestion was continued for the next few days" (p. 51). He did not, however, discuss his thinking about performing or prescribing these procedures or his reasoning behind subsequently giving them up. For a time, he continued to put his hands on patients' foreheads, telling them that at his *touch* they would remember something or something would occur to them. He viewed this as a form of enhanced hypnotic suggestion, abandoned the practice when he abandoned hypnosis, and appeared not to give any thought to what his patients might have derived from his touching them.

The relief of pain and suffering in psychoanalysis

Pain and suffering are two overlapping entities. Both are conditions of the self. Although they can spring from physical or emotional damage to the self, phenomenologically, they are conditions of consciousness; they are felt or experienced. Pain exists in both acute and chronic forms, while suffering, by its very nature, is a chronic or longstanding ailment of the self.

Regrettably, care and relief of suffering (one of its attendant goals) are outside of the ken of many psychoanalysts not only as a matter of temperament,[11] but, as we will see, also on the grounds of clinical theory. Although there is almost no literature on care of the patient, there is a tiny literature on suffering. The bulk of what there is flows from a roundtable discussion on "The Meaning of Suffering in Therapy" held in 1960 (yes, *1960*) at the annual meeting of the American Psychiatric Association and appearing as a series of papers the following year in the *American Journal of Psychoanalysis* (Bieber, 1961; Martin, A. R., 1961; Millet, 1961; Szasz, 1961; Weiss, 1961; Wenkart, 1961). These participants were all psychoanalysts and all physicians. The word *therapy* in the titles of the discussion and the papers is of note. This is 1961 and, in this long-ago time, when these authors said "therapy," that is precisely what they meant – a distinct and lesser god than psychoanalysis. It is unclear to what extent their *praxis* actually cleaved to that distinction. The patient's suffering might also, to these authors, have been of concern in psychotherapy or ignored, on technical grounds, in psychoanalysis.[12]

That said, these analysts display a spectrum of ideas about pain, suffering, and their presumptive roles in assuaging them. Some authors noted that "relief of suffering has remained a chief task of the psychiatrist" (Weiss, 1961, p. 17) and "patients

---

11 A supervisor's bizarre comment, "I prefer to work with negative transference [and therefore provoke it?]," has stayed with me for over 40 years.

12 Lest one imagine that this sort of thinking is a thing of the past, Brusset (2012) offered a discussion of therapeutic action in which he makes a knifelike distinction between psychoanalysis and psychotherapy, worries about symptom removal, and observes in the abstract "the extension of the indications and modifications in the expression of psychic suffering have led to the development of psychotherapies" (p. 427). Although the sentence structure is somewhat obscure, the meaning is unmistakable: Relief of suffering is outside the purview of psychoanalysis proper.

138 Care and suffering

enter psychotherapy because they suffer, whether or not they are aware of it" (Bieber, 1961, p. 5). Wenkart (1961) saw pain and suffering as inevitable aspects of existence: "real suffering, if the truth be known, elevates us; real pain enriches and ennobles us" (p. 21). She appeared to consider these feelings existentially necessary and the place of the analyst not to deprive her patient of them. Bieber put his finger on the problem:

> There is a notion that prevails among some therapists that relief of pain and suffering militates against therapeutic change. They will thus justify the prov-ocation of anxiety and be wary about undue relief of a patient's suffering. I consider such attitudes and practices to be *without scientific basis*. . . . Although pain and suffering may mobilize a patient to act in a constructive direction . . . it may also promote inhibition and resistance to therapy. (p. 5, italics added)

While Bieber was prescient in his concerns in 1961, those attitudes remain alive and well today.

Consistent with a position that continues to have considerable sway, at least for some 21st-century psychoanalysts, Buechler (2010) opined, "a third possibil-ity embraces suffering as not only unavoidable, but as a primary source of wisdom and personal identity" (p. 334). She hypothetically divided analysts into groups depending on their views on suffering in the therapeutic situation and whether it should be alleviated or valued and cherished as an inevitable and important part of life (she clearly privileges this latter position). However, the problem here is that Buechler defined the "early" alleviation of suffering by the analyst or psychothera-pist as accomplished in two ways: by refraining from the interpretation of defense and by medicating the patient out of it. She particularly questioned the use of anti-depressants as depriving a patient of, with the analyst's help, feeling and working with his depression. These are questionable assumptions about the therapist's views concerning suffering and its alleviation. It is, however, uncertain just how widely these views are held.

The problem with Buechler's (2010) understanding of the analyst's differing possible responses to suffering is contained in a brief case illustration she offered. A patient tells her of an instance of her husband's "emotional generosity." (I have no idea what this means; does Buechler?) The patient finds this comforting. Now, Buechler thinks that an analyst who seeks to reduce a patient's suffering would not want to disturb this comfort and as a result would make no comment about it. She sees the comfort as defensive and the issue being one of whether or not the analyst decides to address it. Buechler opted for asking the patient how she was feeling when her husband was being generous; by doing so, she believes she is prioritizing analyzing rather than minimizing pain and "preserv[ing] the patient's equanimity" (p. 339). I think this entirely misstates the distinction. Obviously, one would need to know more about the patient to know what one would do. If this were a schizo-phrenic patient in weekly, largely supportive rather than exploratory psychotherapy

Care and suffering **139**

being treated with an atypical antipsychotic, I *would* say nothing. I would do so not out of any therapeutic desire to spare the patient needless suffering, but rather out of a concern that I might seriously destabilize her. In the normal course of a psychoanalytic psychotherapy or analysis, I would say or ask *something*, in the service of trying to understand why she needed to tell me that, and to do so at that moment. It is clearly important material. Unlike Buechler, I would not usually expect such an intervention to cause particular suffering, and if I had reasons for thinking otherwise in this case, then that – the fact that psychic pain is inherent in questioning the emotional generosity – is the issue I would pursue with appropriate tact and timing. I have gone on at some length about this because it may be symptomatic of a wider misunderstanding of the analyst's role vis-à-vis the patient's suffering.

In "Suffering and Psychotherapy," Strupp (1978) took a contemporary position consistent with Bieber's (1961) thinking and quite different from Buechler's (2010) later views. He uses psychoanalytic psychotherapy as an umbrella term that includes psychoanalysis[13] and asks, or perhaps accuses:

> On commonsense grounds, what is the justification of a treatment that advocates, in the interest of its ultimate therapeutic aims, the prolongation of emotional suffering over periods frequently extending over months or years? Secondly, has sufficiently serious thought been given to viable alternatives? Thirdly, what is the evidence that the classical model is the *via regia* for achieving one's goals? ...Therapists cannot be blamed for the patient's problems prior to therapy, but they are *accountable for their professional activities that are ostensibly designed to ameliorate the problems.* (p. 74, italics added)

He went on to observe that, although the reasons some therapies fail while others succeed are not well understood, "we do know that . . . human interest, warmth, honesty and a desire to understand provide the therapist with powerful leverage in mitigating anxiety, depression and guilt" (p. 74).

The opportunity to share previously unspoken guilt-ridden, shameful, or painful thoughts and secrets with an empathic and accepting "expert" (Strupp, 1978; Tessman, 2003) has been shown to be of central therapeutic importance beyond that of any theoretical orientation. However, as Strupp observed, it has tended, over the decades, to be dismissed, depreciated, or at best afforded secondary importance. It is hardly the stuff upon which a "prestigious scientific discipline" (p. 75) could be built or maintained, requiring instead a treatment based on "*the systematic application of technical procedures based on theoretical principles*" (p. 75, italics added).

Strupp (1978) mistakenly, in my opinion, gives away the store when he asserts that "the factors responsible for the experience of relief from emotional suffering

---

13 I often have difficulty distinguishing a psychotherapy from a psychoanalysis, which I see lying on a spectrum, distinct in the polar areas but ambiguous and uncertain in between.

140 Care and suffering

must be looked for in the area of nonspecific, interpersonal effects resulting from an accepting human relationship" (p. 75). The argument I have been leading up to throughout this book is that for such "interpersonal" factors (the something more than interpretation: Stern et al., 1998) to be effective, a phenomenologically based atheoretical exploration of the self (the *Eigenwelt*) and its connections with the *Mitwelt* and *Umwelt* is also required. Elucidating and quantifying the various factors that lead to relief from suffering is by no means an easy task (or it would have been accomplished long ago). Some of those factors will make for unpleasant reading. In the meantime, it is certainly safe to say that therapists and analysts who do not assign any importance to the relief of suffering in their work are unlikely to perceive very much of that relief.

Suffering as it is encountered in the therapeutic situation comes from two sources: It is brought in by patients from their lives and childhood development, or it arises as a result of their reactions to the various procedures deployed by the therapist. My own view is that a patient should be relieved of suffering as quickly as is possible in a therapeutic process. The qualification that I am inserting here pertains to the therapist's not behaving in a cheerleading or gratifying manner that parts company with reality (the patient's or the therapist's) and that the suffering not be drugged out of the patient for the sake of doing so. Antidepressants, mood stabilizers, and atypical antipsychotics are appropriate for the treatment of major depressive disorder, bipolar disorder, borderline personality disorder, and psychosis. Indeed, rather than interfering with the therapeutic process, they can be a necessary precondition for the establishment of that process. Such conditions, in themselves, are capable of producing great pain and suffering that can be relieved by an appropriate regimen of medication often requiring considerable skill to formulate. The day may have already come when a therapist or psychoanalyst is sued for malpractice for withholding such medications; if not, it will be upon us shortly. I do not find a place for medicating away mild to moderate anxiety with habit-forming antianxiety agents, but this view is based on the ultimate harm such agents can do a patient rather than some theoretical position.

With respect to suffering that is caused or mobilized by the treatment activities of the therapist, my experience, like Szasz's (1961) a half-century earlier, is that I don't see much suffering arise out of my clinical work with patients. What suffering I do see, often considerable, is what they bring in with them. Perhaps the only exception to this is two patients who I have seen over the years who suffered from unrequited eroticized transference, one of whom very correctly observed that the danger of some such occurrence, the appearance of an intense transference reaction, should have been discussed with her to the degree it was predictable, as part of informed consent to undergo treatment.

Sharon offers a fairly typical example of the kinds of pain and suffering that I am talking about, as well as its responsiveness to treatment. She is a 32-year-old graduate student in physics at UCSB. She consulted me because of diffuse feelings that her life was not going well. Multiple attempts at therapy for depression and moderate substance abuse had proved of only limited benefit to her.[14] Although obviously unhappy, she did not speak of this; it was uncertain whether that was because she was not able to formulate it as such or was too proud to admit it. Perhaps both were the case. A question of "How are you?" would immediately elicit a machine gun burst of "Fine-how-are-you?" It emerged that she had many superficial relationships in which she got little and gave a lot. She came from a dysfunctional, even borderline family in which she was often attacked and scapegoated as she tried to connect with siblings and parents. I told Sharon that her place in the family seemed to combine elements of a Cinderella and a Cassandra. Although wealthy, her parents gave her little financial help; she often held two part-time jobs in addition to her work as a graduate student. The care she received from her grandmother and her friends who babysat Sharon for the first six years of her life had preserved her intelligence and appealing spunkiness but could not protect her from considerable damage. Despite her best efforts, I found Sharon easy to like.

The suffering that Sharon brought to her treatment, although she was reluctant to acknowledge it, grew out of her mother's "care" of her, her condoning the abuse she endured at the hands of her siblings, and her father's behavior as a disinterested and absentminded bystander. The therapeutic stance I took with her was to identify this abuse whenever I saw it and to comment on how she must be in great pain as a result of it. She had little to say about my observations, but more when I pointed out that she was repeating the trauma by getting people at work to treat her in the same way. With someone as prickly and defensive as Sharon, I was particularly careful to serve up this mixture of care and meaning with a teaspoon rather than a ladle.

Two things happened about a year in. Sharon became emotionally involved with a kind man; her previous romantic relationships had been infrequent and usually abusive. As she reported this, she became tearful and said to me, "I know you've told me this over and over again but I just now realized that my family will never change and the way they treat me will never change." She said that this awareness had first made her suffer (her choice of words), but then she felt that a great weight had been lifted from her. I thought (but did not say) that the meaning she had derived from her treatment at the hands of a caring witness had made the relationship possible.

But what about the suffering that seems to be a frequent if only implicit component of case reports or presentations? I am left to speculate that therapists cause their patients to suffer by inducing an iatrogenic regression (although controversial, I would insist that it is *not* therapeutic) that serves to make the patient feel helpless, infantile, and the object of the therapist's power manipulations. Strupp (1978) has noted the inconvenient truth that, however much a part of the clinical theories of both the Classical and the British Middle Schools (e.g., Winnicott, 1955), so-called therapeutic regression might be, *there is no hard evidence, clinical or otherwise, that it*

---

14 I suspect that such histories of multiple failed attempts at getting the help they both need and want are far from uncommon.

142 Care and suffering

is either therapeutic or necessary. To the contrary, there *is* ample evidence that such regressions are painful, and to force a patient into one is morally and medico-legally questionable. All that is necessary to start down this road is for the patient to ask a question and the analyst to remain silent. If the analyst either answers the question or offers a short explanation of why she doesn't think it useful to answer or doesn't know the answer, the problem is avoided. Absent these respectful responses, the patient experiences a narcissistic injury and, since he does not like this feeling, *quickly learns to not ask questions.* While an undoubted relief to the analyst bent on unresponsiveness, this should not be considered an instance of therapeutic action but rather of therapeutic misalliance. I do not believe that interpretations, confrontations, and the like have much of a potential to induce suffering in any but the most fragile of patients (although using them to verbally assault the patient certainly does have that potential). Poorly timed, tactless, or premature interpretations are easily shed by the average patient, except perhaps the disappointment they may engender towards the therapist who utters them. Kohut (1984) takes much the same position and, although I have not seen it explicitly discussed, so must at least some relational authors.

Care of the patient

Moving on to the therapist's care of the patient, of which the relief of suffering is one aim, we find almost no psychoanalytic literature. Schafer (2005) offers a paper, "Caring and Coercive Aspects of the Psychoanalytic Situation," in which he argues that the two are interreferential and that patients are, at best, ambivalent about them. Fundamental to this position is his insistence that care is located on the counter-transference/transference axis. By psychoanalytic care, Schafer means something that is different from the usual meaning of "the provision of what is needed for sustaining well-being" (*Merriam-Webster's Dictionary,* 2004, p. 187). The problem is that he never does say just *what* he means by "concerned care" beyond what is to be had that is inherent to the psychoanalytic situation. This failure constitutes a major shortcoming in a paper by a noted author on so important a subject. Schafer suggests that care and coercion both reside in four usual aspects of the therapeutic situation: interpretation, working in a responsible manner, free association, and collaborating with the analyst. He then adds a fifth aspect, reassurance, talking about its having a coercive side.

I do not find either of Schafer's (2005) premises – that care and coercion reside in the transference/countertransference, and that they are inseparably linked – to be sustainable. Unquestionably, care and coercion can be individually driven by elements of countertransference, and a veneer of the former can mask the presence of the latter, but these are quite different assertions. His position on reassurance is also both convoluted and untenable. He describes reassurances as inclusive of certain apologies, appeasement, excessive explanation, and attempts to calm the patient, or to shut down a particular associative thread under the guise of sparing the patient

Care and suffering **143**

from something. What is really going on here is that none of these maneuvers constitute any sort of actual reassurance; rather, they represent attempts by the therapist to hide his countertransference from himself by coercing the patient's complicity in this maneuver. True reassurance consists in the therapist, as a caring expert, providing a patient with ontological information they do not possess, the absence of which is causing them pain or distress (e.g., telling a patient some painful or disturbing state will pass or respond to therapy when it is knowable that it will).

This is perhaps the best place to make explicit something about care of the patient that should be implicit but perhaps isn't. Caring for a patient, and a patient's feeling cared for, should not interfere with his being able to experience and express a broad spectrum of possible negative feelings for the analyst, nor should the analyst be unable to entertain such feelings about the patient. Two clarifications are in order here. The first is that iatrogenic negative feelings engendered in the patient by, for lack of better terms, the analyst's actual bad or uncaring behavior are not relevant to this discussion. The second is that, to the contrary, if an analyst makes use of pseudo-caring as a means of suppressing negative feelings and coercing a patient into not speaking about them, then they are unlikely to appear and the damage to the analytic process will be considerable.

Ingram, in a 1997 paper, made observations about reassurance that are quite similar to my own. He recounts how, at a recent clinical meeting, the guest lecturer responded to a question of what to do with an obviously distressed patient. The presenter responded by saying, "just explain that there is nothing to worry about [!]." This pseudo-reassurance, very much in keeping with Schafer's (2005) ideas about what constitutes analytic reassurance, in effect, dismisses the distress as a subject of analysis. Ingram instead goes on to remind us of Martin's (1949) old definition of reassurance as "to free from fear, anxiety, and terror" (p. 17). He goes on to define false reassurance (again consistent with Schafer's conception of reassurance) as involving a complete disregard of the patient's psychological and emotional reality or concerns. Martin's definition represents aspects of care of the patient.

So what kind of reassurance do I offer my patients? First, I do *not* reassure patients concerning outcomes that I have little basis for predicting. When proposing treatment to a new patient, I tell them specifically that I can work with them to relieve or improve their symptoms and their suffering (in whatever form and words are appropriate to a particular patient). If these are chronic problems and there have been multiple unsuccessful attempts at therapy and/or psychopharmacology but I nevertheless do think I can be of help, I tell the patient that. If I don't feel I have anything to offer, I tell the patient just that, being clear it is not about them and suggest a referral to what I consider a more appropriate sort of therapist or a psychopharmacologist.

Tom, a 20-something young man, returned to college after a hiatus of several years. As his first semester progressed, he found himself able to study, write, and get high grades. As finals approached, he became growingly anxious about his ability to do well, in spite of studying. I said to him something like, "it's clear that you're

144 Care and suffering

working hard at this [he had been] and have done well so far; I think that the finals should go fine." He felt better, and they did.

Although a seeming paradox, saying nothing but listening intently without being phased by a patient's telling their story or telling about something they find deeply painful, putting it into words, sometimes for the first time, supplemented only by a word or two or a nonverbal utterance of understanding on the analyst's part, can sometimes be the most reassuring thing of all.

Telling a patient that they are suffering from a major mental disorder that is likely to be helped by an appropriate regimen of therapy and medication (when inadequate attempts at pharmacotherapy or psychotherapy have failed in the past) can be reassuring when the patient already knows that something beyond his control is happening to him. However, some patients would be terrified by such information and usually offer clues to that effect. I always say, if I believe it to be true, that medication will only deal with a piece of the problem and, although it may be necessary, it is not sufficient. It can only relieve suffering and facilitate the psychotherapy that is also necessary to address the wider problem that I would describe phenomenologically as an illness of the self. On only a couple of occasions have I had patients leave treatment when medication relieves suffering, and rather than viewing this as an illustration of some greater psychodynamic truth, I see it only as the outcome of an additional de facto screening procedure. It is perhaps only stating the obvious to make note of the fact that, like analysis itself, there is no such thing as one-size-fits-all reassurance and that, to be an effective rather than a false reassurance, it must be used as a seasoning rather than a major ingredient of the analytic repast. Although opinions may differ on this, I share the view of the contemporary schools of psychoanalysis that each therapeutic situation is unique, a "one-off" experience for both members of the dyad.

If there is little literature on care, reassurance, and suffering in the therapeutic situation, there is, perhaps surprisingly, more of a literature dealing with physically touching or being touched by a patient. Touch is an aspect of care of the patient about which I acquired a new perspective after my own recent medical hospitalization but never experienced in my personal therapy or analyses. It has only been fairly recently that I have begun to suspect that this might have been part of a larger problem of some consequence. I am quite certain that the great majority of us never even consider this. I have never seen it written about from the perspective of the author-as-patient rather than that of author-as-analyst.

I believe that touch *does* occur in the contemporary therapeutic situation, although I have no idea how frequently. I'm quite sure that the degree to which analysts are comfortable using touch varies enormously with underuse more frequent than overuse. In my own practice, I have infrequently touched some patients. (I have not even considered it with others who I know would find it seductive, erotically stimulating, disorganizing, or some combination of all three.) I have touched patients of both genders. The touch has consisted of handshakes, sometimes holding a patient's hand in both of mine, a hand on the shoulder, and, occasionally, a hug.

Hugs have always started with the patient, and my practice in all cases has been to act semi-spontaneously, with a couple of seconds of reflection. I have never been asked to hold a patient's hand but would certainly do so if it seemed appropriate. I view touching as offering, usually at the end of a session, comfort, care, and a communication of my understanding that something is particularly difficult or painful. The results, as far as I have been able to ascertain, have been entirely positive. The hugs, few and far between, caused me difficulty until I began writing and thinking about them. I had felt them to be forbidden and, while *I* didn't consider them boundary violations, I worried that my colleagues or a licensing body might. I doubt I'm alone in any of this.

A female patient asks for a hug at the end of the last session of a successful analysis; we have the hug and it felt warm, non-sexual, and satisfying. A man talks about whether or not I would ever hug him and his fears that I would not; *I* hug *him* at the end of the session and his eyes tear up as he leaves. In the next session, he confesses that he feared that I considered him too miserable a creature to hug.

I continue to work with some patients from the community in which I used to practice, via telephone (Leffert, 2003) or FaceTime. Once a year, I return to see them in person (they sometimes also come out to see me). The contacts always begin with a little small talk about my trip, and I offer a handshake in which I take the patient's hand in both of mine. I began doing this without thinking about it and only reflected on it after the fact. I recall with some amusement the comment a supervisor, a second-generation analyst, had made to me in the 1970s when I related, with considerable discomfort, that I had shared a hug with a patient at the end of her last session. He mentioned just finishing an analysis with a woman who had kissed him at the end of the last session. It was a "real kiss" on the lips, he told me with satisfaction, not the miserable peck on the cheek she had given him on the eve of some vacation. I was deeply shocked (perhaps that's why he told me about it) at the time, but what it meant to him was that, through the analysis, she had gone from being a little girl to being a woman. I have to think that part of the reason it worked was that he was then as old as the decade, 40 years her senior.

Some analysts deal with the dilemma by resorting to what I would term stealth touch. I listened to a case presentation in another community in which the patient, as the analyst described, reached down to cover herself with the soft blanket that was folded at the foot of the couch. The blanket? I was curious and asked what the blanket was doing at the foot of the couch; the presenter looked at me blankly and said that everyone had such a blanket. Other members of the audience agreed. I don't have such a blanket (I have a little Persian rug, having found that otherwise the fabric of the couch would wear out after a year or two) and have not encountered the practice in other communities. It certainly can serve as a substitute for touch, regulated by the patient as needed.

The psychoanalytic prohibition against touch rests on theoretical grounds and the cautionary tale of Sándor Ferenczi, a combination of justifiable concern and psychoanalytic power relations (Leffert, 2010, Chapter 7). The theoretical issue

146 Care and suffering

hinges on libido theory (Freud, Sigmund, 1905/1953b). If libido theory is the only motivational system you have, then there are only sublimation and neutralization (putative processes, the existence of which is quite difficult to actually prove without using the terms to justify themselves) to guard against direct expression of sexual fantasies. Therapist behaviors in the area of touch then must lie on the so-called "slippery slope" to sexual boundary violations (e.g., Gabbard, 2000). However, moving beyond the hermeneutics of psychoanalytic metapsychology, libido theory, as we have already seen, is *not* the only game in town. As we've already discussed, Panksepp (Panksepp, 2009; Panksepp & Biven, 2012) has described the existence of seven emotional systems (SEEKING, FEAR, RAGE, LUST, CARE, PANIC/ GRIEF, and PLAY), all centered in ancient subcortical regions of mammalian brains, neuroevolutionary in origin, and demonstrated in cross-mammalian studies. If touch occurs in relations between the analyst's CARE system and her patient's FEAR and GRIEF/PANIC systems, the interaction is therapeutic.

Holding, both in its literal and its metaphorical sense, has been a part of psychoanalytic technique with severely regressed patients dating back at least to mid-century. Boss's (1963) work with the patient he calls Dr. Cobling in which he held her and nursed her with a bottle of "sweet milk" that she brought in for that purpose offers us an illustration of it. He viewed this in the context of a necessary, *self-imposed* regression in which he provided her with early maternal experiences she never had and served to reparatively deal with the damaging ones she did. Winnicott (1972) offers a "transcript" of a fragment of an analysis in which he held the patient's hands and describes his emotionally and cognitively holding her. He characterizes the couch as his metaphorical lap. However, Little (1985), in describing his work with her during what she terms states of psychotic anxiety, says that Winnicott did in fact *physically* hold her and had done so with other patients. Slochower (2014) amplifies on Winnicott's views from a contemporary relational perspective. Although not spoken of much or written about, one does, from time to time, hear contemporary reports of analysts non-sexually holding their patients (while I have never had occasion to do so myself, I would if I deemed it therapeutically *necessary*).

Which brings us to *Psychoanalytic Inquiry*, Volume 20, Number 1 (Breckenridge, 2000; Casement, 1982; Fosshage, 2000; Holder, 2000; McLaughlin, 2000; Pizer, 2000; Ruderman, 2000; Schlessinger & Appelbaum, 2000; Shane, Shane, & Gales, 2000), an entire issue devoted to touch in the psychoanalytic situation. The issue is structured as a series of commentaries on a paper by Casement (1982). In it, he describes his work with a patient who at one point desperately begs him to hold her hand. It is the last session of the week; he tells her he will think about it over the weekend and, on Monday, tells her that he has decided not to do it. The patient is severely traumatized by the rejection, and the analysis, according to my reading of it, is irreparably harmed.

All of the authors offer thoughtful discussions of the case and the complexities of touching or being touched by a patient (and the question of touch *can* be quite complex) including appropriate references to what literature there is on the subject.

Care and suffering **147**

They are not judgmental of Casement, citing the times (1982) and the principle that, if a therapist is not comfortable touching a patient, he or she should not do so.[15] That said, the authors fall into a number of groups on the subject. Two of them (Breckenridge, 2000; Fosshage, 2000) treat touch as a usual part of their being with patients. Although I could not speculate on frequency, I get the sense that they are entirely comfortable with a handclasp, a handshake, a hand on the shoulder, and, infrequently, a hug. Shane and colleagues (2000) use their paper primarily for a condensed restatement of their position on therapeutic action (Shane, Shane, & Gales, 1997). A more fully realized discussion of their views on touch would have been of interest. What *is* curious, and speaks to how far behind we are on the subject, is that they are the only authors to recognize and state that *touch is a part of the care of the patient*. Casement (2000), by way of updating his position, describes his work with a terribly depressed patient who tells him good-bye on a Friday, saying that she plans to end her excruciatingly painful life over the weekend. He believes her, spontaneously takes her hand and tells her she *will* get through this and he'll see her on Monday.[16]

The remaining authors convey a sense that touch is a subject with which they are struggling. Their prose has a dense and clotted quality, and they say little or nothing about their own experiences with patients. They try to do the complexity of the subject justice, but what emerges tends to reflect the perceived dangers inherent in touch, the risk of boundary violations, and that, perhaps, words are better until proven otherwise for a given patient. I imagine that most psychoanalysts would be sympathetic to their positions.

So, by a rather long and necessarily roundabout journey, we come again to the subject of the care of the patient in psychoanalytic psychotherapy and psychoanalysis. The most important aspect of care of the patient lies not in some procedure or set of procedures, but rather in how the therapist understands what he or she should be doing and be prepared to do. What we think we are doing always follows from that understanding. However, sometimes what we actually do, for better or worse, differs from what we think we are doing (to the extent that it is knowable) and what the patient experiences.

No discussion of the care of the patient in psychoanalytic therapy could be complete without some clinical illustrations of what I am talking about. What I discovered with some surprise is that caring for my patients had become so much a part of my identity as a psychoanalyst that the specifics of what I *do* in this area proved difficult to isolate. Schachter and Kächele (2007), in a rare paper on what

---

15 None consider the possibility that, if a patient needs to touch or be touched in the therapeutic situation and the therapist is uncomfortable doing so, then perhaps the analytic fit is bad and that needs to be dealt with.

16 I can't help wondering whether prescribing the appropriate antidepressant would have rendered this unnecessary. If not, I would have also offered the patient a phone contact over the weekend. What if this "gratified" the patient and she did it again to get that result? Why, we would *talk* about that.

148 Care and suffering

they term "psychoanalysis-plus," "propose adding to the analyst's armamentarium the use of explicit support, consolation, persuasion, and advice" (p. 430) to understanding. To this list, I would add advertent suggestion (in contrast to inadvertent suggestion, Leffert, 2013, Chapter 1). Their list offers a very reasonable overview, but as I have noted about the work of other authors, they miss the fact that what they are talking about is *care of the patient*.

I can only attribute this general omission to the latent persistence of clinical neutrality as a part of our analytic identity, however much many of us have come to see it as both impossible and counter-productive. Our irreducible subjectivity makes it impossible to separate ourselves from our values, aesthetics, beliefs, and theories; to imagine otherwise is at best an exercise in self-delusion.

There is another argument made by Schachter and Kächele (2007) in defense of their position on psychoanalysis-plus that I have already, in effect, strongly disagreed with. They posit "that as long as the analyst continues to interpret the patient's unconscious feelings, conflicts, and fantasies and explore transference-countertransference interactions, we should defer" (p. 437) questions about these techniques being analytic and consider instead whether they are therapeutic. My disagreement with this position is twofold: I consider these procedures to be entirely analytic, and what I have been arguing for throughout this book is that sometimes things in an analysis are most productively left *unsaid* and that there are times when explicitness can indeed disrupt the therapeutic process or dilute its emotional experience. Put another way, interpretation, like any other element of the psychoanalytic toolbox, is therapeutically useful in some clinical situations and detrimental in others.

There are two criticisms usually leveled against care of the patient: that it is not analysis (perhaps the ultimate contemptuous dismissal of the work of one analyst by another), and that these broad techniques can greatly harm an *analysand* (not a patient). The first critique hinges on what one includes in the definition of analysis, and I will reserve that discussion for the next chapter. As for the second critique, so what? *Anything* we do in the therapeutic situation, either consciously or unconsciously, has the *potential* for harming a patient; all we can do is apply what we think we know and observe the results of what we have done to see if it is good enough. What evidence we have (e.g., Frank, 1973; Strupp, Fox, & Lessler, 1969; Tessman, 2003; Wallerstein, 2006) also suggests that if we convey to our patients that we like, respect, accept them, and privilege the relief of their suffering, our efforts are more likely to succeed and meaning and authenticity to follow.

Adler (2002), in a wider discussion of care in the doctor-patient relationship, makes a number of critical points that are relevant to the therapeutic situation. He posits that such a caring relationship requires an emotional investment on the part of the caregiver as well as the patient and asks if it is worth the trouble. He describes physiological evidence (unstudied in our literature) from two sources that it is and coins the term the "sociophysiology of interpersonal relationships" to account for them. The first is that empathic relationships demonstrate a synchronization of functioning in the autonomic nervous systems of the partners or among members of larger groups sharing empathy. The second is that feeling cared about in an empathic relationship reduces stress hormone levels and returns an individual to a baseline state. These observations are entirely consistent with Panksepp's (Panksepp, 2009; Panksepp & Biven, 2012) findings. It has also been demonstrated that, in the absence of having anything specific to do at some point in a therapy, offering ourselves to a patient in the context of a positive social bond increases feelings of well-being and reduces neuroendocrine activity in the hypothalamic-pituitary-adrenal axis (one would expect to see an increase in circulating oxytocin levels as well). The vehicle for all these salutary effects appears to be responsive listening. (Silence as a psychoanalytic technique of abstinence and neutrality will not work here, but empathic silence in small to moderate doses will.)

To talk about how I see care as a part of my own work with patients, I am going back to Joe and Roger, who we've discussed several times already. As you may recall from the last chapter, Joe came to see me because he was suffering from insomnia and hypochondriasis. Over the course of roughly a year and a half of psychoanalytic therapy, his symptoms disappeared. He left well-pleased with the results, and *I* was left wondering just what I had done. Since those times, it has become clear to me that what I did was to care for Joe. From the first session, I treated his views of himself and his problems with interest and respect. The apparent paradox of his coming to see me because I could prescribe psychotropic medication for his symptoms and then telling me he didn't want to take medication (he found the idea of taking *any* medication highly disturbing) I did not raise with him; to have done so would have implied that his thinking was silly or nonsensical rather than leading us to any useful information. I said instead something like, "I understand your concerns; let's see what we can do by talking without it." It is clear to me now that I intuitively did a number of things here. I treated his concerns about taking drugs with respect (I did see it as simply another aspect of his medically based anxiety). I told him I thought that our talking together could very well treat his symptoms but that I prioritized the relief of his suffering and would come back to the medication question if it didn't improve. I very much approached him as a caring expert without any attendant claims of power or authority.

I was always prepared to discuss his medical worries with him as just that. When he told me that he was having some muscle twitches and had read about amyotrophic lateral sclerosis, I supported his decision to see a neurologist.[17] He did so, and when his EMG studies came back normal, he was able to comfortably let the issue drop. At another time, when he brought in some GI complaints, I suggested instead that it was probably nothing, that we could wait and see if they persisted and only then pursue a referral to a gastroenterologist. He was comfortable with that; his anxiety lessened and the symptoms resolved in ten days or so. Joe's insomnia

---

17 In this particular case, I think it was important that I was a physician and that I had maintained my knowledge base in general medicine.

150 Care and suffering

began to clear (connected to no therapeutic events that I was able to identify) but recurred (also connected with no identifiable issue) on a few occasions, enhanced by his fears of not being able to sleep while he was trying to *get* to sleep. I handled these recurrences with reassurance. I reminded him that the insomnia had already cleared up once and I thought it would do so again. After this had occurred a number of times, he was able to do that for himself, and I stopped saying it. He became able to, on occasion, experience a night in which he had trouble sleeping as simply that. I was unable to come up with a credible hypothesis (distinct from a guess) concerning the origin of his symptoms, but I have since understood that my being there as a solid, concerned, and reassuring presence, focused on and attentive to his suffering, is what made the therapy curative. (I have since begun to see Joe again around some very stressful life issues; although he has struggled with them, the hypochondriasis and insomnia have not recurred.) Was this analysis? I will argue in the next chapter that it was. For now, I will only say that I cared for him while maintaining an exploratory interest in his life, past and present, and offering him phenomenologically based observations on the meaning of what he told me rather than genetic reconstructions of his past that he could experience no connection with.

With Roger, I am quite certain that, had I limited myself to exploring the narrative meanings of what he told me about himself, attributed feelings to him that he did not experience, or confronted him about his present-day actions, the analysis would have been, at best, of intellectual value. Much of what I know about care I learned from Roger and only later found the language that I have been using in this chapter to describe it.

I was able to learn a lot about Roger and about what he needed from me in the early sessions. I took a detailed if preliminary history from him, allowing him to talk as much as he wanted about any topic but spontaneously asking questions whenever he stopped talking or had piqued my analytic curiosity. I asked early on if he was angry with any of the ward staff or the other residents. "Nope, never felt that," he replied, making it clear that those sorts of questions wouldn't be useful. From what he told me about the intensity and unreliability of his mother, I understood at the time that I needed to be present as a reliable, stable, good enough, and usable other for him.[18] I kept this observation to myself but translated it for him by saying I thought I could help him. I tend to be quite regular about the mechanics of my practice; Roger would not have done well with and would have responded with anger to a chronically late analyst (although many patients are able to adapt to such things, a considerable amount may be lost in the process as a result of such "adaptation").

Some months later, he began talking about his time in medical school as one of aloneness, a subject he had not previously broached. He thought that perhaps

---

18 I was offering Roger a new and healing object, not attempting to be a better mother to him than the one he had had.

that had bothered him. At one point, he had gotten himself into a face-off with a department chair who promptly failed him; he was required to repeat the subject. He had considered this an outrage since he knew the subject, had felt great anxiety about it at the time, and still thought about it. I said a number of things to him about these experiences. One was, "those years were horrible for you" (said with feelings of empathy and sadness on my part and without the qualifier "must have been," which would have pulled the punch). When he told me about his long, solitary walks and lonely weekends, I said, "it sounds to me like you were very depressed at the time; do you think that could be true?" as a new way of organizing the meaning and experience of those years for him. He was able to reply (vintage Roger!) by saying that while "he had never thought of it that way, I probably had a point."

Our interaction over his failing and having to repeat a subject was an important turning point in Roger's analysis. I said to him something like, "you know, Roger, the guy was certainly an arrogant jerk, but when someone can do you harm, *for your own protection*, you have to just stuff it and go on." He was silent for a few minutes. I let him be and then looked over at him and saw tears running down his cheek. I had provided him with information he needed in a form he could accept and, in the process, cared for him. I think that the tears were about his feeling that I also cared *about* him. My commenting explicitly about that would have destroyed the intensity of his experience. The fact that I was fairly certain that there was a masochistic component to his actions I also did *not* mention; over time, Roger was able to reach and explore this conclusion for himself.

Over the course of this book and the two that have preceded it, I have described a variety of pieces of the therapeutic situation, some of its foundations, and both enhancements and constraints to be found in interdisciplinary study. I have offered critiques of both past and contemporary ways of psychoanalytically being with patients. These have involved examples of both deconstruction and construction. Many of the positions I have taken are novel and, at times, subversive and edgy. We are now in a place to fit these things together into a way of conceptualizing psychoanalysis and cure.

7

SO WHAT *IS* PSYCHOANALYSIS, REALLY, AND WHAT ARE ITS THERAPEUTIC GOALS AND ACTIONS?

Introduction

Psychoanalysis is no longer, strictly speaking, psycho-analysis at all. Psycho-analysis, the compound noun in widespread usage at least through the 1940s, was coined by Freud and referred to the analysis of an individual psyche, analysis in the sense of identifying its nature, ingredients, or composition.[1] The hyphen was deleted in due course with a change in meaning from something descriptive to a term denoting some wider process. We use it even though this process of identifying is now only a part, perhaps even only a small part, of what we do. As a signifier, what it signifies has changed. Similarly, interpretation was the singular tool of psychoanalysis, be it of "the" unconscious or "the" transference, where to interpret meant something like explain, tell the meaning of, reveal the depth of, or offer a translation of. There are two different meanings of interpretation: translation/analyzing/explaining and a "reading" of a text. (The term *text* in post-structural thought refers to the results of *any* act of representation.) Orthodox psychoanalysis hews to the former; contemporary psychoanalysis is implicitly about the latter. From a post-structural or postmodern point of view, there *is* no single meaning, translation, or explanation of a thing. Each reading is unique. The search for meaning becomes a problem of subjective contextual ontology, if you will, where any interpretation is a one-off reading of a text. As we have been discussing, even this modified definition of interpreting accounts for only a part of what we do in the psychoanalytic situation and, as far as the term *psychoanalysis* goes, there is now broad disagreement as to exactly what it signifies; this elasticity (Sandler, 1983) is not necessarily a bad thing.

Meanwhile, the concept of "something more" (Boston Change Process Study Group, 2005) has become of concern to many, but by no means all, of us. This has

---

1 The hyphenated form remains to this day in the title of the *International Journal of Psycho-Analysis*.

grown out of an interest in non-interpretive mechanisms in psychoanalysis (Stern, D.N. et al., 1998) and in the role of the therapist/analyst as a new object (e.g., Loewald, 1960; Shane, Shane, & Gales, 1997) with whom the patient can engage.

The neurosciences have expanded exponentially over the past few decades so that they now offer possibility but also impose significant constraints on what can be theorized or fantasized about psychoanalytically. As the intervals in which life experience results in documentable changes in brain structure have shortened to hours (Assaf & Pasternak, 2008; Bock et al., 2011; Le Bihan et al., 2001), the distinctions between structure and function have become less meaningful and have metaphorically taken on an air of quantum mechanics. The result is a self that, for good or ill, changes itself (*Eigenwelt*) and is in turn changed by its relationships with the wider world (*Umwelt* and *Mitwelt*). Relationships and meanings change the brain and the self of which it is a part. The brain does not only change itself.

The separation between psychoanalysis and psychotherapy on the one hand, and between insight, support, care, and healing on the other, are becoming more arbitrary and artificial. Orthodox psychoanalysts would claim that what I have been calling care *of* the patient is really transference gratification, while relational analysts are likely to claim that this is what they have been doing for decades.

Patients, broadly speaking, come to us for two reasons: Some aspect(s) of their lives are not going well, and they want help solving the problem(s); and/or they are suffering, an experience of the total self, and are in emotional pain. Our job, then, is to care for them and to heal them, whatever these things mean, and, ultimately, to the extent we are able, to cure them. What these goals look like is another matter.

However, a significant number of psychoanalysts believe that this is not our job at all. They see themselves as purveyors of insight, accompanied or not by emotion, perhaps psychoanalytic change (Compton, 1988; Mendelson, 1995), and psychoanalytic disillusionment both within the transference (Strachey, 1934) and outside of it (Arden, 1993). Some analysts believe that the psychoanalyst has no business with any of the tasks I described above, that "the purpose of psychoanalysis is only to help the patient integrate split-off parts of his personality" (Caper, 1992, p. 289) and that the psychoanalyst "need not worry about the likely therapeutic impact of an interpretation, but only concern himself with giving an accurate, intelligible description of what the patient is doing in the transference and in his internal world" (p. 290).

There is a tendency within orthodox psychoanalysis, present in both clinical writing and theorizing, to discuss the therapeutic situation as if it were comprised of two separate elements: conscious and repressed memory, and the therapeutic relationship made up of mostly transference, "therapeutic" regression, and a (much) lesser quantity of countertransference. The contemporary schools of Relational and Intersubjective psychoanalysis and others before them (e.g., Bromberg, 1996, 2011; Gill, 1982) have upped the quantity of countertransference acknowledged to be present in the therapeutic relationship and moved both from an exclusive focus on the genetic past into the present of analyst/patient relations. Similarly, there has been an expansion of a focus on memory, trauma, and the undoing of repression

154 So what *is* psychoanalysis?

into a quest for narrative and meaning (or, from my own phenomenological perspective, an exploration of the patient's *and* the analyst's being).

The problems in separating the psychoanalytic process into these two unstable categories, analysis of transference and the recovery of repressed memories, are legion. They not only overlap, but are also irreducibly interreferential. In these circumstances, one cannot even speak of something being about a narrative or something else being about a relationship. All that we *can* speak about is viewing the unfolding therapeutic situation and the experience of it from different perspectives. We have, in fact, done this for a long time but have not much acknowledged it.

This requires an expanded, multifactorial perspective, which includes the pursuit of meaning, the various kinds of memory, narrative, and the nature of the being-in-the-world of both members of the therapeutic couple. A reconsideration of a much larger relational perspective is also required. It is hard to imagine now that when Greenson (1967) added the real relationship and the working alliance to transference-with-a-bit-of-countertransference, it was considered highly controversial. Contemporaneous with, but ignored by, orthodox Freudians, the interpersonal perspective (e.g., Bromberg, 1996; Green, 1964; Sullivan, 1950/1971b, 1953/1997) moved the therapeutic situation out of the consulting room and into the world. More recently, the field of Network Studies (Christakis & Fowler, 2009; Leffert, 2013) offers further insights into this interpersonal perspective. The supplementation of the genetic transference with the hear-and-now transference (Gill, 1982) also changed thinking about its analysis but did not then offer relational considerations of how much of that here-and-now was really transference rather than simply a mode of being-with others (albeit configured in part by old patterns) and how much of *that* was iatrogenic rather than therapeutic. I have posited that care of the patient, healing, and relief of pain and suffering draw on both.

The therapeutic opportunity contained in analyzing a *patient's* perspectives on being-in-the-world is not to be missed. To knit concepts together, we can focus on a patient's *dispositif*. All of us possess our individual *dispositifs* (apparatuses comprising rules of knowledge that change throughout life, the record of which, along with the knowledges that have been collected with them, compose a unique personal *archive*; Foucault, 1969 & 1971/1972). However, among individuals, they should have far more in common with each other than difference, and they should mostly reflect the *Mitwelt* and the *Umwelt* more than the *Eigenwelt*. Sometimes, significant individual and collective (in the sense of a social network) differences can and do appear. Joan, a lawyer in her 50s, was raised in a household where an older brother, who she adored, physically abused her. The abuse was denied, and she came to understand the world through church, Sunday school, and her sheltered life in an honors class in primary and secondary school. She believed that if you were nice to people in the world, they would always be nice to you. Her parents were similarly clueless, while her mother was preoccupied by her own much-exaggerated self-importance. Hidden by Joan's sunny narrative was a darker part of herself in which she repeated the early abuse in a series of relationships with men that she blindly entered and, despite her intelligence, failed to understand. In the wider world, she would find herself being exploited by people pursuing their own interests with no regard for her. I was reminded of the animals and birds of the Galapagos Islands living in an environment without natural predators and being helpless as a result. We spent much time going over issues of personal narrative and her religious views of her not being entitled to very much; both were regulated by intense feelings of guilt. This accomplished relatively little beyond establishing an increasing ability to speak up for herself. It was only after I had figured out that I needed to talk to her about the nature of her world, the world *she* lived in, that the analysis began to develop real traction and her world changed for her. Similar deviations in group worlds also occur; segregation in the South come to mind.

An expanded perspective on psychoanalysis

If psychoanalysis is a species of phenomenology, then the clinical pursuit of meaning is achieved primarily through observation (listening to and looking at the patient), deconstruction (discourse aimed at opening and expanding meaning), and our feelings about being-with the patient to the extent to which they are accessible to self-reflection rather than the pursuit of some deeper truth that cannot be grasped simply by referencing experience. It is this deeper truth (whose existence cannot be verified) that requires the existence of some overarching *theory*. To be without a theory is a very uncomfortable place for a psychoanalyst; to even posit such a theory-less state is to provoke accusations of nihilism. Consistent with a phenomenological perspective, the arguments against the existence of an underlying theory of psychoanalysis are overwhelming. In roughly 125 years, no such theory has emerged that some large majority of psychoanalysts and psychotherapists would agree on, and, even if they *were* to agree, there has emerged no way to verify that such theories demonstrate validity.[2] The inconvenient truth that is never considered is that there exist multiple theories, each with its partisans, and that many of us can competently navigate from one to the other without considering just *what* such navigation implies. We are left with two possible positions: that there are many theories with equal standing, or that there are many theories that have their adherents but in mine [sic] resides the higher truth. The only possible conclusion is that these many theories only have standing as local and unstable knowledges (a post-structural reality) that take us back to observation and deconstruction. This leaves us free to make what we will of the therapeutic situation and identify the constants we find in it.

---

2 Unlike agreement or reliability, to demonstrate that a theory is *valid*, one would have to demonstrate from *outside* the theory that it accounts for what it says it does and that there are no other theories that account for the data we observe.

156 So what *is* psychoanalysis?

Desired goals and outcomes of psychoanalysis

Phenomenology offers a completely different perspective on the nature of the goals of psychotherapy and psychoanalysis and how to ascertain that they are being achieved clinically. The first guiding principle is to ask the patient what she wants and, if she doesn't know, help her figure it out.[3] We all (I hope) do something like that when we begin a first session by asking a patient something like "what brings you here?" (the most neutral), "what's troubling you?" (a mild question about suffering), or "how can I help you?" (which speaks to the prospective patient about how a therapist thinks about what she does). Each of these begins *a* process, one that is explicitly or implicitly a mutual interview. However, a problem that often arises is our failure to adequately privilege what the patient is trying to tell us over our clinical theories and heuristics about what we think he is telling us.

As clinicians, we possess some general (hopefully not specific) ideas about what constitutes the good life and how it is lived. If we think phenomenologically, we think about a capacity to live more fully and at some kind of higher level – the mindful rather than the mindless, the thrown rather than the fallen everyday. Somewhat more technical but still phenomenological is to live in the world of the present, influenced to be sure by our own authentic historicity, rather than rooted in earlier epistemes and heuristics. This is not as different as might appear at first glance from Caper's (1992) observation that "the aim of psychoanalysis is to help the patient integrate split-off parts of his personality" (p. 286). However, it is very different from his idea that an analyst's wish to heal or cure a patient is rooted in a reaction formation against his unanalyzed sadism. Guignon (2006) posits the need for human experience to contain some "irreducible moral experience" (p. 206), something entirely foreign to our training as psychoanalysts.

We've talked about care and relief of pain and suffering, but we need to consider the role of healing, cure, and palliation in our work.[4] All of these terms are subjective and contextual; they are entirely about the being-in-the-world, Dasein and its analysis in the therapeutic situation. At least three of these, care, cure, and heal, are verbs and nouns that refer to both a process and a state of being. There is, at this point, some divergence with respect to diseases of the soul or self and diseases of the physical self. The language doesn't work very well here to clarify the distinction, but what I am trying to get at is the difference between illness, damage, or injury and pain or suffering, which are experienced conditions of the conscious self. Healing does not usually result in the disappearance of a wound but rather its replacement

---

3 This should not be taken to preclude a subsequent expansion or change in goals as the situation merits.

4 Perhaps I'm being obtuse, but if we ball-park a four times per week analysis as lasting five years (a conservative figure) at $200 per session, we are looking at an enormous investment of time and money. The idea that a patient would willingly consent to such a therapy in order to be able to integrate disparate, split-off parts of their personality seems ludicrous to me.

So what *is* psychoanalysis? **157**

by a physical or emotional scar. Examples of wounds are trauma and loss. Cure refers to the treatment of some generalized illness of the self and the relief of the suffering that it (directly or indirectly) causes. A successful cure carries with it the likelihood or at least the hope that the condition will not recur. Depression and personality disorders are examples of such illnesses. Palliation would seem to be about *either* the relief of pain connected with a wound or the relief of the suffering attendant on some illness where true healing or cure is not possible or has not yet occurred. In the absence of cure or healing, palliation must be ongoing if is to continue to be effective in treating pain and suffering. As a profession, we have tended to look down on palliation as some lesser thing, and the idea of applying it as a treatment progresses is either not thought about or is thought to be contra-indicated. I have never attended *any* psychoanalytic gathering (be it a class or a case presentation or the delivery of a paper) in which these topics have been discussed.

I have tried to approach these terms (healing, cure, and palliation) phenomenologically after observing that, although authors tend to offer recognizable definitions of them, they differ in ways that result in idiosyncratic usage and ultimately fail because of it. Ornstein (1994), for example, argues that cure is relativistic (by which I think she means that the relative importance of various concrete elements of cure vary from patient to patient) and favors abandoning the term and sticking to *healing*. Shapiro (1995) applies the term *idiosyncratic* to cure as a way of signifying his view (which I am sympathetic to) that each analysis is unique and therefore the nature of the therapeutic "potion" is similarly unique. This position is consistent with more widely held views of clinical theory and therapeutic action (e.g., Bacal, 2006; Bacal, 1998) and my own discussions throughout the present volume. Another way of describing cure that respects its "one-offness" is to say that it is an *emergent property of the therapeutic situation*. This is consistent with what complexity theory has to teach us about psychoanalysis (Leffert, 2008; 2010, Chapter 3): In large, complex systems, unique outcomes cannot be predicted by the behavior of the individual elements of that system (in this case the therapeutic situation). We need to think about these terms, while maintaining their distinctness, their *différance*, without allowing their individual, subjective meanings to slip into their societal, social constructivist (or co-constructivist) meanings. Similarly, there are two definitions of well-being and the good life, the individual and the societal, the patient's and the analyst's, the autocentric and the allocentric.

Dimen (2010), in an otherwise very thoughtful paper aimed at exploring the issues involved in conceptualizing the nature of cure, illness, and healing, nevertheless gets herself caught up in a tangle of one-person and two-person psychologies. She cites Groddeck (1923/1976) as defining *cure* as a voluntary release from an inhibition and the subsequent failure of desire, as opposed to what arises in post-structural thought (my language) that ideas about illness, cure, and health are socially constructed and hence not amenable to objective definition. What these distinctions (and several more in between) represent is a genealogy of these processes, not a temporal replacement of one by another. The referents of what constitutes an illness

158 So what *is* psychoanalysis?

and what constitutes its cure or healing do change. They allow for some plurality of views both internal and societal on the subject, while the nature of what it means to be sick and what it means to be healed or cured stay pretty constant. Whether the illness in question was demonic possession in the Middle Ages, melancholia in the early modern period, or PTSD in contemporary times, and whether the cure involves an exorcism, incarceration, antidepressants, or a psychoanalytic approach to trauma, what is *meant* by describing something as an illness or a cure (regardless of whether the cure actually works) remains the same.

Gordon (1979) would drop the term *cure* not because cures are relativistic, but because she would in part define it as instilling in a patient the capacity to adhere to social norms which in turn raise power issues. This was certainly true for hospitalized patients in past decades (less so now) but one must go back further to the Enlightenment and the Pre-Modern period (Foucault, 1979/1995, 1961/2006a) to encounter it in its unalloyed form. It also should not be used to minimize the importance for an individual of being able to navigate the social milieu in which she finds herself.

It might seem from the above that I imagine some kind of finite, describable (at least individually), and attainable goal or endpoint for therapy or analysis. To the contrary, as clinicians we know that cure is at its best a partial creature. There are a number of possible reasons for such outcomes. The first, following Gill's (1982) observation to the effect that the majority of clinical work is of poor quality, is to say that we are not very good at what we do. However, let's assume that we are mostly knowledgeable, intelligent, and conscientious therapists. The second is to say that we are only in the early stages of using phenomenological and relational knowledge and at the very beginning of thinking about the application of neuroscience in the therapeutic situation. A corollary to this point would be that there are pharmacological or genetic treatments now over the horizon that could make a major difference. Developments in all of these areas have, over the past half-century, already significantly increased what we are able to do. Still a third possibility, perhaps the least optimistic, is that we are bumping up against the limits of the possible. Freud (1937/1964) considered this question 75 years ago. This argument would go something like this. The effects of early experience and trauma are such that they lead to subsequent experiences (sometimes resulting in re-traumatization) that are additive across the life cycle. These experiences and their subsequent encrustations with repetitive events produce a result that is amenable to only some degree of cure or healing. In terms of neuroplasticity, the hardwiring that takes place in a developmentally immature brain and self is only subject to, at best, some modification. This is the only time when the neuroplastic brain can be shaped absent the influence of "higher" structures, with their constant grip on reality, that develop later. The pre-linguistic nature of being in these early times is a fundamental part of the neuroplasticity.[5] We can treat these problems in

---

5 The Right Brain, for example, is initially "burnt in" (Schore, 2003a) before the Left Brain, still unmyelinated, has come "on line."

the present with a combination of emotional availability, great patience, an absence of emotional expectations of the patient, and a joint search for narrative and meaning. What we *cannot* do is to return to the original site(s) of the developmental failures and complete the process that failed or was aborted. We currently lack the data to tell us if these concerns are merited, but at the current pace of progress in psychoanalysis and neuroscience, we might expect answers to these questions over the next decade.

There is a final sort of goal of treatment that has no name and is not spoken of in psychoanalysis and psychoanalytic psychotherapy. This is the ongoing and continued care rendered to a patient suffering from some chronic condition that may be improved but cannot be healed or cured to a degree that allows for the cessation or termination of treatment. This is not the same thing as the belittled concept of support, which it can *include* (as it can be a part of any sort of psychotherapeutic endeavor). We have no way of conceptualizing this kind of ongoing care for a reasonably well-functioning patient as opposed to, say, a chronic schizophrenic. Instead, psychotherapy or psychoanalysis is expected to do the job of healing or curing and then exit. This is distinctly odd, for two reasons. The first is that although we don't name or much discuss this form of treatment, I suspect that we all have two or three patients we are treating in this way and may even feel a bit ashamed of doing so. I certainly do. The second is that in medicine the ongoing care of a patient suffering from a chronic illness, diabetes for example, does not raise an eyebrow, whereas sending the patient off with a five-year supply of prescriptions for insulin certainly would.

In addition to their therapeutic importance, there is also great pedagogic value in our using language signifying healing, curing, managing, and palliating. These terms force us to really *think* about what we are trying to do in a particular therapeutic situation. If we don't, with a patient seeking one or more of the above and the analyst focused on the application of some theory,[6] they are operating at cross purposes. There is language to describe what is taking place in such a state of affairs. In Wittgenstein's (1953) terms, the therapeutic couple are engaged in a series of language games. Even more relevant, however, is Lyotard's (1983/1988) concept of the *différend*. A *différend* describes a situation in which parties are engaged in a discourse involving a dispute between them. However, the parties "operate within such radically different language games that there can be no agreement regarding how an argument could be settled or [even] what rules one would have recourse to in doing so" (Leffert, 2010, p. 35). Unfortunately, the "resolution" of this problem in the therapeutic situation often occurs when the analyst forces a patient to learn and comply with (Lukes, 2005) *his* rules and suppress her own. These behaviors inevitably produce limited therapeutic results.

---

6 It is important to recognize what is and isn't theory. Saying, for example, that the Oedipus "complex" is the essential issue to focus on in the therapeutic situation is theory. To say that therapy or analysis is a two-person psychology (even if one of them says very little and tries to sound flat and neutral) is not about theory; it is simply a description of what is.

160 So what *is* psychoanalysis?

Narrative and meaning

Many of the conditions that lead people to seek us out are in fact diseases of narrative and meaning. They are illnesses of being. One result of such conditions is a failure of desire. It is interesting to reflect on the fact that, although growingly talked about in the present, prior to the millennium these terms were, for most (not all) analysts, like some kind of exotic flower, rarely encountered in clinical thought or the therapeutic situation. Dimen (2010) observes that as the result of a "joint exploration of meaning, the patient's self emerges in its various states, whole and multiple" (p. 258). This is quite similar to Caper's (1992) comments about the goals of analysis.

I believe these to be flawed arguments. The self is a bio-psycho-social being inseparable from its world. What they are talking about is some sort of mental representation of the self, important but different. I would prefer to say that what they are talking about is the capacity to represent the self in a multiplicity of ways that, nevertheless, are consistent and capable of connection to each other and that such representations are, in fact, internal working models (Bowlby, 1973; Craik, 1943/1952). What they and a great majority of us are talking about when we use the term is, sadly, a Cartesian self (Damasio, 1994; Stolorow, 2011) subject to all the errors of a hypothetical mind-body dualism.

Personal meaning and narrative are intimately connected. Narrative is involved in the capacity to represent the self as both a memoir and a genealogy. Both terms appear deceptively easy to understand. While we are, to some degree, conscious of meaning and narrative, they usually lie beyond our awareness. Meaning is a state of being not much perceived in its absence. It applies to larger concerns, such as the meaning of one's life, that are not particularly illuminating. We are talking more about personal meaning and the narrative(s) that is consistent with attaining and maintaining it. They speak to the authenticity of one's life, one's presence and being-in-the-world, and the capacity for aesthetic experience and well-being. Such ideas are not the limited province of intellectual elites but must be formulated in terms that can be understood as parts of wider human experience.

It is curious that concepts that would seem to lie at life's very center are so little discussed or understood by professions that are engaged in the alleviation of emotional illness, pain and suffering. They have only recently become cutting edge ideas in the areas of end-of-life care and palliation (Gwande, 2014). We *are* aware that our thinking about patients' lives needs to be value-neutral. Easier said than done. Clearly, a therapist's values (what constitutes the good life; what is aesthetic) must be the subject of some self-reflection. We have to consider social values from the perspective of societal norms, but we also may not accept the validity of some of these norms (woman are often paid less for doing the same job as men; cannibalism is normative in some New Guinea tribes; it was fine to kill Jews in the Germany of the 1930s and '40s). People frequently evince some values that they do not incorporate into their lives (charitable giving is widely acknowledged to be a societal good, but many people do not participate in it). In spite of the best of neutral intentions, our own values can sometimes unconsciously inform the therapeutic situation (the gold standard is a single, lifelong, heterosexual bond, and, in decades past, orgasms achieved or produced outside of heterosexual intercourse in the "missionary position" were considered perverse).

Neuroscience: selected issues

This final chapter is not the place for any sort of exhaustive survey of the neurosciences and their relevance for psychoanalysis, both topics I have discussed at length in the past (Leffert, 2010, 2013). For our purposes here, I want to take up, for lack of a better term, what I would call the biology of the self and to consider just a few of the ways it bears on healing and cure in the psychotherapeutic enterprise.

A common error in thinking about neuroscience perspectives on the self and their role in psychoanalytic thinking and practice is to view them as underlying the psychological, as deeper, and to either enthusiastically embrace or dismiss them on that basis. If we stay with a phenomenological perspective, all that we are justified in doing given the state of our current knowledge, perhaps all we can assert at *any* level of knowledge, is that we are viewing the activity of the self from different perspectives. No perspective can claim any sort of depth with respect to another, and quantum mechanics *as metaphor* comes to mind as a way of describing their relationship.

Left-brain consciousness gets confused with the self, of which it is only one emergent property. The *experience* of the self is of a consciousness located in the head behind the eyes that experiences emotional and physical perceptions of the world and the physical body. (Conversely, the experience of the location of the self's *boundary* with the world is at its physical surface, its container, the skin.) This experience is not accurate. *Consciousness is an organ of self-experience.* However narcissistically injurious, the overwhelming weight of the evidence supplied by neuroscience supports the view that consciousness is a small, specialized part of the self that includes *some* of its perceptual, evaluative, and executive functions; it also includes an entirely understandable tendency to overestimate its own importance that borders on hubris. The Left Brain's synthetic abilities seamlessly knit its conscious thoughts into a linear, serial experience that is subsequently integrated into narrative. As the neuroscience tells us, nothing could be further from the truth. This kind of cognition, however, does have an important role to play in certain kinds of problem solving (Baars, 1993/2003b); it is just that it is not the whole or a major part of the neurocognitive story.

The self is much more complex than that, and by far the greatest majority of its activities take place beyond left-brain consciousness. Some of it is in and out of consciousness; much of it is incapable of being conscious, incapable for many different reasons (Willingham & Preuss, 1995). Conscious thoughts proceed in the Left Brain over the course of seconds, while right-brain cognition proceeds over milliseconds. At the very least, the Left Brain is grossly unable to keep up with it, and

162 So what *is* psychoanalysis?

consciousness is all about summaries, edited for different purposes. What follows from all of this is that left-brain consciousness is not the be all and end all of "selfhood," just as moving things *into* left-brain consciousness is not the be all or end all of psychoanalysis (although verbal discourse is certainly a significant part of it).

We could certainly use the term *Neuropsychoanalysis* to describe what we do. For example, the neurochemistry of stress, depression, and relief of depression has become fairly well understood in recent years (Panksepp, 1998, 2003; Panksepp & Biven, 2012; Porges, 2009, 2011). From the biological side, stress and loss lead to an activation of the pituitary adrenal system mediated by adrenocorticotrophic hormone (ACTH) and corticotrophin release factor (CRF). The initial result is a compensatory release of biogenic amines, norepinephrine, serotonin, and dopamine. If this condition persists (and emotional experience may lead to this persistence), biogenic amines are ultimately depleted, leading to depression. Depression also mobilizes the GRIEF system, resulting in a depletion of oxytocin and endogenous opioids (the brain's CARE and comfort food) that enhances the depression.[7] The administration of psychotropic agents that either decrease the re-uptake (SSRIs, SNRIs) or the degradation (MAOIs) of these neurotransmitters are often effective in relieving the depression. They do not, however, address either GRIEF or the depletion of oxytocin and endogenous opioids. Although this undoubtedly represents a fruitful area for ongoing psychopharmacological research studying the benefits of externally administered oxytocin, we have other tools that can address this problem right now. Psychoanalysis or psychotherapy can heal and ameliorate GRIEF, but only if the analyst's CARE is involved. We have just spent a chapter discussing what that care looks like and will return to it shortly. For the present, it is worth noting that CARE has been administered and involved in the treatment of depression and GRIEF probably since prehistoric times. The existence of these dual problems of grief and depression, involving as they do different neurochemical and neurohormonal pathways, hypothetically explains why the combination of therapy and pharmacology yield the best results in the treatment of depression (Panksepp & Biven, 2012; Petersen, 2006) and why the theoretical orientation of the therapist appears to be irrelevant to the outcome.

Of particular importance here are the neuropsychological aspects of empathy. It is perhaps useful to repeat the question: Why, as psychoanalysts and psychotherapists, should we concern ourselves with the neuropsychology of empathy? Surpassed perhaps only by transference, psychoanalysis in contemporary times has claimed empathy for its own. Empathy and the understanding of the other that it engenders is central to what we do and an essential component of therapeutic success. The opposite question really makes more sense: Given its centrality and

---

7 In addition to this systemic response to external stressors and loss, an alternative depressive system exists in some individuals. It is either congenitally "wired in" or else neurochemically operationalized or "kindled" by early life experiences such as exposure to maternal depression (Bowlby, 1973; Radke-Yarrow, 1991).

So what *is* psychoanalysis? **163**

importance, how could you *not* want to know how it works and where it came from phylogenetically? Be it the central role of empathy in the therapeutic situation (Kohut, 1984, 2010), the concept of sustained empathic inquiry (Stolorow, 1990; Stolorow, Atwood, & Brandshaft, 1994), or the idea of empathy as intervention (Safran, 2012), empathy has remained central to our therapeutic and collegial discourse. However, over the past couple of decades, there has been an explosion of research on empathy in the fields of development, cognitive neuroscience, and functional neuroanatomy. Inevitably, this work has required some refinement and reconsideration of our views on the subject.

As psychoanalysts and developmental psychologists, we have in recent years come to locate the development of a capacity for empathy in the very young child's successful navigation of his early relationship with a good enough mother. It is true whether we think of the process in terms of secure attachment (Bowlby, 1979[1977]/1984, 1988), the development of primary intersubjectivity (Bråten, 2007; Bråten & Trevarthen, 2007; Ferrari & Gallese, 2007; Trevarthen, 1974, 2009), or the activity and development of the right pre-frontal cortex (Schore, 2009, 2011) in the first year of life. It is no less true if, as Schore does, we are talking about the burning in of the autonomic nervous system or that of the Vagus nerve (Porges, 2009, 2011) through maternal-infant eye contact. This is also true for its failure to develop if the mother's (e.g., Radke-Yarrow, 1991, 1998) or the infant's "hard wiring" (Baron-Cohen, 2000; Baron-Cohen, Leslie, & Frith, 1985) is not up to the job.

Research in all of these areas is, however, still pushing forward. As Morelli and colleagues (Morelli, Rameson, & Lieberman, 2014) note, across multiple models, empathy is comprised of three elements: "congruent affect with the target, perspective taking, and prosocial motivation to help the target" (p. 39). The latter experience occurs as the functional consequence of empathy. It has both cognitive and emotional elements. Recent fMRI evidence suggests the existence of two different systems governing empathy (Shamay-Tsoory, 2011): an emotional and a cognitive system. The former occurs operationally through the activity of the Mirror Neuron System (MNS) (e.g., Iacoboni, 2007, 2008), while the latter has to do with the capacity to develop a Theory of Mind (ToM) (Baron-Cohen, Tager-Flusberg, & Cohen, 2000; Gallagher & Frith, 2003).

The most phylogenetically ancient system, the beginnings of empathy in mammals, manifests itself as emotional contagion (de Waal, 2008). This concept is closely related to that of contagion in Social Network Theory (Christakis & Fowler, 2009), a more general concept that refers to the spread of any information across a social network. The mammalian concept can refer to a herd or a network as small as two individuals. Siegel (2009) offers a neuroanatomical discussion of how the functioning of the emotional and cognitive systems mesh with each other. Empathy is a process whereby two individuals become linked, each experiencing their own versions of what the other is experiencing. The journey by which this information becomes available to us consciously *or* unconsciously is a complex one, not entirely linear as Siegel describes it: "It is through [the] flow from cortical perceptual mirror

164 So what *is* psychoanalysis?

neuron activities to sub-cortical limbic – brainstem – bodily resonance and then back up to cortical representation that we come to feel the feelings of others, to be aware of our own internal state as a reflection of the internal world of another" (pp. 161–162).

If we observe an event, a child's falling or someone smashing a finger, the emotional system operates well on its own to enable us to grasp and experience the feeling. If we observe someone's facial expression, we *can* emotionally grasp in a coarse way whether it is positive or negative. However, coming to a sense of what that person is feeling and why they might be feeling it requires deploying cognitive empathy in the way that Siegel (2009) describes. This involves a process that, as psychoanalysts, we are more comfortable describing as mentalization. The mentalizing of observed action (Spunt, Satpute, & Lieberman, 2010) has been shown to operate in a system that is discrete from the MNS. The operation of this system is usually, but not always, automatic.

No consideration of these issues in 2015 would be complete without a discussion of the linked terms *embodied cognition* and *embodied simulation*. These terms lie in the general area of social cognition (Gallese, 2007; Goldman & de Vignemont, 2009). It must be noted that they and the existence of the processes they signify remain as of this writing controversial. A so far unnoticed element involved in this debate is that the use of the term *embodied* implies a brain self as opposed to a total self and the Cartesian separation of mind and body. A more accurate, Post-Cartesian picture is that of the self using body knowledge and body language and their neural correlates in order to grasp the other and inform self-experience. People navigate their social worlds in part by using a group of functions that have been designated as "folk psychology." They include Theory of Mind, mind reading (a term of art used to signify the acquisition of knowledges about what another person is thinking or feeling), and behavior reading (the ability to grasp, with varying degrees of accuracy, why people do what they do). Folk psychology is not a derogatory term but rather one that locates thought and feeling in terms distant from their functional neuroanatomy. It also subsumes what we as therapists and analysts think about what is going on with our patients and what we should do about it. Social cognition and the mind reading and behavior reading that follow from it stand in stark contrast to the behavior reading of non-human mammalian species that is limited to action-prediction. Developmental research (Bråten & Trevarthen, 2007; Schore, 1994, 2009) strongly suggests that the development of these capacities is pre-linguistic.

It follows from simulation theory (Gallese & Sinigaglia, 2011) that understanding the behavior of others, which begins at the level of the MNS, involves *pretense*: "People first create in themselves pretend desires, preferences and beliefs of the sort they assume others to have" (p. 512). Simulation occurs under conditions of uncertainty (Kahneman et al., 1982; Kahneman & Tversky, 1982) and, although not much thought of by cognitive scientists, makes use of three heuristics: representation, availability, and simulation itself, the latest heuristic to come to the table, so

So what *is* psychoanalysis? **165**

to speak. Simulation of events, and the behavior of objects or internal working models (depending on one's theoretical frame) is also an important component of simulation theory. This aspect of simulation caries people and their relations into the hypothetical future (Leffert, 2013; Schacter et al., 2008).

A problem with the term *embodied* arises in its definition (Gallese & Sinigaglia, 2011) as "body parts, bodily actions, or body representations [that] play a crucial role in cognition" (p. 513). The difficulty here is that then, presumably, there are also cognitions that do not involve the body. However, in the body-brain-self, the body is *always* involved in this way and *always* informs cognition. There is solid neuropsychological evidence (Panksepp, 1998; Panksepp & Biven, 2012; Porges, 2009, 2011) that this is precisely what the self is. What we are left with then is a narrower, less ambitious definition of embodied that simply refers to those cognitions that make reference to the body and that such references can be conscious or not. This, in effect, involves the class of mental representations that exist in bodily formats and are involved in social experience or communication.

Elsewhere, Gallese (2005) offers a more successful, phenomenological definition of embodied simulation as the combined mechanism governing both body awareness (and body modeling) and social understanding. There also now exist identified neural correlates for these processes. What phenomenologists (Husserl, 1925/1977, 1913/1983; Merleau-Ponty, 1945/2012) struggled with decades before the neuroscience became available was how an internally subjective perceptual experience could also be reformatted into a reproducible grasp of the external world that enabled reliable navigation of that world. The neuropsychological tool for this conversion turned out to be bodily-perceptual awareness (when awareness is not meant to imply consciousness, a problem that Husserl, almost a century ago, was unable to solve). The body offers itself as a singular tool for understanding the world. An important element of the *social* navigation of the world is action understanding (Gallese, 2009): the ability to grasp the meaning of actions that we witness. As might be expected, the MNS plays a central role in this understanding and its being automatically followed by action simulation. The operation of these systems can be impaired as a result of structural, developmental, or narcissistic damage.

An expanded relational perspective

It should be obvious that an expanded relational perspective on the therapeutic situation goes beyond that of the Relational School of Psychoanalysis. This is particularly true with respect to those elements of the Relational School who adhere to an exclusively hermeneutic approach to psychoanalysis, eschewing any relevant connection to neuroscience or social theory.

Let's begin with a discussion of healing, cure, the doctor-patient relationship, and what the placebo effect can tell us about them.

How does the therapeutic relationship heal and cure? Three possible answers to this question suggest themselves that, empirically, are hard, perhaps impossible to

166 So what *is* psychoanalysis?

distinguish. The answer that easily has the most literature behind it is that the therapeutic relationship supplies something that the patient either did not get in childhood or experienced in some damaged or distorted fashion. Much time has been spent arguing about whether the therapist provides such things by being themselves, a new and better object (e.g., Green, 1964; Loewald, 1960; Shane et al., 1997), or by actively trying to be some person in the patient's early life (e.g., Alexander & French, 1946; Ferenczi, 1930, 1988) who was remiss. This is not a debate about whether analysis as object relationship is curative – both sides of the debate argue that it is – but simply about theory of technique: how you do it. The second answer that has also been considered in different forms over the years is that the analyst, as the analyst, offers her patient a series of interventions and behaviors aimed at healing the patient in the present as opposed to trying to heal something that happened in the past. In past decades this was seen to be accomplished via transmuting internalization (Kohut, 1984; Strachey, 1934). Thirdly, and more recently, I have argued for the importance of the doctor-patient relationship (Adler, 2002; Leffert, 2013; Schore, 2009) in the here and now and the neuroscience behind it.

Nowhere is the difficulty, if not the impossibility, of making these distinctions more apparent than in the clinical applications of attachment theory. The clinical use of attachment is the latest of the interdisciplinary areas to win acceptance in psychoanalysis and psychotherapy. The question of just how attachment theory can be of use in adult psychoanalysis and psychotherapy is, however, a more complex question. For our purposes, I am using this as a specimen problem to illustrate this general class of theoretical applications. The general arguments for the representations of attachment in adult treatment follow more or less the same course. They begin with Bowlby's (1969, 1988) description of the attachment process in infants and the developing influence of internal working models (Craik, 1943/1952) on that process. They progress to his conclusion that these models could be re-opened in adult psychotherapy. Main's (George, Kaplan, & Main, 1984; Main, 1991) Adult Attachment Interview, offering a view of the archeology of attachment in the adult, became a way of bringing attachment forward and was used by several authors to establish the credentials (it actually cannot do any such thing) of working with attachment in adult therapy. The argument then becomes one of what such work might consist of.

This brings us to Beebe and Lachmann (2002). They set their work on attachment in what might be described as a fairly standard dyadic relational-discursive frame. They identify three organizing aspects of mother-child interaction beginning at four months that remain stable over the life cycle but can be transformed in various contexts or as a result of trauma. They dub these *Lifespan Organizing Principles of Interaction*, and they include vocal rhythm coordination, facial mirroring, and distress regulation. These authors see in the therapeutic situation the opportunity to reorganize early attachment experiences through a combination of implicit unconscious and explicit conscious symbolic communication and argue for the centrality of implicit relational knowing (Boston Change Process Study Group,

So what *is* psychoanalysis? **167**

2005) in the process. They posit that patterns of attachment are subject to emergent transformation throughout the life cycle as opposed to being permanently hardwired in. They offer a case illustration in which Lachmann consciously uses vocal rhythm coordination, facial mirroring, and distress regulation to treat the attachment pathology present in his adult patient, "Karen." The treatment of this difficult patient ultimately goes well and has a successful outcome. The conclusion reached by both authors is that "qualities of attachment, affiliation and intimacy are transmitted in psychoanalysis in the implicit mode through patterns such as vocal rhythm coordination, facial mirroring, and distress regulation" (p. 81). What is *explicit* in their clinical position is that they are offering patients, by design, either a new attachment experience or a continuation of the original one.

The work with Karen illustrates a more generic problem with such formulations of healing and cure. We know what Lachmann *thinks* he was doing with Karen, and it doesn't unduly stretch the boundaries of uncertainty to say that he was, more or less and among other things, performing the therapeutic *actions* he described. It is also safe to say that the therapy was genuinely helpful to, and healing for, her. However, *we have no idea* whether the therapy was helpful to her for the reasons Lachmann thinks it was and even less of an idea of whether he created a new attachment experience for her, accessed her original one, or provided instead a more general positive emotional experience. Nor is it clear how one could even *make* such distinctions, as they would pertain to *any* therapeutic program.[8]

The notion of finding the child in the adult is a venerable one in psychoanalytic theory and technique, and the Adult Attachment Interview appears as a gift from the gods to make this possible. Anna Freud (1965) wrote about the urge to complete development a half-century ago, but she realized that such urges were vastly stronger in the child than they were later in the life cycle. In the intervening years, neuroscience has taught us that attachment in the first 18 months of life is happening to an entirely different brain than the one our adult patients come equipped with. The Left Brain has not yet awakened in these early unmyelinated months; attachment is occurring in the parallel processing Right Brain, unaffected by the slow, serial processing of the left. Without the modulating mental processing that is unavoidable in the adult brain, attachment experiences have a vastly greater effect on the laying in of structure-function in the fluid brain of the very young child. At

---

8 I don't mean for a moment to say that what Lachmann chose to do with Karen wasn't helpful to her but simply that it is impossible to know just *how* it was helpful. Neuroscience, for example, tells us that we possess elaborate functional mechanisms for communicating with each other nonverbally or implicitly. It would make no sense to imagine that these mechanisms did not function in the therapeutic situation but would be hard to specify that they operated exclusively in the area of attachment. Although I have argued that it makes no sense to treat a patient who has suffered early maternal deprivation on the couch, removing the healing face-to-face interaction, there is every reason to do so with a patient who has suffered maternal over-stimulation. We have, however, no basis for attributing the salutary benefits of this technical advice to attachment repair.

168 So what *is* psychoanalysis?

the same time, the increase in circulating oxytocin in the brain of a nursing mother (Freeman, 1995; Panksepp, 1998) makes *her* more attuned and flexibly responsive to her infant.

Another unfortunate mistake is that the AAI (George et al., 1984; Main, 1991) is a research tool developed for the study of attachment, not a therapeutic guide for re-opening it. The proper administration of the interview is a complex process that requires a full-time two-week training for developmental psychologists to master. Since the great majority of therapists lack this background and training, and do not formally administer the AAI to their patients (and have no intention of doing either), we find yet another instance in which what appears at first glance to be a valuable interdisciplinary import in practice becomes simply another metaphor deployed in the therapeutic situation. *At best*, looking at a patient's attachment history (as part of a more general developmental assessment) can provide broad outlines of areas that the analyst should explore contextually in the therapeutic relationship.

In contrast to such problematic assertions, Dozier and Tyrrell (1997) offer a more modest and also more verifiable assessment of how attachment functions in adult therapy and analysis. They posit that, while attachment is attachment, a process taking place early in life, the nature of an adult's Internal Working Models *do* evolve and are elaborated throughout the life cycle and can be modified. If the analyst's usual and normative behavior is positively at odds with a patient's life experience, then the experience of that behavior *accompanied by discourse* centered on the difference can be mutative over time.

The overarching issue here for attachment and other similar approaches is that they are theoretical rather than phenomenal. Psychoanalysis has repeatedly stumbled when it has sought to import theory directly into the clinical situation (as opposed to using it as one source among many that can inform what we do) as a *theoretical* basis for notions of therapeutic action. It is well-known that attempts to predict adult psychopathology from accounts of early development have led to disappointing failures, whereas the *contemporaneous* approach to the individual *in his world* is much more successful. History does have a place as a guide to the pursuit of the contemporary (that it has shaped). It offers, for example, a distinction between the emotionally under-stimulated, under-nurtured infant and the over-stimulated one that does suggest differing clinical approaches to adult patients. How empathy acts in these cases is different; in the latter, less is more, while in the former, more is more. Empathy is very much involved in the analyst's creation of the therapeutic space.

The therapeutic space revisited

Some years ago, the concept of the therapeutic frame as a relationship in which the analyst acted to help the patient maintain appropriate relational boundaries within the therapeutic situation was critiqued and replaced by an application of

So what *is* psychoanalysis?   **169**

field theory. The field delineated a sphere of mutual influence: the relationship between analyst and patient. The field took its rightful place in the understanding of therapeutic discourse, best defined as having implicit as well as explicit components. I have argued that the abandonment of the frame concept was premature, that it remained of explanatory importance, and that it was phenomenologically more accurate to regard field and frame as simultaneous descriptions of the therapeutic situation that co-exist in a dialectical relationship to one another.

At the time, I also offered a discussion of the physical space in which the treatment took place, and it is that discussion that I wish to extend, including not only the physical space, but also its mental representations, as they exist for both patient and analyst. Analysts and patients have markedly different perceptions of the physical space of the therapist's office. Beyond liking or indifference,[9] the former take the office pretty much for granted, while for the latter, it offers an opportunity for very different kinds of experience. To get a sense of the patient's view, close your office door and have a seat in the waiting room. One immediately feels that the door, which we experience as either transparent, non-existent, or a part of the therapeutic container, has become an impenetrable barrier, to be opened only by the therapist, never the patient. The office setup itself can have wildly different meanings for patient and therapist.

June, an attorney in her mid-50s, sought analysis because a life that looked good on paper was becoming more and more unsatisfying to her. Two to three years into the analysis, she walked in one day, observed that the weather had finally turned pleasant, and suggested we have the session on a walk. June had never made such a request before, and I was nonplussed. I responded without any time to think it over that I didn't think it was a good idea and, without comment, she lay down on the couch. At the time, she was unable to say anything more about the request or to voice any thoughts about it. Over the next weeks, a series of events of singular importance took place in the analysis. June gradually remembered that, as a child, she had witnessed the sexual abuse of a sibling. She was able to tell me that the invitation to take a walk had been a seductive test of my boundaries; had I agreed, she told me, I would have seen the last of her. Although she had had nothing to say about it over the course of the analysis, she now told me that the only reason she was able to tolerate the couch was that it was adjacent to the door and, as I was seated behind her, she would not need to get by me if she needed to flee in the face of danger. It was then easy for both of us to see that the *Angst* she had felt on

---

9 Offices range from being thoughtfully decorated, to being furnished with castoffs from home, to attempting to be as "neutral" and as unrevealing about its occupant as possible. Nonetheless, they reveal a lot. Anecdotally, the early American psychoanalyst A.A. Brill was unduly fond of pointing to a chair in his office as the one Freud sat in when he visited in 1909. A supervisor of mine had a large office, perhaps 10 x 20 feet. He had placed his chair in one corner, "the" couch halfway down the adjacent long wall, and the "patient" chair in the opposite corner, roughly 22 feet away. Not surprisingly, he was a fairly silent, although well-meaning, analyst.

170 So what *is* psychoanalysis?

witnessing the abuse had been transferred to the therapeutic situation, to emerge in the context of the newly formulated memory. I had had no idea that the way I had arranged my office space was having such a profound effect.

There is, as it turns out, postmodern literature on the subject of space, an important piece of which is Gaston Bachelard's (1958/1994) *The Poetics of Space*. I (Leffert, 2010) have previously observed that "the analytic office is not experienced in isolation but rather as inseparably embedded in a social and historical matrix" (p. 49). As we can see with June, that historicity was twofold; it included what a psychoanalytic space is procedurally about and what patient or therapist brings to it from their respective pasts.

At the time, I focused primarily on the positive, poetic meaning of the therapeutic space, never empty, and inhabited by the analyst as anchorite. Such a view of the analyst/analytic office embodies an image of a beacon, illuminating the darkness between sessions. While undoubtedly true for some patients, it was certainly not true for June, and although we don't name it as such, for some patients, some of the time the office can feel like something akin to a surgery or torture chamber.

One can make broad, phenomenological characterizations of patients that do not flow from any theoretical constructs or metapsychologies. Patients appear who, during their development, were over-stimulated (think of Roger, who we have been returning to over the course of this book), or given no quiet space for solitary reverie (think of Mr. Z, Kohut, 1979), or were grossly under-stimulated (think hospitalism, Spitz, 1965), or were emotionally abandoned (think children of depressed mothers, Radke-Yarrow, 1998). An even broader distinction can be made between working with patients who were traumatized (and could be said to suffer from a form of PTSD) by either over- or under-stimulation and those who weren't. Again, one can, in broad strokes, delineate both the emotional tone and the amount of activity on the analyst's part that is most suited to working with these classes of patient. It should be obvious that patients change over the course of a therapy and the therapist's stance needs to change with them.

With Roger, I felt that I faced just such a choice of how to be and what to say. Had I limited myself to genetic interpretations and confrontations against a mostly silent backdrop, I could easily have precipitated a deeply regressive negative transference that would have taken up much of the analysis. It might even be erroneously characterized as a negative therapeutic reaction, the old idea that blames the patient for an analysis gone wrong for many possible reasons. My sense was that this would have been of very limited therapeutic value and, while it might have provided him with some insight, would have mostly re-traumatized him with its masochistic elements providing an even greater narcissistic injury. I thought, as I do with most patients, that what Roger needed was a new relationship with an entire, relatively constant, caring human being who would explore with him these feelings as they came up as only a part of the therapeutic situation. My busy, cluttered office was just what he needed. There are, of course, some (only some) patients who spontaneously develop these regressive transferences, even in the face of the kind of therapist activities I have been describing with Joe and Roger. I believe that in those cases, one does have to follow the transference while *remaining in the present*, being careful about premature interpretations and not behaving, however well-intentioned, in a way consistent with the early behavior of parental figures that can't help but exacerbate the regression.

Healing and cure in the doctor-patient relationship

The term *doctor-patient relationship* is a curious one. It seems to come up infrequently if at all in collegial discourse, yet a search for it in PEP-Web yielded 542 "hits" in 2014. The great majority of these papers use the term only in passing and do not consider it as signifying any particular group of curative factors. Meanwhile, Relational Psychoanalysts have come to currently think of the patient-therapist relationship as the product of a series of discursive shifts reflecting the influence of postmodernist thought on psychoanalysis (Goldner, 2002). This discursive relation-ship is seen as curative with empathy playing a role in the process as intervention (Safran, 2012) rather than simply setting a therapeutic tone. Currently, there is at best only limited interest in the question of whether or not the term *doctor-patient relationship* is a better signifier for the therapeutic situation than one involving ther-apists and clients. This is unfortunate because it involves a debate that speaks to the very core of what we do.

The very language becomes problematic here, and I'm going to suggest a couple of admittedly arbitrary conventions to try to make it less so. The vast take-no-prisoners power struggle that involved medical psychoanalysts' attempts to deny their psychologist colleagues the analytic franchise and imprimatur took up much of the last century and left the latter with an understandably bad taste in their mouths for anything medical. I want to relate "doctor" to the ancient Greek *iatroi*, a more general term for healers, rather than the contemporary "physician." Perhaps it is impossible, but I'm trying to move the focus away from the letters following therapists' names to the nature of the identity they subscribe to if a treatment is to realize its full potential. I also will use "heal" as referring to the repair of some specific damage to the self and "cure" to the successful treatment of the self that is ill or impaired. The two, healing and cure, should not be considered to be entirely discrete categories (nor as identity categories with all the artificiality such signifiers entail) as they display some blurring and interreferentiality. This is in no way meant to suggest that healing and cure erase these conditions from the self as if they never were; metaphorically, there remain scars and can manifest sequelae.

Before going further, let us briefly consider the question: If not the doctor-patient relationship, what then? We have the general terms *psychologist*, *psychiatrist*, and *psy-choanalyst*. If we consider the folkloric definitions of these categories, it should be fairly obvious that they are problematic. In a general way, psychologists are viewed as treating lesser life problems that talking about will dissipate or offering alterna-tive approaches to dealing with them. It is seen as a user-friendly, low anxiety,

172 So what *is* psychoanalysis?

stigma-free discipline. Psychiatry is another matter. It is perceived as dealing with major mental problems; there is some degree of stigmatization (lessening) associated with consulting a psychiatrist, and one does so usually to receive medication and maybe a little supportive therapy. These are *serious*, scary mental problems. Talk therapy is seen as the province of psychologists who send patients to psychiatrists for medication, should it prove necessary. Psychoanalysts are often seen as using the dangerous and oft-caricatured couch to offer intellectual insight into the distant past rather than help with feelings or life problems in the present. This process is seen as interminable.

I'm going to touch on a few papers to get at what I want to say about the doctor-patient relationship. Kafka (1992) posits a distinction between healing and curing, taking exception to the latter for its supposed connection to the medical model. There are two problems here. One is that while her definitions of healing and curing sound entirely reasonable, her choice of the distinctions she wishes to draw between them – that cure means erasure and is medical, while healing involves reintegration of the self and is psychological – are arbitrary rather than epistemic. Worse is to follow. As Kafka puts it at the very beginning, "the emphasis on cure in psychoanalysis is a carryover from the medical model of disease. It connotes the analyst's authority: it denotes doctor-patient inequality" (p. 110). The medical model, which *does* connote a practitioner performing a treatment on a subject while maintaining a psychological if not a physical distance, is, however, *distinct* from the doctor-patient relationship.

Authority and inequality are, alas, problems in any sort of sustained therapeutic interaction. Inequality in a therapeutic relationship is inevitable; the roles of the participants and their relationship to the damage suffered by one of them make it inevitable. The problem is rather an abuse of authority growing out of the mistaken application of power relations in the therapeutic situation, however conceived. The analyst's authority should not derive from the mechanics of power or membership in some particular school of psychoanalytic belief, but rather from her clinical expertise, wisdom, and ultimately, I'm afraid, from what kind of human being she is. Such care does not prevent the patient from making the analyst into an authority figure. For example, a patient prefaces telling me about a problem with a relationship by saying, "I know you won't like this, but . . ." The technical issue here then became one of when and how I could *return* the authority to him. People who identify themselves as therapists can stumble into this just as easily as those who identify themselves as doctors.

Strupp (Strupp, 1978; Strupp, Fox, & Lessler, 1969) was an astute observer of the psychoanalytic situation. He (1982) expressed concerns about what he termed the "remedicalization of psychotherapy in general and psychoanalysis in particular" (p. 123) and a return to the medical model designed to make these treatment modalities more appealing to the health insurance industry. Strupp posits "the medical model, with its authoritarian conception of the doctor-patient relationship [allowing for the possibility of a doctor-patient relationship *not so grounded*], of

So what *is* psychoanalysis?   **173**

course leaves no doubt as to how power is distributed in the treatment situation" (p. 128). This allows us to accept a critique of the medical model without having to abandon the doctor-patient relationship, but it does not address other questions, such as what we are doing when we refer a patient for a medication consultation or prescribe psychotropic drugs ourselves. For this we need to turn to Adler (2002) and the "sociophysiology of caring."

On the face of it, Herbert Adler (2002, 2007), a psychiatrist writing for the *Journal of General Internal Medicine*, would seem most likely to be writing about the medical model of relationships between patients and their physicians and least likely to be writing about care and the bio-psycho-social nature of relationships between therapists and their patients.

Adler (2007) describes the doctor-patient relationship in terms of an emergent, psychosocial relational process whose evolving nature is best understood on a moment-by-moment basis through the lens of complexity theory. It reflects complex psychosocial actions; the outcome of reciprocal influences occurring in the container of the therapeutic space (Bachelard, 1958/1994). These relationships cannot, however, be considered symmetrical (however much we might like to think of them that way) "because [both] patients and society grant *clinicians* the responsibility to focus attention and treat biological and psychological aspects of a patient's disease" (Adler, 2007, p. 282, italics added). Treatment is interpersonal, informative, and at times prescriptive. The use of empathy is a clinical procedure in the psychoanalytic situation. In contrast to how it is usually thought of in contemporary psychoanalytic circles, it has characteristics that go beyond its being an emotional element of discourse. Empathy involves the activation of two psychobiological processes: emotional contagion and cognitive perspective taking (de Waal, 2008). There are specific indications for its overt use, it is a skilled interpersonal technique that must be learned by therapists possessing innate capacities for its development, and it seeks to affect a positive change in a patient's psychobiology.

On a neurobiological level, psychological or physical suffering results in an activation of the hypothalamic-pituitary-adrenal axis (Adler, 2007; Panksepp & Biven, 2012) that can be treated by a secure attachment bond with an attuned caregiver (Simpson, 1994). Infant-caregiver relationships offer a phenomenological *model* for this process rather than a theoretical reactivation of the original attachment situation.

For me, the process looks something like this. Sarah, an extremely intelligent and self-observant young woman with a history of substance abuse, anxiety, and depression, came to see me because of an emptiness in her life, severe emotional pain, and a lack of any sort of vocational direction.[10] While she *was* able to control

---

10 For what it's worth, although I did not conduct a formal Adult Attachment Interview (George, et al., 1984), I thought that Sarah did fit the adult criteria for a childhood experience of ambivalent attachment.

174 So what *is* psychoanalysis?

her substance abuse, trials of both therapy and psychotropic medication (antidepressants and antianxiety agents) had done nothing for her remaining severe illness. After getting to know her a bit (and observing what just talking did and didn't do for her), I reached two conclusions about her care. I have found that patients with significant depressions who are refractory to therapy with or without standard antidepressant therapy respond to a combination of psychoanalysis and a medication regimen of mood stabilizers similar to that used with bipolar patients. I discussed these options with Sarah and told her that successful pharmacotherapy would make an analytic process possible. I also thought that, for an intelligent patient who already understood so much of her personal narrative, the therapeutic relationship (the doctor-patient relationship) would make or break the analysis rather than the attainment of some so far elusive further insight.

I employed two sorts of empathic procedures, one autocentric and one allocentric, that I learned over the years. I consciously made two sorts of comments in the former mode. I would ask Sarah to help me understand something, or whether I had gotten something right, or, if I asked a question, tell her that I didn't already have an answer in mind (if I *had* an answer, I would just tell her). If, between sessions, I thought about some dilemma relating to her life or struggles (once considered a sure sign of countertransference), I would tell her so. All these procedures served the purpose of explicitly conveying my presence as a human being and an expert, and my interest in understanding her. The second sort of activity, although in common usage by sensitive contemporary analysts (e.g., Goldner, 2002; Stern, D.B., 1997), is not generally understood in terms of specific empathic procedures. In a session with Sarah, I found myself feeling intensely frustrated and alone while she *seemed* to be feeling nothing at all. When I realized what was happening, that these were *her* feelings, I told her so. She then felt them deeply. She began to cry quietly, and my (her) feelings became much more intense. Such experiences of shared attunement have neurohormonal (Panksepp, 2009; Panksepp & Biven, 2012) correlates and involve the brain, heart, face, and vagal circuits (Porges, 1998, 2009, 2011). This complete sequence (I don't think calling it projective identification really adds much) is infrequent; usually, only some part of it happens. Mathews and colleagues (Mathews, Suchman, & Brandt Jr, 1993) used the term "connexional moments," as manifestations of effective empathy.

Schachter and Kächele (2007) approached these issues from a different angle in their paper "The Analyst's Role in Healing: Psychoanalysis-Plus." They discuss the importance of including techniques such as "explicit support, consolation, suggestion, persuasion, and advice" (p. 429) in Contemporary Psychoanalysis and note their exclusion from Classical Psychoanalysis. Implicit in their argument is the premise that the purpose of psychoanalysis is to heal. They offer the frequently made but infrequently honored observation that the effectiveness of psychotherapy or psychoanalysis depends on the person and not the theoretical views of the therapist (e.g., Strupp et al., 1969; Tessman, 2003). Frank and Frank (1993), in a new edition of a now classic work, argue that such treatments cannot be separated from the "personal influence" of their practitioners and, to be considered a psychotherapy, that influence must include a healing subject, a sufferer seeking relief from that suffering, and a structured relationship between healer and sufferer in which healing takes place. Central to this process is helping patients "to feel and function better by encouraging appropriate modifications in their assumptive worlds, thereby transforming the meanings of experiences to more favorable ones" (p. 30). We have lots of interdisciplinary language with which to describe these assumptive worlds: Metacognitive modeling (Main, 1991), Theories of Mind (ToM) (Baron-Cohen, 2000), emotional and conceptual priming (Schacter, 1996), Network Systems (Christakis, 2004; Christakis & Fowler, 2009), Internal Working Models (IWMs) (Bowlby, 1969; Craik, 1943/1952), embodied simulation (Gallese, 2005, 2007, 2009), episodic simulation (Schacter et al., 2008), and the reconfiguration of the *Eigenwelt* in the context of the *Mitwelt* and *Umwelt* (Heidegger, 1927/2010).

The converse of this is feeling what the patient is feeling *without* processing it, or even being unaware of what is taking place. Generally, this failure on the part of the therapist to metabolize his patient's feelings results in their intensification, fostering alienation and mistrust.

There is also a rapidly evolving literature on the neurobiology of interpersonal relationships generally, the doctor-patient relationship (Adler, 2002, 2007; Benedetti, 2011) particularly, and empathy (de Waal, 2008; Shamay-Tsoory, 2011) and the placebo effect (Benedetti, 2009; Benedetti, Mayberg, Wager, Stohler, & Zubieta, 2005) even more particularly. Benedetti (2011) observes that "the basic idea of the biopsychosocial model is not so much to deny biomedical research but rather to criticize its narrow focus on [its] anatomical, physiological, and molecular mechanisms" (p. 39). A similar critique can be mounted against the narrow focus on verbal discourse maintained in most psychoanalytic circles. The biological and the psychological are interreferential beyond simply denoting two different views of mental function; each exerts an influence on the general biological and psychological health or illness of the self. This holism maintains the locus of care as residing in the whole self, regardless of what combination of physical and psychological care may be required to heal or to cure. Reflecting both the psychological and the biological is the observation that the ritual itself through which therapeutic acts (Benedetti) of whatever sort are conducted changes the patient's brain.

On meeting the therapist for the first time, if not before based on expectations, the immediate implicit or explicit question facing the patient is whether the therapist is trustworthy and competent, or merits fear, suspicion, and watchful waiting. The second question is whether the therapist has anything to offer. Roger, for example, began his analysis from a position of watchful waiting and soon progressed to trust. Therapist behaviors that inspire trust include perceived competence, "compassion, confidentiality, reliability, and communication" (Benedetti, 2011, pp. 125–126). Trust decisions are made in the amygdala; the therapist's facial expression and choice of language are of particular importance in reaching these decisions. Assessment takes place rapidly, in time frames on the order of 100

176 So what *is* psychoanalysis?

msec. If the face is judged untrustworthy, increasing activity in the amygdala results; conversely, a judgment that a person is trustworthy results in the production of oxytocin in the hypothalamus and its secretion by the pituitary. Oxytocin is a pro-social hormone that increases feelings of safety and well-being. It does so in part by binding to receptors in the amygdala that inhibit the latter's activity. Oxytocin has also been shown (Panksepp, 1998, 2003) to be a "therapy hormone" in that it loosens conceptual priming (Schacter, 1996) and facilitates change through interpersonal (here patient-therapist) contact.

While we know that all therapies, regardless of their theoretical basis, can be curative, several studies suggest (Benedetti, 2011) that psychotherapy (and psychoanalysis) "work only through a benign positive interaction" (p. 125) that inspires trust and hope. Unfortunately, it takes only a moment's consideration to realize that psychoanalysts and psychoanalytic psychotherapists seem largely unaware of the importance of these procedures. The fact that we deliberately break off face-to-face contact with some of our patients through making them lie on the couch can cause problems facilitating and maintaining trust and hope. A colleague recently remarked to me that he thought that the middle phase of analysis was characterized by analysands depreciating both the process and their analysts. I found this particularly disturbing given that the evidence overwhelmingly supports the conclusion that positive feelings about the therapist and the therapeutic process correlate most strongly with a positive therapeutic outcome. The converse, that negative perceptions of process and therapist correlate with a negative therapeutic outcome, has not been studied. My colleague's observation could easily be viewed as a rationalization of bad therapy, bad technique, and character problems in the therapist; it merits a certain skepticism. Again, this should not for a moment be taken to suggest that there isn't a place or even a necessity for negative spectrum feelings in a therapy or analysis. What I do want to posit is that if such feelings are sustained over time, they should raise concerns that the therapist is missing something and should look for it, or that the feelings are iatrogenic.

The placebo effect

Perhaps nothing stands more on the cusp of the psychological and the biological in the doctor-patient relationship than the lowly and much denigrated placebo. A placebo can be defined as a) a sugar pill or otherwise therapeutically inert procedure with which you trick the patient into imagining he's feeling better or prove that there was never anything wrong with him in the first place, or b) healing effects of feeling cared for focused on a particular kind of transaction. A further possibility is to study the effect of psychosocial factors on therapeutic efficacy by administering a therapeutically inert procedure. This last option is confounded by the likelihood that the most effective treatment involves combining a therapeutically active intervention with a positive psychosocial context. Over the past few decades, a growing

So what *is* psychoanalysis? **177**

body of research (Benedetti, 2009; Benedetti et al., 2005; Frank & Frank, 1993)[11] into the neurobiology of the placebo effect points to b). The evidence is even more compelling if it is compounded by that of the Lessebo effect (Colloca, Lopiano, Lanotte, & Benedetti, 2004; Mestre, Prakesh, Marras, Tomlinson, & Lang, 2014), in which a treatment of proven effectiveness has its efficacy reduced or eliminated if the patient is told in advance that the treatment is ineffective. Another variant of the placebo effect can be seen in open-hidden studies (Benedetti et al., 2003). If Valium, a benzodiazepine anti-anxiety agent, is administered to an anxious patient without his knowledge, it proves to be totally ineffective; if it is administered *with* the patient's knowledge, a marked diminution of anxiety results. In effect, a placebo can be thought of as a sort of elixir distilled from the doctor-patient relationship.

It is mostly very difficult to tease apart the placebo component from the specific effects of a psychotherapy (Benedetti, 2009). However, while Prozac and placebo affect the same area of the brain, this is different from the areas affected by interpersonal or cognitive-behavioral therapy (CBT). Both forms of psychotherapy exert effects on the pre-frontal cortex while they individually affect other areas of the brain. So far, this work is still in its early stages with much not yet understood and still to be elucidated. We do know that psychotherapy, the placebo effect, and psychotropic medication influence different parts of the brain, yet all of them can be brought to bear on problems like anxiety and depression. How they alter the way the self processes information arising internally and from being-in-the-world that leads to broader changes in capacities for feeling and acting is not at all understood, but the doctor-patient relationship lies at the center of all of these processes.

Patient selection

I want to end with a caveat. At the macro level, this book has followed the path taken by books written to offer a critique of psychoanalytic business as usual. These books suggest different or novel ways of thinking about clinical and theoretical issues that attempt to push the edge of that thinking to a greater or lesser extent. Among them, this book has tended to lie on the more radical end of the spectrum, as did *Contemporary Psychoanalytic Foundations* (2010) and *The Therapeutic Situation in the 21st Century* (2013) before it, and as will the provisionally titled *Psychoanalysis, Aesthetics, and Well-Being* after it. Be that as it may, we all offer critiques of current thinking with some clinical examples and then go on to either introduce new ideas

---

11 For our purposes, a problem with much (a search of PubMed for the term *placebo* obtains 120,000 hits) but not all of this research is that, for simplicity of study, it tends to focus on pain and conditions like Parkinson's disease. As with psychotherapy research, simplification tends to limit the usefulness of the knowledge gain from the results that are obtained. That said, there is evidence (Wager, et al., 2004) obtained from fMRI studies that shows characteristic activity in certain areas of the brain when placebo is administered along with an expectation of analgesia.

178 So what *is* psychoanalysis?

or further explicate old ones. There has been a constant dialectic between explication and introduction with one or the other in the forefront over the course of our history. However, we all write about the successful nature of our work and how we view the reasons for that success. To a lesser extent, we also offer examples of unsuccessful work in terms of what we failed to understand, how the clinical theory (even a phenomenological one) failed us, or what mistakes we made.

Instead, I want to consider two sorts of people (I can call only some of them patients) who seek us out for a variety of reasons. The more engaged group is made up of people who come to see us seeking some kind of help with their lives, often suffering from pain, depression, and anxiety. We regularly start out in some kind of psychoanalytic process that proves genuinely helpful to them. Such therapies take place at frequencies ranging from one to five sessions per week and may last weeks (less commonly), months, or years. At some point, this process of exploration and change comes to an end, usually, à la Freud (1937/1964), with a sense of some things left undone.[12] Although some of these patients choose to terminate their treatment, others, however, choose to remain in therapy, usually at a lesser frequency of sessions. Ellen, a woman in her early 50s, lives a somewhat difficult life. I had seen her twice weekly for two years, resulting, in the language I have been using, in some change in the nature of her Internal Working Models and the nature of the Heuristics she relies on. As a consequence, her life, which had been wildly out of control, had improved to a point where it was from time to time only a bit chaotic. As a measure of this change, it was no longer possible to isolate her role in making it so. Ellen chose to continue seeing me at a frequency ranging from monthly to twice monthly. In these sessions I would listen carefully to what she said, chat with her about her life, and usually made a suggestion or two. She found this enormously helpful and soothing. I was relationally present for her and also filled in with some functions she was unable to fully manage for herself. I have no sense or concern (financing the therapy at this level is not a problem) about how long we will continue like this. A second group of patients come seeking this second kind of therapeutic situation from the start.

Still another group are unable to either engage the therapist as a usable object (Winnicott, 1965) or lack a Theory of Mind (Baron-Cohen et al., 2000), or to even grasp the fact that the therapist *is* an object as opposed to some two-dimensional need-satisfying paper cutout. The great majority of these people disappear after a session or a few sessions when they do grasp that the therapist, like others, is not dispensing whatever commodity they are interested in. Such people may appear confusing when the therapist fails to deduce that they are not patients at all. A subgroup of *these* people come in appearing to be patients (this becomes a matter of definitions). They present with problems in their lives that are addressable in

---

12 This group is distinct from those patients with whom it is possible to identify an obstacle to overcome or those for whom simply more time does the trick.

So what *is* psychoanalysis? **179**

therapy and wish to pursue them. They tend not to be in great emotional pain about these problems and want weekly therapy, rarely twice weekly therapy, and almost never psychoanalysis (however defined). They appear to be involved in the process, make therapeutic progress and *seem* to recognize that the therapist is a person. Ultimately, however, they reveal their inability to grasp that the therapist *is* a person in the same way they are. This can be subtle and easily escapes our notice as we unconsciously fill in these blanks as we work with them. Sometimes such therapy can go on for a year or two but ends in some kind of rupture or disappearance. I had seen Adam, a 40-year-old oncologist, on a weekly basis for over a year. The therapy had been of great help to him in relieving some disabling psychosomatic symptoms, and he seemed involved in both the therapy and his relationship with me. I had told him at the start that I had a 24-hour cancellation policy but would try to find alternative times for him if he gave me enough notice when the need arose. A scheduling conflict led to his cancelling an appointment an hour before its scheduled time, leaving me a message that he would see me the next week. When I billed him for the time, he called, leaving a message that I had mistakenly charged him for the session. In the next session, when I reminded him of my cancellation policy, he erupted, saying that, although I had been of help to him, I could bill him for it but he wouldn't pay and would "just get another therapist." He stormed out. The latent therapist-as-commodity problem had appeared, surprising me. In retrospect, threads of anger and a certain shallowness in his perceptions of friends and lovers became obvious. This was not about the meaning of the charge in the context of our relationship as one could easily imagine. He just didn't want to pay, whatever we had said about the mutuality of the therapeutic endeavor. He made no attempt to contact me or to pay his outstanding bill, even minus the offending session. I did not pursue him.

Other patients who appear to be involved in therapy suddenly disappear without any particular signals or emotions. Kohut (1971) described this problem with narcissistic patients who just disappeared after a separation, sometimes after a vacation of either patient or analyst or, rarely, after a weekend. He found that he had quite simply ceased to exist emotionally for them. I have suggested over the course of this book that we can say more about the situation than to simply term these patients "narcissistic." Robert, a postdoctoral fellow in chemistry at the local university, came to see me because he was unable to do the research he needed to do if he was to progress in his career. Secondarily, a multiyear relationship with a woman who clearly loved him had not led anywhere (for him), and he wanted to move on. He came from a family lacking in emotion, where there had been little care to be had. I thought that an analysis was required here but, since it was not clear if he would be staying in the area, we agreed to start once a week. With Robert, I was clear from the start about his relational deficits and his attachment pathology. He seemed to make some progress. He felt more like working and spoke of valuing our sessions. I expected a long-term process here and did not think anything was amiss. At the end of the academic year, he left on a month's vacation; he disappeared and

180   So what *is* psychoanalysis?

I never heard from him again. Although I did not want to intrude,[13] I felt it was important to do *something* to at least show my continuing interest in him. I wasn't sure what I thought would be best. After a month or so, I settled on emailing him a simple question mark. While his disappearance was unexpected, the fact that Robert would do something like this was not surprising but was entirely consistent with his deficits. I never heard from him again.

It is possible, of course, that any or all of these situations could have resulted from technical failings or some emotional blindness on my part. I can only say that I think not and that I have worked my way through such issues with other patients, usually as part of a productive therapeutic situation but sometimes only after a therapy had ended in a planned or unplanned way.

I have attempted to offer new, interdisciplinary ways of looking at what we do and how we do it. To paraphrase an old aphorism, I have tried to offer new wine in new bottles. Such an effort cannot be without its limitations, as our work always has its limitations. We are not always successful and sometimes we fail. I have focused particularly on care, healing, relief of suffering, and cure, all from a phenomenological perspective. Therapeutic actions and results are always partial and incomplete, at least to some degree. Grandiosity remains a dangerous companion, and there will always be limits in what we and our patients are able to accomplish.

---

13 He had chosen not to call. Contacting a patient in such circumstances and trying to get them to come in and at least "talk it over" (in practice often a euphemism for employing power tactics to keep them in treatment) has never, in my experience, proven truly useful.

REFERENCES

Adams, M. V. (2000). Compensation in the service of individuation – Phenomenological essentialism and Jungian dream interpretation: Commentary on a paper by Hazel Ipp. *Psychoanalytic Dialogues, 10,* 127–142.

Addis, D. R. (2008). Constructive episodic simulation: Temporal distance and detail of past and future events modulate hippocampal engagement. *Hippocampus, 18,* 227–237.

Adler, H. M. (2002). The sociophysiology of caring in the doctor-patient relationship. *Journal of General Internal Medicine, 17,* 883–890.

Adler, H. M. (2007). Toward a biopsychosocial understanding of the patient-physician relationship: An emerging dialogue. *Journal of General Internal Medicine, 22,* 280–285.

Ainsworth, M. D. S., Bell, S. M., & Stayton, D. J. (1974). Infant-mother attachment and social development: "Socialization" as a product of reciprocal responsiveness to signals. In M. P. M. Richards (Ed.), *The introduction of the child into a social world* (pp. 99–135). Cambridge: Cambridge University Press.

Ainsworth, M. D. S., Blehar, M. C., Waters, E., & Wall, S. (1978). *Patterns of attachment: The psychological study of the strange situation.* Hillsdale, NJ: Lawrence Erlbaum Associates.

Alexander, F., & French, T. M. (1946). *Psychoanalytic therapy principles and applications.* New York: Ronald Press.

Allik, T. (2003). Psychoanalysis and the uncanny: Take two OR when disillusionment turns out to be an illusion. *Psychoanalysis and Contemporary Thought, 26,* 3–37.

Anonymous. (1969). Archives of General Psychiatry. XIV, 1966: An experimental approach to dream and telepathy. Montague Ullman. pp. 605–613. *Psychoanalytic Quarterly, 38,* 343.

Apter-Levy, Y., Feldman, M., Valcart, A., Ebstein, R. B., & Feldman, R. (2013). Impact of maternal depression across the first 6 years of life on the child's mental health, social engagement, and empathy: The moderating role of oxytocin. *American Journal of Psychiatry, 170,* 1161–1168.

Arbesman, S., & Christakis, N. A. (2010). Leadership insularity: A new measure of connectivity between central nodes in networks. *Connectivity, 30,* 4–10.

Arden, M. (1993). Thoughts on the healing process. *International Forum of Psychoanalysis, 2,* 149–154.

Arlow, J. A., & Brenner, C. (1964). *Psychoanalytic concepts and the structural theory.* New York: International Universities Press.

182 References

Asimov, I. (1974). The last question. *The best of Isaac Asimov* (pp. 157–169). Garden City, NY: Doubleday. (Original work published 1956)

Askay, R., & Farquhar, J. (2006). *Apprehending the inaccessible: Freudian psychoanalysis and existential phenomenology*. Evanston, IL: Northwestern University Press.

Askay, R., & Farquhar, J. (2012). Psychoanalysis. In S. Luft & S. Overgaard (Eds.), *The Routledge companion to phenomenology* (pp. 596–610). London: Routledge.

Assaf, Y., & Pasternak, O. (2008). Diffusion tensor imaging (DTI)-based white matter mapping in brain research: A review. *Journal of Molecular Neuroscience, 34*(1), 51–61.

Baars, B. J. (2003a). The fundamental role of context: Unconscious shaping of conscious information. In B. J. Baars, W. P. Banks, & J. B. Newman (Eds.), *Essential sources in the scientific study of consciousness* (pp. 761–775). Cambridge, MA: MIT Press. (Original work published 1988)

Baars, B. J. (2003b). How does a serial, integrated, and very limited stream of consciousness emerge from a nervous system that is mostly unconscious, distributed, parallel and of enormous capacity? In B. J. Baars, W. P. Banks, & J. B. Newman (Eds.), *Essential sources in the scientific study of consciousness* (pp. 1123–1129). Cambridge, MA: MIT Press. (Original work published 1993)

Bacal, H. A. (Ed.). (1998). *Optimal responsiveness: How therapists heal their patients*. Northvale, NJ: Jason Aronson.

Bacal, H. A. (2006). Specificity theory: Conceptualizing a personal and professional quest for therapeutic possibility. *International Journal of Psychoanalytic Self Psychology, 1*, 133–155.

Bach, S. (1975). Narcissism, continuity and the uncanny. *International Journal of Psychoanalysis, 56*, 77–86.

Bachelard, G. (1994). *The poetics of space* (M. Jolas, Trans.). Boston, MA: Beacon Press. (Original work published 1958)

Balint, M. (1955). Notes on parapsychology and parapsychological healing. *International Journal of Psychoanalysis, 36*, 31–35.

Barabási, A.-L. (2003). *Linked*. London: Plume Books.

Barabási, A.-L. (2005). Network theory – the emergence of the creative enterprise. *Science, 308*, 639–641.

Baron-Cohen, S. (2000). Theory of mind and autism: A fifteen-year review. In S. Baron-Cohen, H. Tager-Flusberg, & D. J. Cohen (Eds.), *Understanding other minds: Perspectives from developmental cognitive neuroscience* (2nd ed., pp. 3–20). Oxford: Oxford University Press.

Baron-Cohen, S., Leslie, A. M., & Frith, U. (1985). Does the autistic child have a "theory of mind"? *Cognition, 21*, 37–46.

Baron-Cohen, S., Tager-Flusberg, H., & Cohen, D. J. (2000). *Understanding other minds: Perspectives from developmental cognitive science* (2nd ed.). Oxford: Oxford University Press.

Bass, A., Ipp, H., & Seligman, S. (Eds.). (2013). *Psychoanalytic dialogues* (Vol. 23, pp. 1–128). New York: Taylor & Francis.

Bauer, W. D. (2003). Comment on Natterson. *Psychoanalytic Psychology, 20*, 522–527.

Beebe, B., & Lachmann, F. (2002). Organizing principles of interaction from infant research and the lifespan prediction of attachment: Application to adult treatment. *Journal of Infant, Child, and Adolescent Psychotherapy, 2*, 61–89.

Benedetti, F. (2009). *Placebo effects: Understanding the mechanisms in health and disease*. Oxford: Oxford University Press.

Benedetti, F. (2011). *The patient's brain: The neuroscience behind the doctor-patient relationship*. Oxford: Oxford University Press.

Benedetti, F., Maggi, G., Lopiano, L., Lanotte, M., Rainero, I., Vighetti, S., & Pollo, A. (2003). Open versus hidden medical treatments: The patient's knowledge about a therapy affects the therapy outcome. *Prevention and Treatment, 6*(1). doi:10.1037/1522-3736.6.1.61a

Benedetti, F., Mayberg, H. S., Wager, T. D., Stohler, C. S., & Zubieta, J. (2005). Neurobiological mechanisms of the placebo effect. *Journal of Neuroscience, 25*, 10390–10402.

Benjamin, J. (1988). *The bonds of love.* New York: Pantheon.

Benjamin, J. (2000). Intersubjective distinctions: Subjects and persons, recognitions and breakdowns: Commentary on paper by Gerhardt, Sweetnam and Borton. *Psychoanalytic Dialogues, 10*, 43–55.

Bieber, I. (1961). The meaning of suffering in therapy. *American Journal of Psychoanalysis, 21*, 5–8.

Binswanger, L. (1958). The existential analysis school of thought (E. Angel, Trans.). In R. May, E. Angel, & H. F. Ellenberger (Eds.), *Existence* (pp. 191–213). New York: Simon & Schuster.

Blanton, S. (1971). *Diary of my analysis with Sigmund Freud.* New York: Hawthorne Press.

Bock, D. D., Wei-Chung, A. L., Kerlin, A. M., Andermann, M. L., Hood, G., Wetzel, A. W., . . . Reid, R. C. (2011). Network anatomy and *in vivo* physiology of visual cortical neurons. *Nature, 471*(7337), 177–182.

Bogen, J. E. (2000). Split-brain basics: Relevance for the concept of one's other mind. *Journal of the American Academy of Psychoanalysis and Dynamic Psychiatry, 28*, 341–369.

Bogen, J. E., & Vogel, P. J. (1962). Cerebral commisurotomy in man: preliminary case report. *Bulletin of the Los Angeles Neurological Society, 27*, 169–172.

Boris, E., & Klein, J. (2012). *Caring for America: Home health workers in the shadow of the welfare state.* Oxford: Oxford University Press.

Bornstein, B. H., & Emler, A. C. (2001). Rationality in medical decision making: A review of the literature on doctors' decision-making. *Journal of Evaluation in Clinical Practice, 7*, 97–107.

Boss, M. (1963). *Psychoanalysis and Daseinanalysis.* New York: Basic Books.

Boston Change Process Study Group. (2005). The "something more" than interpretation revisited: sloppiness and co-creativity in the psychoanalytic encounter. *Journal of the American Psychoanalytic Association, 53*, 693–729.

Bowlby, J. (1969). *Attachment and loss: Vol 1. Attachment.* New York: Basic Books.

Bowlby, J. (1973). *Attachment and loss: Vol. 2. Separation: Anxiety and anger.* New York: Basic Books.

Bowlby, J. (1984). The making and breaking of affectional bonds. In *The making and breaking of affectional bonds* (pp. 126–160). London: Tavistock. (Original work published 1979[1977])

Bowlby, J. (1988). *A secure base: Parent-child attachment and healthy human development.* New York: Basic Books.

Bowlby, J. (1991). Ethological light on psychoanalytic problems. In P. Bateson (Ed.), *The development and integration of behaviour: Essays in honor of Robert Hinde* (pp. 301–313). Cambridge: Cambridge University Press.

Brandt, L. W. (1966). Process or structure? *Psychoanalytic Review, 53C*, 50–54.

Bråten, S. (Ed.). (2007). *On being moved: From mirror neurons to empathy* (Vol. 68). Amsterdam: John Benjamins.

Bråten, S., & Trevarthen, C. (2007). Prologue: From infant intersubjectivity and participant movements to simulation and conversation in cultural common sense. In S. Bråten (Ed.), *On being moved: From mirror neurons to empathy* (Vol. 68, pp. 21–34). Amsterdam: John Benjamins.

Breckenridge, K. (2000). Physical touch in psychoanalysis: A closet phenomenon? *Psychoanalytic Inquiry, 20*, 2–20.

Brentano, F. (1995). *Psychology from an empirical standpoint* (L. L. McCalister, Trans.). London: Routledge. (Original work published 1874)

Breuer, J., & Freud, S. (1955). Studies in hysteria. In J. Strachey (Ed.), *Standard edition* (Vol. 2, pp. 1–319). London: Hogarth Press. (Original work published 1893–1895)

184 References

Brody, S. R. (2013a). Entering the night country: Reflections on self-disclosure and vulnerability. *Psychoanalytic Dialogues, 23*, 45–58.

Brody, S. R. (2013b). Response to commentaries on entering night country: Analytic self-disclosure as divergent conflict. *Psychoanalytic Dialogues, 23*, 75–79.

Bromberg, P. M. (1996). Standing in the spaces: The multiplicity of self and the psychoanalytic relationship. *Contemporary Psychoanalysis, 32*, 509–535.

Bromberg, P. M. (2011). The Gill/Bromberg correspondence. *Psychoanalytic Dialogues, 21*, 243–252.

Brooke, R. (1991). Psychic complexity and human existence: A phenomenological approach. *Journal of Analytical Psychology, 36*, 505–518.

Bruch, H. (1962). Perceptual and conceptual disturbances in anorexia nervosa. *Psychosomatic Medicine, 24*, 187–194.

Brusset, B. (2012). The therapeutic action of psychoanalysis. *International Journal of Psychoanalysis, 93*, 427–442.

Buechler, S. (2010). No pain, no gain? Suffering and the analysis of defense. *Contemporary Psychoanalysis, 46*, 334–354.

Cacioppo, J. T., Christakis, N. A., & Fowler, J. H. (2009). Alone in the crowd: The structure and spread of loneliness in a large social network. *Journal of Personality and Social Psychology, 97*, 977–991.

Caper, R. (1992). Does psychoanalysis heal? A contribution to the theory of psychoanalytic technique. *International Journal of Psychoanalysis, 73*, 283–292.

Carman, T. (2006). The principle of phenomenology. In C. B. Guignon (Ed.), *The Cambridge companion to Heidegger* (pp. 97–119). Cambridge: Cambridge University Press.

Casement, P. J. (1982). Some pressures on the analyst for physical contact during the re-living of an early trauma. *International Review of Psychoanalysis, 9*, 279–286.

Casement, P. J. (2000). The issue of touch: A retrospective overview. *Psychoanalytic Inquiry, 20*, 160–184.

Cassell, E. J. (2004). *The nature of suffering and the goals of medicine* (2nd ed.). Oxford: Oxford University Press.

Christakis, N. A. (2004). Social networks and collateral health effects. *British Medical Journal, 329*, 184–185.

Christakis, N. A., & Fowler, J. H. (2007). The spread of obesity in a large social network over 32 years. *New England Journal of Medicine, 357*, 370–379.

Christakis, N. A., & Fowler, J. H. (2008). The collective dynamics of smoking in a large social network. *New England Journal of Medicine, 358*, 2249–2258.

Christakis, N. A., & Fowler, J. H. (2009). *Connected: The surprising power of our social networks and how they shape our lives*. New York: Little, Brown.

Cicchetti, D., & Toth, S. L. (1995). Child maltreatment and attachment organization: Implications for intervention. In S. Goldberg, R. Muir, & J. Kerr (Eds.), *Attachment theory: Social, developmental, and clinical perspectives* (pp. 279–308). Hillsdale, NJ: Analytic Press.

Coan, J. A. (2008). Toward a neuroscience of attachment. In J. Cassidy & P. R. Shaver (Eds.), *Handbook of attachment: Theory, research, and clinical applications* (2nd ed., pp. 241–265). New York: Guilford Press.

Coburn, W. J. (2002). A world of systems: The role of systemic patterns of experience in the therapeutic process. *Psychoanalytic Inquiry, 22*, 655–677.

Colloca, L., Lopiano, L., Lanotte, M., & Benedetti, F. (2004). Overt versus covert treatment for pain, anxiety and Parkinson's disease. *Lancet Neurology, 3*, 679–684.

Coltrera, J. T. (1962). Psychoanalysis and existentialism. *Journal of the American Psychoanalytic Association, 10*, 166–215.

Compton, A. (1988). Psychoanalytic cure. *Psychoanalytic Review, 75*, 217–229.

Cooper, P. (2002). Between wonder and doubt: Psychoanalysis in the goal-free zone. *Journal of the American Psychoanalytic Association, 62*, 95–118.

Cooper, S. H. (1993). Interpretive fallibility and the psychoanalytic dialogue. *Journal of the American Psychoanalytic Association, 41*, 95–126.

Craik, K. (1952). *The nature of explanation.* Cambridge: Cambridge University Press. (Original work published 1943)

Damasio, A. (1994). *Descartes's error: Emotion, reason, and the human brain.* New York: Grosset/ Putnam.

Dastur, F. (2012). Dasein. In S. Luft & S. Overgaard (Eds.), *The Routledge companion to phenomenology* (pp. 318–326). London: Routledge.

de Jong, T. R., Measor, K. R., Chauke, M., Harris, B. N., & Saltzman, W. (2010). Brief pup exposure induces Fos expression in the lateral habenula and serotonergic caudal dorsal raphe nucleus of paternally experienced male California mice (*Peromyscus californicus*). *Neuroscience, 169*, 1094–1104.

de Waal, F. B. M. (2008). Putting the altruism back into altruism: The evolution of empathy. *Annual Review of Psychology, 59*, 279–300.

Derrida, J. (1978). *Writing and difference* (A. Bass, Trans.). Chicago, IL: University of Chicago Press.

Derrida, J. (1982). *Margins of philosophy* (A. Bass, Trans.). Chicago, IL: University of Chicago Press. (Original work published 1972)

Descartes, R. (1999). *Meditations and other metaphysical writings* (D. M. Clarke, Trans.). New York: Penguin Books. (Original work published 1641)

Dimen, M. (2010). Reflections on cure, or "I/Thou/It." *Psychoanalytic Dialogues, 20*, 254–268.

Dozier, M., & Tyrrell, C. (1997). The role of attachment in therapeutic relationships. In J. A. Simpson & W. S. Rholes (Eds.), *Attachment theory and close relationships* (pp. 221–248). New York: Guilford Press.

Dunbar, R. (1993). Coevolution of neocortex size, group size and language in humans. *Behavioral and Brain Sciences, 16*, 681–735.

Eagle, M. N. (2003). Clinical implications of attachment theory. *Psychoanalytic Inquiry, 23*, 27–53.

Edelson, M. (1984). *Hypothesis and evidence in psychoanalysis.* Chicago, IL: University of Chicago Press.

Ehrenwald, J. (1974). The telepathy hypothesis and schizophrenia. *Journal of the American Academy of Psychoanalysis and Dynamic Psychiatry, 2*, 159–169.

Eisenbud, J. (1946). Telepathy and problems of psychoanalysis. *Psychoanalytic Quarterly, 15*, 32–87.

Eisenbud, J. (1948). Telepathy and medical psychology: By Jan Ehrenwald, M.D. New York: W. W. Norton, 1948. 212 pp. *Psychoanalytic Quarterly, 17*, 545–548.

Eisler, K. R. (1968). The relationship of explaining and understanding in psychoanalysis. *Psychoanalytic Study of the Child, 23*, 141–177.

Erikson, E. (1963). *Childhood and society* (2nd ed.). New York: W. W. Norton. (Original work published 1950)

Fairfield, S., Layton, L., & Stack, C. (Eds.). (2002). *Bringing the plague: Toward a postmodern psychoanalysis.* New York: Other Press.

Faye, E. (2009). *Heidegger: The introduction of Nazism into philosophy* (M. B. Smith, Trans.). New Haven, CT: Yale University Press.

Feifel, D., Macdonald, K., Nguyen, A., Cobb, P., Warlan, H., Galangue, B., . . . Hadley, A. (2010). Adjunctive intranasal oxytocin reduces symptoms in schizophrenia patients. *Biological Psychiatry, 68*, 678–680.

186 References

Ferenczi, S. (1930). The principle of relaxation and neocatharsis. *International Journal of Psychoanalysis, 11*, 428–443.

Ferenczi, S. (1988). *The Clinical Diary of Sándor Ferenczi* (M. Balint & N. S. Jackson, Trans.). Cambridge, MA: Harvard University Press.

Ferrari, P. F., & Gallese, V. (2007). Mirror neurons and intersubjectivity. In S. Bråten (Ed.), *On being moved: From mirror neurons to empathy* (pp. 73–88). Amsterdam: John Benjamins.

Finzi, E., & Wasserman, E. A. (2006). Treatment of depression with Botulinum Toxin A: A case series. *Dermatologic Surgery, 32*, 645–650.

Flavell, J. H. (1986). The development of children's knowledge about the appearance-reality distinction. *American Psychologist, 41*, 418–425.

Flavell, J. H. (1993). The development of children's understanding of false belief and the appearance-reality distinction. *International Journal of Psychology, 28*, 595–604.

Fonagy, P. (1999). Memory and therapeutic action. *International Journal of Psychoanalysis, 80*, 215–223.

Fonagy, P., & Bateman, A. (2013). Mentalization-based treatment. *Psychoanalytic Inquiry, 33*, 595–613.

Fosshage, J. L. (2000). The meanings of touch in psychoanalysis: A time for reassessment. *Psychoanalytic Inquiry, 20*, 21–43.

Foucault, M. (1972). *The archeology of knowledge & The discourse on language* (A. M. S. Smith, Trans.). New York: Pantheon. (Original work published 1969 & 1971)

Foucault, M. (1980). The confession of the flesh (C. Gordon, L. Marshall, J. Mepham, & K. Soper, Trans.). In C. Gordon (Ed.), *Power/knowledge: Selected interviews & other writings* (pp. 194–228). New York: Pantheon Books. (Original work published 1977)

Foucault, M. (1994). *The birth of the clinic: An archaeology of medical perception* (A. M. Sheridan Smith, Trans.). New York: Vintage Books. (Original work published 1973)

Foucault, M. (1995). *Discipline and Punish: The Birth of the Prison* (A. Sheridan, Trans.). New York: Vintage Books. (Original work published 1979)

Foucault, M. (2000). *Power* (R. Hurley & Others, Trans.). New York: New Press.

Foucault, M. (2006a). *History of madness* (J. Murphy & J. Khalfa, Trans.). London: Routledge. (Original work published 1961)

Foucault, M. (2006b). *Psychiatric Power: Lectures at the College de France 1973–1974* (G. Burchell, Trans., J. Langange, Ed.). New York: Palgrave Macmillan. (Original work published 2003)

Frank, J. D. (1973). *Persuasion and healing: A comparative study of psychotherapy*. Baltimore, MD: Johns Hopkins Press.

Frank, J. D., & Frank, J. B. (1993). *Persuasion & Healing: A comparative study of psychotherapy* (3rd ed.). Baltimore, MD: Johns Hopkins Press.

Freed, P. J., Yanagihara, T. K., Hirsch, J., & Mann, J. J. (2009). Neural mechanisms of grief regulation. *Biological Psychiatry, 66*, 33–40.

Freeman, A. (Ed.). (2006). *Consciousness and its place in nature: Does physicalism entail panpsychism?* Exeter: Imprint Academic.

Freeman, W. J. (1995). *How brains make up their minds*. London: Weidenfeld & Nicolson.

Freeman, W. J., & Barrie, J. M. (2001). Chaotic oscillations and the genesis of meaning in cerebral cortex. In W. Sulis & I. Trofimova (Eds.), *Nonlinear dynamics in the life and social sciences* (pp. 13–37). Amsterdam: IOS Press.

Freeman, W. J., Chang, H. J., Burke, B. C., Rose, P. A., & Badler, J. (1997). Taming chaos: Stabilization of aperiodic attractors by noise. *IEEE Transactions on Circuits and Systems – I: Theory and Applications, 44*, 989–996.

Freud, A. (1965). *The writings of Anna Freud: Vol. 6. Normality and pathology in childhood: Assessments of development*. New York: International Universities Press.

Freud, S. (1953a). The interpretation of dreams. In J. Strachey (Ed.), *Standard edition* (Vols. 4 & 5). London: Hogarth Press. (Original work published 1900)

Freud, S. (1953b). Three essays on the theory of sexuality. In J. Strachey (Ed.), *Standard edition* (Vol. 12, pp. 130–243). London: Hogarth Press. (Original work published 1905)

Freud, S. (1955a). Dreams and telepathy. In J. Strachey (Ed.), *Standard edition* (Vol. 18, pp. 177–193). London: Hogarth Press. (Original work published 1941 [1922])

Freud, S. (1955b). Lines of advance in psycho-analytic therapy. In J. Strachey (Ed.), *Standard edition* (Vol. 17, pp. 157–168). London: Hogarth Press. (Original work published 1919 [1918])

Freud, S. (1955c). Notes upon a case of obsessional neurosis. In J. Strachey (Ed.), *Standard edition* (Vol. 10, pp. 155–318). London: Hogarth Press. (Original work published 1909)

Freud, S. (1955d). The "uncanny." In J. Strachey (Ed.), *Standard edition* (Vol. 17, pp. 219–256). London: Hogarth Press. (Original work published 1919)

Freud, S. (1957). The unconscious. In J. Strachey (Ed.), *Standard edition* (Vol. 14, pp. 166–215). London: Hogarth Press. (Original work published 1915)

Freud, S. (1959a). An autobiographical study. In J. Strachey (Ed.), *Standard edition* (Vol. 20, pp. 7–74). London: Hogarth Press. (Original work published 1925)

Freud, S. (1959b). Inhibition, symptom, and anxiety. In J. Strachey (Ed.), *Standard edition* (Vol. 20, pp. 87–178). London: Hogarth Press. (Original work published 1926)

Freud, S. (1961a). The ego and the id. In J. Strachey (Ed.), *Standard edition* (Vol. 19, pp. 12–66). London: Hogarth Press. (Original work published 1923)

Freud, S. (1961b). Some additional notes on dream interpretation as a whole. In J. Strachey (Ed.), *Standard edition* (Vol. 19, pp. 127–138). London: Hogarth Press. (Original work published 1925)

Freud, S. (1964). Analysis terminable and interminable. In J. Strachey (Ed.), *Standard edition* (Vol. 23). London: Hogarth Press. (Original work published 1937)

Freud, S. (2005). *The unconscious* (G. Frankland, Trans.). London: Penguin Books. (Original work published 1911, 1915, 1925, 1927, 1940)

Freud, S. (2006). *Interpreting dreams* (J. A. Underwood, Trans.). London: Penguin Books. (Original work published 1899)

Frommer, M. S. (2013). When the analyst's protected space is breached: Commentary on paper by Stephanie R. Brody. *Psychoanalytic Dialogues, 23*, 59–71.

Gabbard, G. O. (2000). Consultation from the consultant's perspective. *Psychoanalytic Dialogues, 10*, 209–218.

Gaensbauer, T. J. (2011). Embodied simulation, mirror neurons, and the reenactment of trauma in early childhood. *Neuropsychoanalysis, 13*, 91–107.

Galin, D. (1974). Implications for psychiatry of left and right cerebral specialization: A neurophysiological context for unconscious processes. *Archives of General Psychiatry, 31*, 572–583.

Gallagher, H. L., & Frith, C. D. (2003). Functional imaging of "theory of mind." *Trends in Cognitive Sciences, 7*, 77–83.

Gallese, V. (2005). Embodied simulation: From neurons to phenomenal experience. *Phenomenology and the cognitive sciences, 4*, 23–48.

Gallese, V. (2007). Before and below "theory of mind": Embodied simulation and the neural correlates of social cognition. *Philosophical Transactions of the Royal Society Biological Sciences, 362*, 659–669.

Gallese, V. (2009). Mirror neurons, embodied simulation, and the neural basis of social identification. *Psychoanalytic Dialogues, 19*, 519–536.

Gallese, V., Fadiga, L., Fogassi, L., & Rizzolatti, G. (1996). Action recognition in the premotor cortex. *Brain, 119*, 593–609.

188 References

Gallese, V., & Goldman, A. (1998). Mirror neurons and the simulation theory of mind-reading. *Trends in Cognitive Sciences, 2*, 493–501.

Gallese, V., & Sinigaglia, C. (2011). What is so special about embodied simulation? *Trends in Cognitive Sciences, 15*, 512–519.

George, C., Kaplan, N., & Main, M. (1984). *Adult attachment interview protocol.* Unpublished manuscript, University of California at Berkeley.

George, C., & Solomon, J. (2008). The caregiving system: a behavioral systems approach to parenting. In J. Cassidy & P. R. Shaver (Eds.), *Handbook of attachment: Theory, research, and clinical application* (2nd ed., pp. 833–856). New York: Guilford Press.

Gerson, S. (2004). The relational unconscious: A core element of intersubjectivity, thirdness, and clinical process. *Psychoanalytic Quarterly, 73*, 63–98.

Gill, M. M. (1982). *Analysis of transference: Vol. 1. Theory and technique.* New York: International Universities Press.

Gill, M. M., & Holtzman, P. S. (Eds.). (1976). *Psychology versus metapsychology: Essays in honor of George S. Klein.* New York: International Universities Press.

Gilovich, T., & Griffin, D. (2002). Heuristics and biases: Then and now. In T. Gilovich, D. Griffin, & D. Kahneman (Eds.), *Heuristics and biases: The psychology of intuitive judgment* (pp. 1–18). Cambridge: Cambridge University Press.

Gilovich, T., & Savitsky, K. (2002). Like goes with like: The role of representativeness in erroneous and pseudo-scientific beliefs. In T. Gilovich, D. Griffin, & D. Kahneman (Eds.), *Heuristics and biases: The psychology of intuitive judgment* (pp. 617–624). Cambridge: Cambridge University Press. (Original work published 1996)

Goldman, A., & de Vignemont, F. (2009). Is social cognition embodied? *Trends in Cognitive Sciences, 13*, 154–159.

Goldner, V. (2002). Relational theory and the postmodern turn. In S. Fairfield, L. Layton, & C. Stack (Eds.), *Bringing the plague toward a postmodern psychoanalysis* (pp. 157–165). New York: Other Press.

Gordon, R. (1979). Reflections on curing and healing. *Journal of Analytical Psychology, 24*, 207–217.

Green, M. R. (1964). Her life. In M. R. Green (Ed.), *Interpersonal psychoanalysis: The selected papers of Clara M. Thompson* (pp. 345–377). New York: Basic Books.

Green, M. R. (Ed.). (1964). *Interpersonal psychoanalysis: The selected papers of Clara M. Thompson.* New York: Basic Books.

Greenson, R. R. (1967). *The technique and practice of psychoanalysis.* New York: International Universities Press.

Gregory, R. L. (1997). *Eye and brain: The psychology of seeing* (5th ed.). Princeton, NJ: Princeton University Press.

Groddeck, G. (1976). *The book of the it* (V. M. E. Collins, Trans.). New York: International Universities Press. (Original work published 1923)

Grotstein, J. S. (1979). Who is the dreamer who dreams the dream and who is the dreamer who understands it – A psychoanalytic inquiry into the ultimate nature of being. *Contemporary Psychoanalysis, 15*, 110–169.

Grotstein, J. S. (2004). Spirituality, religion, politics, history, apocalypse and transcendence: An essay on a psychoanalytically and religiously forbidden subject. *International Journal of Applied Psychoanalytic Studies, 1*, 82–95.

Grünbaum, A. (1984). *The foundations of psychoanalysis.* Berkeley: University of California Press.

Guignon, C. B. (2006). Authenticity, moral values, and psychotherapy. In C. B. Guignon (Ed.), *Cambridge companion to Heidegger* (2nd ed., pp. 268–292). Cambridge: Cambridge University Press.

Gwande, A. (2014). *Being mortal*. New York: Metropolitan Books.

Hanly, C. (1979). *Existentialism and psychoanalysis*. New York: International Universities Press.

Heidegger, M. (1982). *The basic problems of phenomenology* (Rev. ed., A. Hofstadter, Trans.). Bloomington: Indiana University Press. (Original work published 1975)

Heidegger, M. (2001). *Zollikon seminars: Protocols-conversations-letters* (F. Mayr & R. Askay, Trans.). Evanston, IL: Northwestern University Press. (Original work published 1987)

Heidegger, M. (2008). *Being and time* (J. Macquarrie & E. Robinson, Trans.). New York: Harper Perennial. (Original work published 1927)

Heidegger, M. (2010). *Being and time* (J. Stambaugh & D. J. Schmidt, Trans.). Albany: State University of New York. (Original work published 1927)

Hoffman, I. Z. (1987). The value of uncertainty in psychoanalytic practice. *Contemporary Psychoanalysis, 23*, 205–214.

Hoffman, I. Z. (1992). Some practical implications of a social-constructivist view of the psychoanalytic situation. *Psychoanalytic Dialogues, 2*, 287–304.

Hoffman, I. Z. (1996). The intimate and ironic authority of the psychoanalyst's presence. *Psychoanalytic Quarterly, 65*, 102–136.

Hoffman, I. Z. (1998). *Ritual and spontaneity in the psychoanalytic process*. Hillsdale, NJ: Analytic Press.

Holder, A. (2000). To touch or not to touch: That is the question. *Psychoanalytic Inquiry, 20*, 44–64.

Hollander, E. (2013). Social synchrony and oxytocin: From behavior to genes to therapeutics. *American Journal of Psychiatry, 170*, 1086–1089.

Holmes, D. S. (1990). The evidence for repression: An examination of sixty years of research. In J. L. Singer (Ed.), *Repression and dissociation: Implications for personality theory, psychopathology and health* (pp. 85–102). Chicago, IL: University of Chicago Press.

Holmes, E. A., & Mathews, A. (2010). Mental imagery in emotion and emotional disorders. *Clinical Psychology Review, 30*, 349–362.

Holmes, J. (2010). *Exploring in security: Towards an attachment-informed psychoanalytic psychotherapy*. London: Routledge.

Holt, R. R. (1967). The development of the primary process: a structural view. In R. R. Holt (Ed.), *Motives and thought: Psychological essays in honor of David Rapaport* (pp. 344–383). New York: International Universities Press.

Homer (1998). *The Iliad* (R. Fagles, Trans.). New York: Penguin Books.

Hoppe, K. D. (1977). Split brains and psychoanalysis. *Psychoanalytic Quarterly, 46*, 220–244.

Husserl, E. (1970). *The crisis of European sciences and transcendental phenomenology* (D. Cairns, Trans.). Evanston, IL: Northwestern University Press. (Original work published 1937)

Husserl, E. (1977). *Phenomenological psychology: Lectures, summer semester; 1925* (J. Scanlon, Trans.). The Hague: Martinus Nijhoff. (Original work published 1925)

Husserl, E. (1983). *Ideas pertaining to a pure phenomenology and to a phenomenological philosophy. First book. General introduction to a pure phenomenology* (F. Kersten, Trans.). New York: Springer. (Original work published 1913)

Husserl, E. (1999). *Cartesian Meditations* (D. Cairns, Trans.). Dordrecht: Springer. (Original work published 1931)

Iacoboni, M. (2007). Face to face: The neural basis of social mirroring and empathy. *Psychiatric Annals, 37*(4), 236–241.

Iacoboni, M. (2008). *Mirroring people: The new science of how we connect with people*. New York: Farrar, Strauss and Giroux.

Iacoboni, M., Molnar-Szakacs, I., Gallese, V., Buccino, G., Mazziotta, J. C., & Rizzolatti, G. (2005). Grasping intentions of others with one's own mirror neuron system. *PloS Biology, 3*, e79.

190 References

Iacoboni, M., Woods, R. P., Brass, M., Bekkering, H., Mazziotta, J. C., & Rizzolatti, G. (1999). Cortical mechanisms of human imitation. *Science, 286*(5449), 2526–2528.

Ingram, D. H. (1997). Reassurance in analytic therapy. *American Journal of Psychoanalysis, 57*, 221–241.

James, W. (2007). *Principles of psychology* (Vol. 1). New York: Cosimo. (Original work published 1893)

Jaynes, J. (1977). *The origins of consciousness in the breakdown of the bicameral mind.* Boston, MA: Houghton Mifflin.

Jung, C. G. (1968). *The archetypes and the collective unconscious* (Vol. 9, R. F. C. Hull, Trans.). Princeton, NJ: Princeton University Press. (Original work published 1933)

Kafka, H. (1992). To cure or to heal? A clinical and theoretical study of healing processes within psychoanalysis. *International Forum of Psychoanalysis, 1*, 110–118.

Kahneman, D., Slovic, P., & Tversky, A. (Eds.). (1982). *Judgment under uncertainty: Heuristics and biases.* Cambridge: Cambridge University Press.

Kahneman, D., & Tversky, A. (1982a). The simulation heuristic. In D. Kahneman, P. Slovic, & A. Tversky (Eds.), *Judgment under uncertainty: Heuristics and biases* (pp. 201–208). Cambridge: Cambridge University Press.

Kahneman, D., & Tversky, A. (1982b). Variants of uncertainty. *Cognition, 11*, 143–157.

Kahneman, D., & Tversky, A. (2000). Prospect theory: An analysis of decisions under risk. In D. Kahneman & A. Tversky (Eds.), *Choices, values, and frames* (pp. 17–43). Cambridge: Cambridge University Press. (Original work published 1979)

Kandel, E. R. (2001). The molecular biology of memory storage: A dialogue between genes and synapses. *Science, 294*, 1030–1038.

Kandel, E. R. (2006). *In search of memory.* New York: W. W. Norton.

Kandel, E. R., & Tauc, L. (1965). Mechanism of heterosynaptic facilitation in the giant cell of the abdominal ganglion of *Aplysia depilans. Journal of Physiology (London), 181*, 28–47.

Kardiner, A. (1977). *My analysis with Freud.* New York: W. W. Norton.

Kearney, R. (2003). *Strangers, gods, and monsters.* Abingdon: Routledge.

Kinsley, C. H., Bardi, M., Karelina, K., Rima, B., Christon, L., Friedenberg, J., & Griffin, G. (2008). Motherhood induces and maintains behavioral and neural plasticity across the lifespan in the rat. *Archives of Sexual Behavior, 37*, 43–56.

Kinsley, C. H., & Lambert, K. G. (2008). Reproduction-induced neuroplasticity: Natural behavioural and neuronal alterations associated with the production and care of offspring. *Journal of Neuroendocrinology, 20*, 515–525.

Klein, G. S. (1970). *Perception, motives, and personality.* New York: Alfred A. Knopf.

Klein, G. S. (1976). *Psychoanalytic theory.* New York: International Universities Press.

Klein, J. G. (2005). Five pitfalls in decisions about diagnosis and prescribing. *British Medical Journal, 330*, 781–783.

Kohut, H. (1971). *The analysis of the self.* New York: International Universities Press.

Kohut, H. (1977). *The restoration of the self.* New York: International Universities Press.

Kohut, H. (1979). The two analyses of Mr. Z. *International Journal of Psychoanalysis, 60*, 3–27.

Kohut, H. (1984). *How does analysis cure?* (A. Goldberg, Ed.). Chicago, IL: University of Chicago Press.

Kohut, H. (2010). On empathy: Heinz Kohut (1981). *International Journal of Psychoanalytic Self Psychology, 5*, 122–131.

Laszlo, E. (1996). *The systems view of the world: A holistic vision for our time.* Cresskill, NJ: Hampton Press. (Original work published 1972)

Latour, B. (1999). *Pandora's hope: Essays on the reality of science studies.* Cambridge, MA: Harvard University Press.

Latour, B. (2005). *Reassembling the social: An introduction to Actor-Network-Theory*. Oxford: Oxford University Press.

Latour, B., & Woolgar, S. (1986). *Laboratory life: The construction of scientific facts*. Princeton, NJ: Princeton University Press.

Lazar, S. G. (2001). Knowing, influencing, and healing: Paranormal phenomena and implications for psychoanalysis and psychotherapy. *Psychoanalytic Inquiry, 21*, 113–131.

Le Bihan, D., Mangin, J.-F., Poupon, C., Clark, C. A., Pappata, S., Molko, N., & Chabriat, H. (2001). Diffusion tensor imaging: concepts and applications. *Journal of Magnetic Resonance Imaging, 13*, 534–564.

Leffert, M. (2003). Analysis and psychotherapy by telephone: Twenty years of clinical experience. *Journal of the American Psychoanalytic Association, 51*, 101–130.

Leffert, M. (2007). A contemporary integration of modern and postmodern trends in psychoanalysis. *Journal of the American Psychoanalytic Association, 55*, 177–197.

Leffert, M. (2008). Complexity and postmodernism in contemporary theory of psychoanalytic change. *Journal of the American Academy of Psychoanalysis and Dynamic Psychiatry, 36*, 517–542.

Leffert, M. (2010). *Contemporary psychoanalytic foundations*. London: Routledge.

Leffert, M. (2013). *The therapeutic situation in the 21st century*. New York: Routledge.

Leshan, L. (1965). Discussion. *American Journal of Psychoanalysis, 25*, 55–60.

Lichtenberg, J. (2003). A clinician's view of attachment theory and research: A discussion of the papers in three issues of *Psychoanalytic Inquiry*. *Psychoanalytic Inquiry, 2003*, 151–206.

Little, M. I. (1985). Winnicott working in areas where psychotic anxieties predominate: A personal record. *Free Associations, 1*, 9–42.

Loewald, H. W. (1960). On the therapeutic action of psycho-analysis. *International Journal of Psychoanalysis, 41*, 16–33.

Luft, S., & Overgaard, S. (Eds.). (2012). *The Routledge companion to phenomenology*. New York: Routledge.

Lukes, S. (2005). *Power: A radical view* (2nd ed.). New York: Palgrave Macmillan.

Lyons, R. (2011). The spread of evidence-poor medicine via flawed social-network analysis. *Statistics, Politics, and Policy, 2*(1), 1–26.

Lyotard, J. (1988). *The differend* (G. V. D. Abbeele, Trans.). Minneapolis: University of Minnesota Press. (Original work published 1983)

Main, M. (1991). Metacognitive knowledge, metacognitive monitoring, and singular (coherent) vs. multiple (incoherent) model of attachment. In C. M. Parkes, J. Stevenson-Hinde, & P. Marris (Eds.), *Attachment across the life cycle* (pp. 126–159). London: Routledge.

Main, M., Kaplan, N., & Cassidy, J. (1985). Security in infancy, childhood, and adulthood: A move to the level of representation. *Monographs of the Society for Research in Child Development, 50*, 66–104.

Major, R., & Miller, P. (1981). Empathy, antipathy and telepathy in the analytic process. *Psychoanalytic Inquiry, 1*, 449–470.

Malabou, C., & Derrida, J. (2004). *Counterpath* (D. Wills, Trans.). Stanford, CA: Stanford University Press. (Original work published 1999)

Marion, R. (1999). *The edge of organization: Chaos and complexity theories of formal social systems*. Thousand Oaks, CA: Sage.

Martin, A., Wiggs, C. L., Ungerleider, L. G., & Haxby, J. U. (1996). Neural correlates of category-specific knowledge. *Nature, 379*, 649–652.

Martin, A. R. (1949). Reassurance in therapy. *American Journal of Psychoanalysis, 11*, 17–29.

Martin, A. R. (1961). The meaning of suffering in therapy: A roundtable discussion. *American Journal of Psychoanalysis, 21*, 3–4.

192 References

Masschelein, A. (2011). *The unconcept: The Freudian uncanny in late-twentieth-century-theory.* Albany: State University of New York.

Mathews, D. A., Suchman, A. L., & Brandt, W. T., Jr. (1993). Making "connexions": Enhancing the therapeutic potential of patient-clinician relationships. *Annals of Internal Medicine, 118,* 973–977.

May, R. (1958a). The origins and significance of the existential movement in psychology. In R. May, E. Angel, & H. F. Ellenberger (Eds.), *Existence* (pp. 3–36). New York: Simon & Schuster.

May, R. (1958b). Contributions of existential psychotherapy. In R. May, E. Angel, & H. F. Ellenberger (Eds.), *Existence* (pp. 37–91). New York: Simon & Schuster.

May, R. (1964). Creativity and encounter. *American Journal of Psychoanalysis, 24,* 39–43.

May, R. (1966). The problem of will and intentionality in psychoanalysis. *Contemporary Psychoanalysis, 3,* 55–70.

May, R., Angel, E., & Ellenberger, H. F. (Eds.). (1958). *Existence.* New York: Simon & Schuster.

Mayerhoff, M. (1990). *On caring.* New York: Harper Perennial. (Original work published 1971)

McClelland, J. L., & Rumelhart, D. E. (1986). *Parallel distributed processing* (Vol. 2). Cambridge, MA: MIT Press.

McLaughlin, J. T. (2000). The problem and place of physical contact in analytic work: Some reflections on handholding in the analytic situation. *Psychoanalytic Inquiry, 20,* 65–81.

Meehl, P. (1954). *Clinical versus statistical prediction.* Minneapolis: University of Minnesota Press.

Meehl, P. (1991a). Some methodological reflections on the difficulties of psychoanalytic research. In C. A. Anderson & K. Gunderson (Eds.), *Paul E. Meehl: Selected philosophical and methodological papers* (pp. 272–283). Minneapolis: University of Minnesota Press.

Meehl, P. (1991b). Subjectivity in psychoanalytic inference: The nagging persistence of Wilhelm Fliess's Achensee question. In C. A. Anderson & K. Gunderson (Eds.), *Paul E. Meehl: Selected philosophical and methodological papers* (pp. 284–337). Minneapolis: University of Minnesota Press. (Original work published 1983)

Mendelson, M. D. (1995). Psychoanalysis: Healing agent or catalyst? *Contemporary Psychoanalysis, 31,* 106–112.

Merriam-Webster's Collegiate Dictionary (11th ed.). (2005). Springfield, MA: Merriam-Webster.

Merleau-Ponty, M. (2012). *Phenomenology of perception* (D. A. Landes, Trans.). London: Routledge. (Original work published 1945)

Mestre, T. A., Prakesh, S., Marras, C., Tomlinson, G., & Lang, A. E. (2014). Another face of placebo: The lessebo effect in Parkinson disease. *Neurology, 82,* 1402–1409.

Millet, J. P. (1961). The meaning of suffering in therapy. *American Journal of Psychoanalysis, 21,* 8–12.

Mitchell, S. A. (1991). Contemporary perspectives on self: Toward an integration. *Psychoanalytic Dialogues, 1,* 121–147.

Mitchell, S. A. (1992). Commentary on Trop and Stolorow's "Defense analysis in self psychology". *Psychoanalytic Dialogues, 2,* 443–453.

Molière. (1959). *The misanthrope and other plays.* London: Penguin Books.

Molnar-Szakacs, I., & Arzy, S. (2009). Searching for an integrated self-representation. *Communicative and Integrative Biology, 2,* 365–367.

Montgomery, K. (2006). *How doctors think: Clinical judgment and the practice of medicine.* Oxford: Oxford University Press.

Morelli, S. A., Rameson, L. T., & Lieberman, M. D. (2014). The neural components of empathy: Predicting daily prosocial behavior. *Social Cognitive and Affective Neuroscience, 9,* 39–47.

References **193**

Murphy, M. (2013). Navigating night country: Self-disclosure, mortality, community. *Psychoanalytic Dialogues, 23*, 72–74.

Newirth, J. (2003). *Between emotion and cognition: The generative unconscious*. New York: Other Press.

Nisbett, R. E., & Ross, L. (1980). *Human inference: Strategies and shortcomings of social judgment*. Englewood Cliffs, NJ: Prentice Hall.

Nisbett, R. E., & Wilson, T. (1977). Telling more than we can know: Verbal reports on mental processes. *Psychological Review, 84*, 231–259.

Noel, H., & Nyhan, B. (2011). The "unfriending" problem: The consequences of homophily in friendship retention for causal estimates of social influence. *Social Networks, 33*, 211–218.

Nunez, P. L. (2000). Toward a quantitative description of large-scale neocortical dynamic function and EEG. *Behavioral and Brain Sciences, 23*, 371–398.

Ogden, T. H. (1994). The analytic third: Working with intersubjective clinical facts. *International Journal of Psychoanalysis, 75*, 3–19.

Orange, D. (1995). *Emotional understanding: Studies in psychoanalytic epistemology*. New York: Guilford Press.

Orange, D. (2000). Zeddies's relational unconscious: Some further reflections. *Psychoanalytic Psychology, 17*, 488–492.

Orange, D. (2009). Psychoanalysis in a phenomenological spirit. *International Journal of Psychoanalytic Self Psychology, 4*, 119–121.

Orange, D., Atwood, G. E., & Stolorow, R. D. (1997). *Working intersubjectively: Contextualism in psychoanalytic practice*. Hillsdale, NJ: Analytic Press.

Ornstein, A. (1994). Empathy, the interpretive process, and the relativity of psychoanalytic cure. *Canadian Journal of Psychoanalysis, 2*, 103–117.

The Oxford English Dictionary (2nd ed.). (1989). Oxford: Clarendon Press.

Palumbo, S. R. (1999). *The emergent ego: Complexity and coevolution in the psychoanalytic process*. Madison, WI: International Universities Press.

Panksepp, J. (1998). *Affective neuroscience: The foundations of human and animal emotions*. Oxford: Oxford University Press.

Panksepp, J. (2003). At the interface between the affective, behavioral, and cognitive neurosciences: Decoding the emotional feelings of the brain. *Brain and Cognition, 52*, 4–14.

Panksepp, J. (2009). Brain emotional systems and qualities of mental life: From animal models of affect to implications for psychotherapeutics. In D. Fosha, D. J. Siegel, & M. F. Solomon (Eds.), *The healing power of emotion: Affective neuroscience, development, and clinical practice* (pp. 1–26). New York: W. W. Norton.

Panksepp, J., & Biven, L. (2012). *The archaeology of mind: Neuroevolutionary origins of human emotions*. New York: W. W. Norton.

Petersen, T. J. (2006). Enhancing the efficacy of antidepressants with psychotherapy. *Journal of Psychopharmacology, 20*, 19–28.

Petzet, H. W. (1993). *Encounters and dialogues with Martin Heidegger, 1929–1976* (P. Emad & K. Maly, Trans.). Chicago, IL: University of Chicago Press. (Original work published 1983)

Pizer, B. (2000). Negotiating analytic holding: Discussion of Patrick Casement's learning from the patient. *Psychoanalytic Inquiry, 20*, 82–107.

Porges, S. W. (1998). Love: An emergent property of the mammalian autonomic nervous system. *Psychoneuroendocrinology, 23*, 837–861.

Porges, S. W. (2009). Reciprocal influences between body and brain in the perception and expression of affect: A polyvagal perspective. In D. Fosha, D. J. Siegel, & M. F. Solomon (Eds.), *The healing power of emotion: Affective neuroscience, development, and clinical practice* (pp. 27–54). New York: W. W. Norton.

194 References

Porges, S. W. (2011). *The polyvagal theory: Neurophysiological foundations of emotions, attachment, communication, and self-regulation.* New York: W. W. Norton.

Proulx, E. A. (1994). *The shipping news.* New York: Scribner.

Radke-Yarrow, M. (1991). Attachment patterns in children of depressed mothers. In C. M. Parkes, J. Stevenson-Hinde, & P. Marris (Eds.), *Attachment across the life cycle* (pp. 115–126). London: Routledge.

Radke-Yarrow, M. (1998). *Children of depressed mothers.* Cambridge: Cambridge University Press.

Rapaport, D. (1960). *The Structure of Psychoanalytic Theory: A Systematizing Attempt.* New York: International Universities Press.

Rapaport, D. (1967). *A theoretical analysis of the superego concept* (M. M. Gill, Ed.). New York: Basic Books. (Original work published 1957)

Rapaport, D., & Gill, M. M. (1959). The points of view and assumptions of metapsychology. *International Journal of Psychoanalysis, 40,* 153–162.

Ratcliffe, M. (2009). Phenomenology, neuroscience, and intersubjectivity. In H. L. Dreyfus & M. A. Wrathall (Eds.), *A companion to phenomenology and existentialism* (pp. 329–345). Chichester: Wiley-Blackwell. (Original work published 2006)

Raune, D., MacLeod, A., & Holmes, E. A. (2005). The simulation heuristic and visual imagery in pessimism for future negative events in anxiety. *Clinical Psychology & Psychotherapy, 12,* 313–325.

Renik, O. (1985). Existentialism and psychoanalysis: Charles Hanly. New York: International Universities Press. 1979. 446 pp. *International Journal of Psychoanalysis, 66,* 516–517.

Renik, O. (1993). Analytic interaction: Conceptualizing techniques in the light of the analyst's irreducible subjectivity. *Psychoanalytic Quarterly, 62,* 553–371.

Renik, O. (2000). Subjectivity and unconsciousness. *Analytic Psychology, 45,* 3–20.

Renik, O. (2007). Intersubjectivity, therapeutic action, and analytic technique. *Psychoanalytic Quarterly, 76S,* 1547–1562.

Risse, G. L., & Gazzaniga, M. S. (1978). Well-kept secrets of the right hemisphere: A carotid amytal study of restricted memory transfer. *Neurology, 28,* 487–495.

Rizzolatti, G., Fadiga, L., Fogassi, L., & Gallese, V. (1996). Premotor cortex and the recognition of motor actions. *Cognitive Brain Research, 3,* 131–141.

Romdenh-Romluc, K. (2012). Maurice Merleau-Ponty. In S. Luft & S. Overgaard (Eds.), *The Routledge companion to phenomenology* (pp. 103–112). New York: Routledge.

Rosenblatt, A. D., & Thickstun, J. (1970). A study of the concept of psychic energy. *International Journal of Psychoanalysis, 51,* 265–278.

Rosenblatt, A. D., & Thickstun, J. T. (1977). *Modern psychoanalytic concepts in a general psychology* (Vols. 42/43). New York: International Universities Press.

Ross, M., & Sicoly, F. (1982). Egocentric biases in availability and attribution. In D. Kahneman, P. Slovic, & A. Tversky (Eds.), *Judgement under uncertainty: Heuristics and biases* (pp. 177–189). Cambridge: Cambridge University Press. (Original work published 1979)

Royle, N. (2003). *The uncanny.* Manchester: Manchester University Press.

Rozin, P., Millman, L., & Nemeroff, C. (1986). Operation of the laws of sympathetic magic in disgust and other domains. *Journal of Personality and Social Psychology, 50,* 703–712.

Rozin, P., & Nemeroff, C. (2002). Sympathetic magical thinking: The contagion and similarity "heuristics". In T. Gilovich, D. Griffin, & D. Kahneman (Eds.), *Heuristics and biases: The psychology of intuitive judgement* (pp. 201–216). Cambridge: Cambridge University Press.

Ruderman, E. G. (2000). Intimate communications: The values and boundaries of touch in the psychoanalytic setting. *Psychoanalytic Inquiry, 20,* 108–123.

Rumelhart, D. E., & McClelland, J. L. (1986). *Parallel distributed processing* (Vol. 1). Cambridge, MA: MIT Press.

Safran, J. D. (2006). The relational unconscious: The enchanted interior, and the return of the repressed. *Contemporary Psychoanalysis, 42*, 393–412.

Safran, J. D. (2012). *Psychoanalysis and psychoanalytic therapies (Theories of psychotherapy)*. Washington, DC: American Psychological Association.

Safranski, R. (2002). *Martin Heidegger: Between good and evil* (E. Osers, Trans.). Cambridge, MA: Harvard University Press. (Original work published 1999)

Sagi, Y., Tavor, I., Hofstetter, F., Tzur-Moryosef, S., Blumenfeld-Katzir, T., & Assaf, Y. (2012). Learning in the fast lane: new insights into neuroplasticity. *Neuron, 73*, 1195–1203.

Sandler, J. (1983). Reflections on some relations between psychoanalytic concepts and psychoanalytic practice. *International Journal of Psychoanalysis, 64*, 35–45.

Sartre, J.-P. (2003). *Being and nothingness* (H. Barnes, Trans.). London: Routledge. (Original work published 1943)

Schachtel, E. (1959). *Metamorphosis*. New York: Basic Books.

Schachter, J., & Kächele, H. (2007). The analyst's role in healing: Psychoanalysis-plus. *Psychoanalytic Psychology, 24*, 429–444.

Schacter, D. L. (1992). Understanding implicit memory: A cognitive neuroscience approach. *American Psychologist, 47*, 559–569.

Schacter, D. L. (1996). *Searching for memory*. New York: Basic Books.

Schacter, D. L. (2001). *The seven sins of memory*. Boston, MA: Houghton Mifflin.

Schacter, D. L., Addis, D. R., & Buckner, R. L. (2008). Episodic simulation of future events: Concepts, data, and applications. *Annals of the New York Academy of Science, 1124*, 39–60.

Schafer, R. (1976). *A new language for psychoanalysis*. New Haven, CT: Yale University Press.

Schafer, R. (1979). On becoming a psychoanalyst of one persuasion or another. *Contemporary Psychoanalysis, 15*, 345–360.

Schafer, R. (2005). Caring and coercive aspects of the psychoanalytic situation. *Journal of the American Psychoanalytic Association, 53*, 771–787.

Schlessinger, H. J., & Appelbaum, A. H. (2000). When words are not enough. *Psychoanalytic Inquiry, 20*, 124–143.

Schneider, K. J., Galvin, J., & Serlin, I. (2009). Rollo May on Existential psychotherapy. *Journal of Humanistic Psychology, 49*, 419–434.

Schore, A. N. (1994). *Affect regulation and the origin of the self*. Hillsdale, NJ: Lawrence Erlbaum Associates.

Schore, A. N. (2002). Neuropsychoanalysis, attachment theory, and trauma research: Implications for self psychology. *Psychoanalytic Inquiry, 22*, 433–484.

Schore, A. N. (2003a). *Affect dysregulation and disorders of the self*. New York: W. W. Norton.

Schore, A. N. (2003b). *Affect regulation and the repair of the self*. New York: W. W. Norton.

Schore, A. N. (2005). A neuropsychoanalytic viewpoint: Commentary on paper by Steven H. Knoblauch. *Psychoanalytic Dialogues, 15*, 829–854.

Schore, A. N. (2009). Right-brain affect regulation: An essential mechanism of development, trauma, dissociation, and psychotherapy. In D. Fosha, D. J. Siegel, & M. F. Solomon (Eds.), *The healing power of emotion: Affective neuroscience, development, and clinical practice* (pp. 112–144). New York: W. W. Norton.

Schore, A. N. (2011). The right brain implicit self lies at the core of psychoanalysis. *Psychoanalytic Dialogues, 21*, 75–100.

Scott, C. M. (1962). Symposium: A reclassification of psychopathological states. *International Journal of Psychoanalysis, 43*, 344–350.

196 References

Serres, M., & Latour, B. (2011). *Conversations on science, culture, and time* (R. Lapidus, Trans.). Ann Arbor: University of Michigan Press. (Original work published 1990)

Shalizi, C. R., & Thomas, A. C. (2011). Homophily and contagion are generically confounded in observational social network studies. *Sociological Methods and Research, 40*, 211–239.

Shamay-Tsoory, S. (2011). The neural basis for empathy. *Neuroscientist, 17*, 18–24.

Shane, M., Shane, E., & Gales, M. (1997). *Intimate attachments: Towards a new self psychology.* New York: Guilford Press.

Shane, M., Shane, E., & Gales, M. (2000). Psychoanalysis unbound: A contextual consideration of boundaries from a developmental systems self psychology perspective. *Psychoanalytic Inquiry, 20*, 144–159.

Shapiro, R. (1995). The idiosyncratic nature of cure. *Contemporary Psychoanalysis, 31*, 133–139.

Sharpe, E. F. (1968). *Collected papers on psycho-analysis.* London: Hogarth Press. (Original work published 1950)

Shevrin, H. (2003). The consequences of abandoning a comprehensive psychoanalytic theory: revisiting Rapaport's systematizing attempt. *Journal of the American Psychoanalytic Association, 51*, 1005–1020.

Siegel, D. J. (2009). Emotion as integration. In D. Fosha, D. J. Siegel, & M. F. Solomon (Eds.), *The healing power of emotion: Affective neuroscience, development & clinical practice* (pp. 145–171). New York: W. W. Norton.

Simon, H. A. (1956). Rational choice and the structure of the environment. *Psychological Review, 63*, 129–138.

Simpson, J. A. (1994). Stress and secure base relationships in adulthood. In K. Bartholomew & D. Perlman (Eds.), *Advances in personal relationships* (Vol. 5, pp. 181–204). London: Kingsley.

Singer, J. L. (Ed.). (1990). *Repression and dissociation: Implications for personality theory, psychopathology and health.* Chicago, IL: University of Chicago Press.

Skolnikoff, A. Z. (2004). The quest for a unified psychoanalytic theory: A retreat from uncertainty. *Psychoanalytic Inquiry, 24*, 86–105.

Slade, A. (1999a). Attachment theory and research: Implications for the theory and practice of individual psychotherapy with adults. In J. Cassidy & P. R. Shaver (Eds.), *Handbook of attachment: Theory, research, and clinical applications* (pp. 575–594). New York: Guilford Press.

Slade, A. (1999b). Representation, symbolization, and affect regulation in the concomitant treatment of a mother and child: Attachment theory and child psychotherapy. *Psychoanalytic Inquiry, 19*, 797–830.

Slochower, J. (2014). *Holding and psychoanalysis: A relational perspective* (2nd ed.). London: Routledge.

Slovic, P., Finucane, M., Peters, E., & MacGregor, D. G. (2002). The affect heuristic. In T. Gilovich, D. Griffin, & D. Kahneman (Eds.), *Heuristics and biases: The psychology of intuitive judgment* (pp. 397–420). Cambridge: Cambridge University Press.

Sperry, R. W., Gazzaniga, M. S., & Bogen, J. E. (1969). The neocortical commissures: Syndromes of hemisphere disconnection. In P. J. Vinken & G. W. Bruyn (Eds.), *Handbook of clinical neurology* (Vol. 4). Amsterdam: North Holland.

Spezzano, C. (1995). "Classical" vs. "contemporary" theory: The differences that matter clinically. *Contemporary Psychoanalysis, 31*(1), 20–45.

Spitz, R. (1965). *The first year of life.* New York: International Universities Press.

Sporns, O. (2011). *Networks of the brain.* Cambridge, MA: MIT Press.

Spreng, R. N., Mar, R. A., & Kim, A. S. N. (2008). The common neural basis of autobiographical memory, prospection, navigation, theory of mind, and the default mode: A quantitative meta-analysis. *Journal of Cognitive Neuroscience, 21*, 489–510.

Spunt, R. P., Satpute, A. B., & Lieberman, M. D. (2010). Identifying the what, why, and how of an observed action: An fMRI study of mentalizing and mechanizing during action observation. *Journal of Cognitive Neuroscience, 23*, 63–74.

Stern, D. B. (1991). A philosophy for the embedded analyst – Gadamer's hermeneutics and the social paradigm of psychoanalysis *Contemporary Psychoanalysis, 27*, 51–80.

Stern, D. B. (1997). *Unformulated experience*. Hillsdale, NJ: Analytic Press.

Stern, D. B. (2012). Implicit theories of technique and the values that inspire them. *Psychoanalytic Inquiry, 32*, 33–49.

Stern, D. N., Sander, L. W., Nahum, J. P., Harrison, A. M., Lyons-Ruth, K., Morgan, A. C., . . . Tronick, E. Z. (1998). Non-interpretive mechanisms in psychoanalytic therapy: The "something more" than interpretation. *International Journal of Psychoanalysis, 79*, 903–921.

Stern, S. (2002). The self as a relational structure: A dialogue with multiple-self theory. *Psychoanalytic Dialogues, 12*, 693–714.

Stolorow, R. D. (1990). Converting psychotherapy to psychoanalysis: A critique of the underlying assumptions. *Psychoanalytic Inquiry, 10*, 119–130.

Stolorow, R. D. (2002). From drive to affectivity: Contextualizing psychological life. *Psychoanalytic Inquiry, 22*, 678–685.

Stolorow, R. D. (2011). *World, affectivity, trauma*. New York: Routledge.

Stolorow, R. D., & Atwood, G. E. (1992). *Contexts of being*. Hillsdale, NJ: Analytic Press.

Stolorow, R. D., Atwood, G. E., & Brandshaft, B. (1994). *The intersubjective perspective*. Northvale: Jason Aronson.

Stolorow, R. D., Orange, D., & Atwood, G. E. (2002). *Worlds of experience: Interweaving philosophical and clinical dimensions in psychoanalysis*. New York: Basic Books.

Strachey, J. (1934). The nature of the therapeutic action of psycho-analysis. *International Journal of Psychoanalysis, 15*, 127–159.

Strawson, G. (2006). Realistic monism: Why physicalism entails panpsychism. *Journal of Consciousness Studies, 13*(10–11), 3–31.

Strupp, H. H. (1978). Suffering and psychotherapy. *Contemporary Psychoanalysis, 14*, 73–97.

Strupp, H. H. (1982). Is the medical model appropriate for psychoanalysis? *Journal of the American Academy of Psychoanalysis and Dynamic Psychiatry, 10*, 123–128.

Strupp, H. H., Fox, R. E., & Lessler, K. (1969). *Patients view their psychotherapy*. Baltimore, MD: Johns Hopkins Press.

Sullivan, H. S. (1970). *The psychiatric interview*. New York: W. W. Norton. (Original work published 1954)

Sullivan, H. S. (1971a). The data of psychiatry. In *The fusion of psychiatry and the social sciences* (pp. 32–55). New York: Wiley. (Original work published 1938)

Sullivan, H. S. (1971b). The illusion of personal individuality. In *The fusion of psychiatry and the social sciences* (pp. 198–226). New York: W. W. Norton. (Original work published 1950)

Sullivan, H. S. (1997). *The interpersonal theory of psychiatry*. New York: W. W. Norton. (Original work published 1953)

Szasz, T. S. (1961). The meaning of suffering in therapy. *American Journal of Psychoanalysis, 21*, 12–17.

Taylor, S. E., Pham, L. B., Rivkin, I. D., & Armor, D. A. (1998). Harnessing the imagination: Mental simulation, self-regulation, and coping. *American Psychologist, 53*, 429–439.

Taylor, S. E., & Schneider, S. K. (1989). Coping and the simulation of events. *Social Cognition, 7*, 174–194.

Teicholz, J. G. (1999). *Kohut, Loewald and the postmoderns*. Hillsdale, NJ: Analytic Press.

Tessman, L. H. (2003). *The analyst's analyst within*. Hillsdale, NJ: Analytic Press.

198 References

Trevarthen, C. (1974). Conversation with a two-month-old. *New Scientist, 2,* 230–235.

Trevarthen, C. (2009). The function of emotion in infancy: The regulation and communication of rhythm, sympathy and meaning in human development. In D. Fosha, D. J. Siegel, & M. F. Solomon (Eds.), *The healing power of emotion: Affective neuroscience, development & clinical practice* (pp. 55–85). New York: W. W. Norton.

Tulving, E. (2003). Memory and consciousness. In B. J. Baars, W. P. Banks, A. Tversky, D. Kahneman, & J. B. Newman, (Eds.), *Essential sources in the scientific study of consciousness* (pp. 575–591). Cambridge, MA: MIT Press. (Original work published 1985)

Tversky, A., & Kahneman, D. (1982a). Belief in the law of small numbers. In D. Kahneman, P. Slovic, & A. Tversky (Eds.), *Judgement under uncertainty: Heuristics and biases* (pp. 23–31). Cambridge: Cambridge University Press. (Original work published 1971)

Tversky, A., & Kahneman, D. (1982b). Judgment under uncertainty: Heuristics and biases. In D. Kahneman, P. Slovic, & A. Tversky (Eds.), *Judgment under uncertainty: Heuristics and biases* (pp. 3–20). Cambridge: Cambridge University Press. (Original work published 1974)

Tversky, A., & Kahneman, D. (2000a). Advances in Prospect Theory: Cumulative representation of uncertainty. In D. Kahneman & A. Tversky (Eds.), *Choices, values, and frames* (pp. 44–65). Cambridge: Cambridge University Press. (Original work published 1992)

Tversky, A., & Kahneman, D. (2000b). Rational choice and the framing of decisions. In D. Kahneman & A. Tversky (Eds.), *Choices, values, and frames* (pp. 209–223). Cambridge: Cambridge University Press. (Original work published 1986)

Uddin, L. Q., Iacoboni, M., Lange, C., & Keenan, J. P. (2007). The self and social cognition: the role of cortical midline structures and mirror neurons. *Trends in Cognitive Sciences, 11,* 153–157.

von Senden, M. (1960). *Space and sight: The perception of space and shape in the congenitally blind before and after operation* (S. Schweppe, Trans.). London: Methuen. (Original work published 1932)

Waelder, R. (1963). Psychic determinism and the possibility of predictions. *Psychoanalytic Quarterly, 32,* 15–42.

Wager, T. D., Rilling, J. K., Smith, E. E., Sokolic, A., Casey, K. L., Davidson, R. J., Cohen, J. D. (2004). Placebo induced changes in fMRI in anticipation and experience of pain. *Science, 303,* 1162–1167.

Wallerstein, R. S. (2006). The relevance of Freud's psychoanalysis in the 21st century. *Psychoanalytic Psychology, 23,* 302–326.

Watson, J. (1985). *Nursing: The philosophy and science of caring.* Niwot: University of Colorado. (Original work published 1979)

Watt, D. (2007). Toward a neuroscience of empathy: Integrating affective and cognitive perspectives. *Neuropsychoanalysis, 9,* 119–140.

Weiss, F. A. (1961). The meaning of suffering in therapy. *American Journal of Psychoanalysis, 21,* 17–21.

Wenkart, A. (1961). The meaning of suffering in therapy. *American Journal of Psychoanalysis, 21,* 21–26.

Wheeler, J. A., & Zurek, H. (1983). *Quantum theory and measurement.* Princeton, NJ: Princeton University Press.

Wheelis, A. (1956). Will and psychoanalysis. *Journal of the American Psychoanalytic Association, 4,* 285–303.

Willingham, D. B., & Preuss, L. (1995). The death of implicit memory. *Psyche, 2*(15).

Winnicott, D. W. (1955). Metapsychological and clinical aspects of regression within the psycho-analytical set-up. *International Journal of Psychoanalysis, 36,* 16–26.

Winnicott, D. W. (1965). *The maturational processes and the facilitating environment*. New York: International Universities Press.

Winnicott, D.W. (1972). *Holding and interpretation: Fragment of analysis*. New York: Grove Press.

Winnicott, D. W. (1975a). Anxiety associated with insecurity. In Winnicott, D. W. (Ed.), *Through paediatrics to psycho-analysis* (pp. 97–100). New York: Basic Books. (Original work published 1952)

Winnicott, D. W. (1975b). Primitive emotional development. In Winnicott, D. W. (Ed.), *Through paediatrics to psycho-analysis* (pp. 145–156). New York: Basic Books. (Original work published 1945)

Winnicott, D. W. (1975c). Withdrawal and regression. In Winnicott, D. W. (Ed.), *Through paediatrics to psycho-analysis* (pp. 255–261). New York: Basic Books. (Original work published 1954)

Wittenberg, E. G. (1987). Clinical innovations and theoretical controversy. *Contemporary Psychoanalysis, 23*, 183–198.

Wittgenstein, L. (1953). *Philosophical investigations* (G. E. M. Anscombe, Trans.). Oxford: Blackwell.

Wolford, G., Miller, M. B., & Gazzaniga, M. S. (2004). Split decisions. In M. S. Gazzaniga (Ed.), *The cognitive neurosciences III* (pp. 1189–1209). Cambridge, MA: MIT Press.

Wollmer, M. A., de Boer, C., Kalak, N., Beck, J., Götz, T., Schmidt, T., . . . Kruger, T. H. (2012). Facing depression with botulinum toxin: A randomized controlled trial. *Journal of Psychiatric Research, 46*, 574–581.

Yalom, I. D. (1980). *Existential psychotherapy*. New York: Basic Books.

Yalom, I. D., & Elkin, G. (1974). *Every day gets a little bit closer: A twice-told therapy*. New York: Basic Books.

Zahavi, D. (2012). Intersubjectivity. In S. Luft & S. Overgaard (Eds.), *The Routledge companion to phenomenology* (pp. 180–189). London: Routledge.

Zaidel, E., & Iacoboni, M. (Eds.). (2003). *The parallel brain: The cognitive neuroscience of the corpus callosum*. Cambridge, MA: MIT Press.

Zajonc, R. B. (1980). Feeling and thinking: Preferences need no inferences. *American Psychologist, 35*, 151–175.

Zeddies, T. J. (2000). Within, outside and in between: The relational unconscious. *Psychoanalytic Psychology, 17*, 467–487.

INDEX

action intension 43
Adjustment Heuristic 112, 118
Adler, Herbert 148, 173
adrenocorticotrophic hormone
(ACTH) 162
Adult Attachment Interview (AAI) 166–8
Affect Heuristic 119–20
Ainsworth, M.D.S. 129
Allik, T. 85
American Psychiatric Association 137
American Psychoanalytic Association
(APsaA) 31, 48
amygdala 70
analysis *see* psychoanalysis
analysts *see* therapists
anchoring 112
Angst 59; *see also* anxiety
anxiety 59, 107, 115, 177, 178; from a
phenomenological standpoint 58–60
appearances 38
Arendt, Hannah 35
Arzy, S. 25
Askay, R. 51, 76
Asperger's syndrome 20
attachment 23–4, 32; deficient 20; healthy
vs. pathological forms 129; insecure 22,
117; research on 129; secure 24, 121, 127,
129, 163, 173
attachment theory 166–8
Atwood, G.E. 75
autonomic nervous system 43, 59, 77,
148, 163

autres 15
Availability Heuristic 110–13, 115, 118,
120, 164

Baars, Bernard J. 69, 82
Bachelard, Gaston 170
Balint, M. 132
Baron-Cohen, S. 3
The Basic Problems of Phenomenology
(Heidegger) 57
Beebe, B. 166
behavior reading 164
Being and Time (Heidegger) 35, 57
being-in-the-world 4, 24, 30, 37, 43, 51–2,
55, 63–4, 86, 115, 132, 135, 154, 156,
160, 177; explained 44–6
Benjamin, J. 52
Between Good and Evil (Safranski) 33
biases, egocentric 111
Bieber, I. 138, 139
Binswanger, Ludwig 49
biogenic amines 162
biology 26; *see also* psychobiology
Biven, L. 127, 128
bodily-perceptual awareness 165
body awareness 165
body modeling 165
bonding 17, 127, 128, 130
Boss, Medard 2, 48, 49, 51, 55,
61, 146
boundary violations 145, 146
Bowlby, J. 3, 127, 166

202 Index

brain: laterality of 70–1; physiology of 16, 39, 69, 153; *see also* cerebral hemispheres; Left Brain; Right Brain
brain-heart-face circuit (BHFC) 17, 42
Brandt, L.W. 52
Brentano, F. 54, 74
Bromberg, P.M. 12
Bronx Municipal Hospital Center 31
Buddhist teachings 54
Buechler, S. 138, 139
bulimia 29

Caper, R. 156, 160
care: in the context of relationship 132; diagnosis and 133; examples of 130–1; of the medical patient 130–6; of patients 124–5, 142–51; nature of 126; phylogeny of 126–30; in psychoanalysis and psychotherapy 8, 126, 136–7
care studies 126
"Caring and Coercive Aspects of the Psychoanalytic Situation" (Schafer) 142
Carman, T. 37
Cartesian dualism *see* mind-body (Cartesian) dualism
case studies: Adam 179; Bill 87; Carol 55–6; Ellen 178; Joan 154–5; Joe 97–8, 149–50, 171; June 169–70; Peter 116–17; Robert 179–80; Roger 21–4, 63–7, 105, 109, 150–1, 170–1; Sarah 173–4; Sharon 140–1; Tom 143–4
Casement, P.J. 146–7
Cassell. E.J. 134–5
Celan, Paul 35
cerebral hemispheres 25, 42, 68, 70–1, 73–4, 77–8, 88; *see also* Left Brain; Right Brain
Childhood and Society (Erikson) 46
Christakis, N.A. 27–8, 45, 78, 88, 92
chronic conditions 159
Citalopram 107
Clinical Versus Statistical Prediction (Meehl) 102, 107
Coan, J.A. 128
cognition: embodied 164; primary process 117
cognitive-behavioral therapy (CBT) 177
cognitive sciences 37, 39
collective unconscious 88; *see also* unconscious
Coltrera, J.T. 96
commisurectomies 70
complexity 32, 39
Complexity Theory 1, 100
conceptual priming 175–6

consciousness 161; directedness of 36; and the self 11; and unconsciousness 79
contagion 26, 27–9, 88, 90–1, 111, 163; emotional 163; magical 119
Contagion Heuristic 117, 118–19
Contemporary Psychoanalytic Foundations (Leffert) 1–2, 177
contextuality 27
Cooper, P. 125
Cooper, S.H. 99
coping 115
corpus callosum 78
Cortical Midline Structures (CMS) 3, 25–6, 88
countertransference 142–3, 148, 153, 154, 174
Craik, Kenneth 3, 20
creativity 48
cross-mammalian studies 127
cultural studies, and the uncanny 87
cure(s) 165–6; in the doctor-patient relationship 171–6; in psychoanalysis 8, 70, 97, 98, 103n13, 108, 124, 130–4, 136, 151, 153, 156–8, 161; transference 6, 98; *see also* healing

Damasio, Antonio 15, 16
Dasein 2, 4, 30, 37, 39, 43, 51, 52, 55, 56, 57, 60, 69, 74, 86, 91, 94, 156; explained 44–6
Daseinalysis 47–9
Dastur, F. 44
death, challenge of 46, 60
decision-making: and the importance of affect 120; under risk 103–5
deconstruction 3, 11, 32, 38, 40, 61, 62, 100, 151, 155
demonic possession 158
depression 18, 107, 109, 157, 174, 177, 178; maternal 129; neurochemistry of 162
depth, and time 56–8
Depth Psychology 11, 49
Derrida, Jacques 35
Descartes, René 14, 16, 51
diagnosis 22, 112, 129; and care 133
Dialectical Behavior Therapy (DBT) 124
Die Traumdeutung (Freud) 54, 61
différance 10, 15, 136, 157
différends 10, 159
diffusion tensor imaging (DTI) 10, 16
Dimen, M. 157
disautonomy 26
discourse: collegial 163, 171; philosophical 33, 36, 44, 54, 95; therapeutic 3, 5, 7, 10, 18, 61, 75, 76, 81, 84, 95, 98, 99, 100, 108, 110, 112, 122, 125, 133, 135, 136, 155, 162, 163, 168, 169, 173, 175

disease, vs illness 135–6
dispositifs 154
distress vocalizations (DVs) 129, 130
distributed processing systems 25
doctor-patient relationship: development
  of 175–6; healing and cure in 171–6;
  neurobiology of 175
dopamine 162
Dozier, M. 168
dreams: meaning of 54; uncanniness in 88
"Dreams and Telepathy" (Freud) 89–90
Dunbar, R. 92

economics: and the study of uncertainty
  120; view of decision-making by 101
Edelson, M. 50
ego psychology 58
Eigenwelt 4, 55, 136, 140, 153, 154, 175;
  see also being-in-the-world
Eisler, K.R. 96
Ellis, Albert 102
embodied cognition 164
embodied simulation 42, 115, 164
embodiment 36, 164–5
emotion(s) 115; primary process 126;
  role of 17–18
emotional contagion 163
emotional priming 175
emotional systems 127, 146; relational 60
empathy 41, 127–9, 149, 151, 162–4, 168,
  171, 173–5
end-of-life care 160
endogenous opioids 129, 162
epidemiology 26
epilepsy 42, 70
episodic simulation 175
epistemes 58
epistemology, postmodern 133
Erikson, E. 46, 58
everydayness 45–6, 55–7, 60, 63, 65,
  75, 125
Existence and other works (May) 49
Existentialism 26, 48, 51; and
  phenomenology 35–7; and
  psychoanalysis 50
experience, first-person 36

fantasy 57
Farquhar, J. 51, 76
Ferenczi, Sándor 145
Ferrari, P.F. 42
field theory 169
first-person experience 36
first-person ontology 36
flashbacks 115

fMRI 10, 163
folk psychology 41, 164
Foucault, Michel 58
Fowler, J.H. 27–8, 45, 78, 88, 92
Framingham Study 27
Frank, J.B. 174
Frank, J.D. 174
Freeman, Walter 14, 18
Freud, Anna 167
Freud, Sigmund 9, 14, 31 39, 51, 52–3, 56,
  59, 75, 76, 89, 127, 136, 152, 158, 178;
  on dreams 89; on telepathy 89; three
  major discoveries of 54; on the uncanny
  85–6; on uncertainty 95; and the
  unconscious 74
functional brain imaging (fMRI) 10, 163
functional neuroanatomy 39

Galin, D. 73
Gallese, V. 42, 165
gambler's fallacy 106
general utility theory 101
genetic treatments 158
germ theory of infectious disease 119
Gerson, S. 78, 80
Gesammelte Werke (Freud) 53
Gill, M.M. 1, 158
Gilovich, T. 108
glabellar frown lines 17
goals: phenomenological 48; of
  psychotherapy 47
god and spirituality 91–3
Goldner, V. 52
Gordon, R. 158
Greenson, R.R. 154
Groddeck, G. 157
Grotstein, J.S. 79
Grünbaum, A. 50
Guignon, C.B. 53, 156

healing 10n3, 62, 108, 117, 123–7, 131–2,
  136, 150n18, 153–4, 156–9, 161, 165–7;
  in the doctor-patient relationship 171–6;
  phenomenological perspective 157, 180
Heidegger, Martin 2, 4, 30, 32, 33, 35,
  49–55, 61, 76, 79, 132; on Dasein and
  being-in-the-world 44–6; compared
  to Husserl 37–8; and Nazism 33–5;
  on the subject of time 57; theory of
  phenomenology 34; on the uncanny
  85–6; on the unconscious 76; and the
  Zollikon Seminars 48, 49, 51–2, 74, 76
Heisenberg, Werner 96
Heisenberg Uncertainty Principle 5,
  96, 100

204 Index

Helmholz, Hermann von 51
here-and-now transference 154
hermeneutics 30, 38
heuristics 63, 103, 108, 115, 178; adjustment 112, 118; affect 119–20; availability 110–13, 115, 118, 120, 164; cognitive 117–19; contagion 117, 118–19; representation 164; representativeness 109–10, 112–13, 118, 120, 122; similarity 117–18; simulation 113–17, 164–5
Heuristics and Biases (H & B) 102, 105, 108, 112, 122
hippocampus 16, 70, 72
Hoffman, I.Z. 97–9
Holmes, D.S. 73
Holmes, E.A. 115
Holtzman, P.S. 1
homophily 27, 28, 29
Hoppe, K.D. 73
hormones, pro-social 176
human error 103
human inference 103
Husserl, E. 2, 32, 35, 51, 54; compared to Heidegger 37–8; on intersubjectivity 40
hyperdyadic spread 27
hypnotic suggestion 137
hypochondria 97, 149–50
hypothalamic-pituitary-adrenal axis 173
hypothalamus 17

illness, vs. disease 135–6
infectious disease, germ theory of 119
Ingram, D.H. 143
inhibitions, nature of 54
insomnia 97, 149–50
intentionality 36, 54, 64
Internal Working Models (IWMs) 20–1, 23, 24, 168, 175, 178
internalization 166
interpersonal perspective 154
Interpersonal Psychoanalysis 49, 154, 177
The Interpretation of Dreams (Freud) 54, 61
interreferentiality 5, 17, 26, 40
intersubjectivity 43, 112, 163; as phenomenology 40–1
Intersubjectivity Theory 31
intuition 102–3, 106; clinical 102

James, William 9–12
Jaynes, Julian 92
Jung, Carl 49, 51, 80

Kächele, H. 147, 148, 174
Kafka, H. 172
Kahneman, D. 104, 106, 108, 113–14

Klein, George 13, 74
Klein, Melanie 51
knowability 5, 38; *see also* unknowability
knowledge(s): accumulation and deployment of 100; local 32; relationship with power 32; of the subjective 33
Kohut, Heinz 11, 13, 14, 142, 179

Lachmann, F. 166–7
laterality, of the brain 70–1
Latour, Bruno 4, 40
law of large numbers 105
law of small numbers 105–8
laws of sympathetic magic 117
Lazar, S.G. 132
Leffert, Mark 52
Left Brain 3, 92, 108, 111, 112, 114, 158n5, 161–2, 167; and brain laterality 70; and the uncanny 86–7; and the unconscious 73, 74, 77–8, 81; *see also* cerebral hemispheres; Right Brain
Lessebo effect 177
libido theory 58, 146
Lifespan Organizing Principles of Interaction 166–7
limbic system 70, 72
Little, M.I. 146
Lyons, R. 28
Lyotard, J. 159

MacLeod, A. 115
magical contagion 119
magical thinking 117
magnetic resonance images (MRI) 16
Main, M. 3, 166
Major, R. 90
Major Depressive Disorder (MDD) 107n18
MAOIs 162
Martin, A.R. 143
Mathews, D.A. 115, 174
May, Rollo 2, 48, 49, 50, 54, 58, 61, 62, 63
Mayerhoff, M. 132
meaning, co-construction of 99, 100
Meehl, Paul 101–2, 113
melancholia 158
memory(ies) 153; auditory 72; conceptual 72; distortion of 113; encoded 2–3; episodic 5, 72; priming of 72–3; procedural 72; repressed 154; retrieval of 2, 72; semantic 72; unconscious 71–2; visual 72
mental time travel 57
Merleau-Ponty, M. 35, 37
metacognitive modeling 175

metapsychology(ies) 1–2, 11, 14, 38–9, 121; psychoanalytic 32, 68
Miller, M.B. 90
mind-body (Cartesian) dualism 3, 14, 36, 53, 92, 160, 164
mind reading 164
mirror neuron system (MNS) 25–6, 42–3, 76, 82, 88, 163, 164, 165
Mitchell, Stephen 12, 32
Mitwelt 4, 52, 55, 58, 60, 69, 136, 140, 153, 154, 175; *see also* being-in-the-world
modernism 39
Molnar-Szakacs, I. 25
Montgomery, K. 132
mood stabilizers 174
Morell, S.A. 163
mother-child dyad 38n13, 60, 77, 166

narcissistic conditions 20, 21, 179
narrative(s): analysis of 32; and the cerebral hemispheres 42, 87, 108; of Heidegger's life 34, 35; and meaning 160–1; and memory 72, 75, 114; parental 23; of patients 5, 24, 47, 52, 61, 64–7, 75, 83n9, 87, 89, 100, 108, 111, 122, 150, 154–5, 159, 174; of physicians 130, 135; and the uncanny 87
National Socialism (Nazism) 33–5, 41
The Nature of Explanation (Craik) 20
Nazism *see* National Socialism (Nazism)
Nemeroff, C. 117
neocortical brain regions 127
Neo-Kantianism 51
neo-pragmatism 26
networks: single-contagion mid level 27; social 26, 27–30
Network Studies 10, 26–7, 29, 70, 76, 90–1, 154
network theory 27–8; critiques of 28
neuroanatomy 16, 39, 69, 153
neuropeptides 128–9
neuroplasticity 129, 158
Neuropsychoanalysis 15
neuroscience(s) 1, 3, 10, 25, 26, 32, 33, 74, 120, 153, 159, 161–5; affective 126; and attachment theory 128; cognitive 39; foundations of care in 126–30; integration of phenomenology into 37, 38, 39–40; as phenomenology 42–3; recent findings in 42; of the unconscious 77, 80
neurotransmitters 162
Newirth, J. 81
Newton, Isaac 51, 53
Nisbett, R.E. 83, 108, 109–10

nodes 26, 28
Noel, H. 28
norepinephrine 162
Nyhan, B. 28

Object Relations theory 31
Oedipal triangle 26
Oedipus complex 52
Ogden, T.H. 78
ontogeny 3
ontology(ies) 39; of being 9; first-person 36; post-Cartesian 36
Orange, D. 30, 52, 75, 80
The Origins of Consciousness in the Breakdown of the Bicameral Mind (Jaynes) 92
Ornstein, A. 157
oxytocin 17, 128–9, 162, 176

pain 178; and psychoanalysis 8; relief of 137–42
palliation 123, 125, 131, 157
Panksepp, Jaak 126, 127, 128, 149
parahippocampus 16
parallel processing 74
patient selection 178–80
patients: care of 142–51; goals of 6–7, 153; needs of 153; phenomenological approach to 61–2; therapists' relationships with 29, 171–6
personal meaning 160
personality disorders 157
pharmacological treatments 158
pharmacotherapy 174
phenomena, study of 38; *see also* phenomenology
phenomenological psychoanalysis 2; American 49–50; goals and substance 50–1
phenomenology 2, 8, 13, 31, 33, 51; according to Heidegger 34, 37–8; according to Husserl 37–8; and anxiety 58–60; clinical 53–6; as different from metapsychology 38–9; existential 37–8; and existentialism 35–7; and the goals of psychotherapy and psychoanalysis 156; and intersubjectivity 39–40; intersubjectivity as 40–1: neuroscience as 42–3; psychoanalytic 32; and social networks 30; three paradigms central to 36; and the unconscious 72
philosophy: and the study of uncertainty 120; and the uncanny 87
phobias 118
phylogeny 3

206 Index

physical sciences, and the study of uncertainty 120
Placebo Effect 8, 175–7
Poetics of Space (Bachelard) 170
Polyvagal Theory 16–17
Porges, Stephen 16–17, 43
positivism, scientific 51
postmodernism 26, 32, 33, 35, 39, 100, 133
Post-Traumatic Stress Disorder (PTSD) 115, 158, 170
power: in the doctor-patient relationship 172–3; perversion of 34; relationship with knowledge 32
prediction 102
pre-frontal cortex 163, 177
Preuss, L. 73
primary process cognition 117
Prospect Theory 69, 104–5
psyche 53
Psychiatric Inquiry 146
psychiatry 172
psychic determinism 53
psychoanalysis 1–2, 8, 10, 38; clinical 60–3; concept of 152–3; desired goals and outcomes of 7, 47, 156–9; and existentialism 50; expanded perspective on 155–61; expanded relational perspective 165–8; Neuro-15; phenomenological and existential critiques of 51–3; and phenomenology 39; vs. psychotherapy 139n13, 153; relief of pain and suffering in 137–42; uncertainty in 94; unconscious 82–4
psychoanalytical styles: British Middle School 13, 31, 141; classical 32, 84, 141, 174; Contemporary 1–2, 7, 9, 11, 14, 27, 40n15, 48n2, 51, 52, 59, 60, 61, 67, 68, 81, 84, 94, 95–6, 99–101, 123, 127, 133, 134, 136, 144, 146, 152, 154, 162, 173–4; existential 33; Freudian 50, 52, 96, 99, 100, 154; interpersonal 49, 54, 177; Intersubjective 69, 84, 153; Kleinian 99, 100; metaphysical 61; non-Freudian 101–2; phenomenological 2, 49–51; Relational 2, 13, 31, 69, 76–84, 96–7, 153, 166, 171; Self- 100
psychobiology 173; *see also* biology
psychology 2, 171–2; ego 58; empirical 101; folk 41, 164; radical ego 12; view of decision-making by 101
psychopathology 5, 32, 129; developmental 20; and the unconscious 68
psychopharmacology 107, 143–4, 177
psychosexual development 59

psychotherapy *see* psychoanalysis; psychoanalytical styles
psychotropic medication *see* psychopharmacology
PTSD *see* Post-Traumatic Stress Disorder (PTSD)
purification 40

Radke-Yarrow, M. 129
Rapaport, D. 12–13
Raune, D. 115
reassurance 143
reconstruction 75, 100–1, 150
regression 21, 55, 75, 102, 142, 146, 171; therapeutic 141, 153
Relational Psychoanalysis *see* psychoanalytical styles, Relational
relational unconscious 70, 78–84
relationships: care in the context of 132; doctor-patient 126, 166, 169; formation of 17; interpersonal 148, 175; inequality in 172; therapeutic 2, 4, 5, 7, 61, 80, 124, 126, 132, 136, 153, 165–6, 168, 172, 174
Renik, O. 97
representation heuristic 164
Representativeness Heuristic 109–10, 112–13, 118, 120, 122
repression 3, 4, 21, 56, 68, 71–6, 79–80, 85–7, 153
research: on attachment 128–9; cross-mammalian 127; in neuroscience 120
Right Brain 5, 38n13, 90, 98, 108, 111, 112, 114, 118, 120, 158n5, 161, 167; and brain laterality 70; and the uncanny 86–7; role of the unconscious 73, 77–8, 81; *see also* cerebral hemispheres; Left Brain
right-brain-to-right-brain communication 98, 112
risk, in psychoanalysis 103–5
Rogers, Carl 102
Ross, M. 108, 109–10
The Routledge Companion to Phenomenology (Luft & Overgaard eds) 36
Rozin, P. 117, 118

Safran, J.D. 80, 81
Safranski, R. 33–5
San Diego Psychoanalytic Institute 31
Sartre, Jean-Paul 35, 37, 49, 50, 51, 53, 61, 76
Savitsky, K. 108
Schachter, J. 2, 113, 147, 148, 174
Schafer, Roy 11, 13, 50, 142
Schneider, K.J. 114
Schore, Allan 15–16, 77

scientific positivism 51
self: contexts of 9; differing views of 11–12; emotions as properties of 18; holistic 14–18, 136; intrapsychic 9; nature of 165; as psychic structure 3, 11; in psychoanalysis 12–14; and self-perception 18–21, 24–5; Post-Cartesian 3–4, 9–10; relationship with consciousness 11; and self-representation 12–13, 18–21, 24–5; as unknowable 15; as unstable identity category 26
self-disclosure, forced 84
self objects 11
self-perception 18–21, 24–5
Self-Psychology 15–16, 31
self-reflection 155
self-regulation 115
self-representation 12–13, 18–21, 24–5
serial processing 74
serotonin 162
sexuality 17
Shalizi, C.R. 28
Shane, M. 147
Shapiro, R. 157
Shevrin, H. 97
Siegel, D.J. 163–4
Similarity Heuristic 117–18
simulation, embodied 42, 115, 164
Simulation Heuristic 113–17, 164–5
simulation theory 164
Skolnikoff, A.Z. 97
Slade, A. 65
Slochower, J. 146
Slovic, P. 120
SNRIs 162
social anxiety 116
social bonding 130
social cognition 164
social embedding 26
Social Network Theory 88, 163
social networks 26, 27–8, 39, 69, 93; clinical considerations about 29–30; and the collective unconscious 88
social science 26
social understanding 165
Society for Psychical Research 89
sociology: and the study of uncertainty 120; view of decision-making by 101
sociophysiology of caring 173
space, and the therapeutic relationship 169–70
Spezzano, C. 76
spirituality and god 91–3
split-brain studies 73
SSRIs 162
Stern, D.B. 12, 53, 80

Stolorow, R.D. 14, 30, 45, 52, 61, 75
Strachey, J. 59
Strange Situation 129
stranger anxiety 116
stress, neurochemistry of 162
stress hormones 149
Strupp, H.H. 139, 141, 172
subjectivity 26, 38, 97, 101, 148
suffering: in psychoanalysis and psychotherapy 136–7; relief of 133–5, 137–42
"Suffering and Psychotherapy" (Strupp) 139
suicidal ideation 110
Sullivan, H.S. 12
superorganism 88, 92
support 159
synapses 72, 120
systems theory 32
Szasz, T.S. 140

Taylor, S.E. 114
Teicholz, J.G. 14
telepathy 88–91
temporality 56–8
thalamus 70
theories, need for 155
Theory of Mind (ToM) 20, 23, 43, 115, 163, 164, 175, 178
therapeutic partners 58
The Therapeutic Situation in the 21st Century (Leffert) 1–2, 47, 177
therapists: care of patients by 42–51; goals of 75; as healers 125; relationships with patients 29, 171–6; role of 53–5; values of 6, 160–1
therapy *see* psychoanalysis
thermodynamics, laws of 53
Thomas, A.C. 28
thought transference 88–91
"thrownness" 45–6, 48, 54, 60, 86, 125, 130, 135
ToM *see* Theory of Mind (ToM)
touch, in patient care 144–7
tragic man 11
transference 142, 148, 153, 154; genetic 154; here-and-now 154; regressive 170; thought 88–91
transference cures 6, 98
transference gratification 153
"transference" relationship 58
transference wishes 7
translation 40
trauma 19, 45–6, 57, 58, 60, 66, 70, 72, 76, 80, 115, 117, 136, 141, 146, 153, 157, 158, 170

208 Index

Tulving, E. 2, 57
Tversky, A. 104, 106, 108, 113–14
Tyrrell, C. 168

Umwelt 4, 55, 136, 140, 153, 154, 175;
    see also being-in-the-world
uncanny 5, 87; in dreams 88; and the
    unconscious 84–8
uncertainty 6, 69; in contemporary
    psychoanalysis 95–101; in psychoanalysis
    94; study of 120; theoretical vs. clinical
    97; why psychoanalysts need to study
    121–2; *see also* unknowability
Uncertainty Principle 96, 100
unconscious 3–5; collective 88; Freud's
    discovery of 54; neuropsychology
    of 71–3; neuroscience of 70–1,
    77, 80; phenomenological 74–6;
    phenomenology of 68–9; and relational
    psychoanalysis 76–84; and the uncanny
    84–8; *see also* unconsciousness
unconscious experience 33
"The Unconscious" (Freud) 52
unconsciousness: in the cerebral
    hemispheres 71; and consciousness 79;
    directedness of 36; neuropsychology of
    71–3; as phenomenon of existence 74;
    see also unconscious
Unheimlich 85–6; *see also* uncanny
unknowability 26, 94; *see also* knowability;
    uncertainty

Vagus 16–17
Valium 177
value system, of therapist 6, 160–1
vasopressin 17, 129
venlafaxine 107
visual imagery 115

Watson, J. 131
Watt, D. 127
Wenkart, A.138
white matter architecture 16
will, concept of 54
William Alanson White Psychoanalytic
    Society 49
Willingham, D.B. 73
Wilson, T. 83
Winnicott, D.W. 13, 146
Wittenberg, E.G. 97–9
Wittgenstein, Ludwig 159
Wollmer, M.A. 18
Wolpe, Joseph 102

X Cranial Nerve 16–17

Yalom, I.D. 52

Zahavi, D. 41, 42
Zajonc, R.B.120
Zeddies, T.J. 79, 80
Zollikon Seminars (Heidegger) 48, 49, 51–2,
    74, 76